The Portland GuideBook

Linda Lampman & Julie Sterling

The Writing Works
Division of Morse Press, Inc.
Seattle, WA

Library of Congress Cataloging in Publication Data

Lampman, Linda, 1936-
    The Portland Guidebook.

    Includes index.
    1.   Portland, Or.—Description—Guide-books.
I.   Sterling, Julie, 1929—   Joint author.
II.   Title.
F884.P83L35   1980   917.95'49   80-26308
ISBN 0-916076-42-3

Published by The Writing Works
               Division of Morse Press, Inc.
               417 East Pine St.
               Seattle, WA 98122

Library of Congress Catalog Card Number: 80-26308
ISBN: 0-916076-42-3

For Don and for Jack—
but especially for Portland.
Her name will always mean home.

Follow the Stars

★ Throughout the book this symbol appears following
names or places which are covered elsewhere in the book as
well. Refer to the Index for page numbers.

Acknowledgments

This guide would not have been compiled without the
cooperation of the businesses and agencies mentioned in its
various sections. We wish to express our special thanks to
them for helping make this the most comprehensive book of
this nature available on Portland.

Thanks also to Doug Baker, Martin Clark, Spencer Heinz,
Tom McAllister, Bill Mulflur, and Andy Rocchia of the *Oregon
Journal* and to Bill and Jane Hilliard, Ted Mahar, and John
Wendeborn of *The Oregonian* for assistance in their special
fields; to Tri-Met for its Fareless Square map and route notes,
with special thanks to Pam Dunham and Robert Prowda; to the
Portland Chamber of Commerce and the Greater Portland
Convention and Visitors' Assn. for excellent resource material;
to Warren Iliff of the Washington Park Zoo; to Gail Meredith
and Ross Walker of the Bureau of Parks and Recreation; to
Bob Cramer, master of minutiae; to T. E. Hogg, sports consultant; to Patti Jacobsen, Julie Rogers, and Don Barber for help
on neighborhoods and safety, respectively; to Kay Corbett of
Portland State University and Marge Floren, Reed College.

About the Authors

Linda Lampman McIsaac and Julie Courteol Sterling met when both joined *The Oregonian* staff within two weeks in 1960. They are also authors of *Oregon For All Seasons*.

Linda comes by her writing talents from her mother, Evelyn Sibley Lampman, author of 40 books for young people. Her grandfather was Ben Hur Lampman, poet laureate of Oregon. At *The Oregonian* she was a general assignment reporter. She is the mother of two boys, part-time veterinarian to her farm animals, and public school volunteer in West Linn. Before *The Oregonian* Linda worked in public relations for the Georgia-Pacific Corp. She has also done PR assignments for the Oregon Historical Society. She is married to Jack L. McIsaac, an executive of the Pacific Power and Light Co. and golf consultant for *The Portland GuideBook*.

Julie was also a reporter, first covering police and political news for *The Evanston Review* and then clubs for *The Oregonian*. Along with researching and writing *The Portland Guide Book*, she promotes good public education in Portland as a full-time volunteer. She has three children and is married to Donald J. Sterling, Jr., editor of the *Oregon Journal* who designed the indexes for both *The Portland GuideBook* and *Oregon For All Seasons*.

Photo and Illustration Credits

Cover: James Torson—67, 68
Photos: David Falconer—viii
    Greater Portland Convention and Visitors' Assn.—216
    Maps: Hartwig Petersen, Jack Pierce

CONTENTS

About the Artists

Native Portlander Jim Torson who was commissioned to do the cover art for the first *Portland GuideBook*, paints a fresh bloom to mark a new decade for the City of Roses. His gift of a rose for this third edition is but one of several of his reflections of the city which appear in this book.

Before becoming a graphic artist in Portland, Jim served in the U.S Marine Corps' combat art program. His courtroom drawings have been seen on KATU (Channel 2). He free-lances illustrations from his home studio.

He and his wife, Jane, have two sons, and when Jim's not at his drawing board, he's coaching soccer.

Photographer David Falconer uses his camera as Carl Sandburg used his pen, to capture the many moments which bring America alive.

From sunrise over Mt. Hood to a single tear on the sticky face of a tired six-year-old, no detail escapes the sensitive Falconer eye.

Portland is Dave Falconer's hometown, and although he spent a week at the White House as a personal guest of President Gerald Ford, he remains a hometown boy. Some of his best shots have been captured on his way to and from work when he spots a moment too good to allow time to steal. His camera has caught and held the essence of the city for all of us, who from time to time forget to look up, look down, or even see at all. Many more of his photographs enliven *Oregon For All Seasons,* of which he is a joint author with Lampman and Sterling.

SIGHTSEEING
Places to Visit—Things To See

THE SUN had set on the city by the time his plane touched down. He had seen the Williamette River slipping smoothly between the sparkling shore lights, and it looked just as it had when he left Portland five years ago. It was good to be home.

Friends had told him to expect a new airport in Portland, and he wasn't surprised. It was pleasant to walk through the new, lush corridors. But he was ready to visit his old haunts. He stepped into a waiting cab and asked to go downtown.

As he expected, Portland was alive and well and just as he had left it. He paid his cab fare and climbed out on Broadway for a short walk on old familiar streets. Making a quick turn, he decided to leave his bags at his favorite hotel. He pulled up short at the door to the Congress. It was boarded up, the windows dark and dusty. His hotel was empty, abandoned, closed forever. I'll just check my bag at Trailways, he said to himself, then I'll decide where to stay for the night. But the next corner had no busses, no neon. Just a sign announcing the future home of Orbanco. Suddenly he felt very old and very tired.

I'll just get a room at the Y for the night. A good night's sleep is all I need, he thought; but he was beginning to wonder if he was already asleep and this entire night was a bad dream. He walked downhill to the corner of 6th and Taylor. And he stood looking down at a deep hole where the YMCA had been. Had he been gone that long?

It doesn't pay to turn your back on Portland, as native sons have noted. Just when the hometown kid or traveler thinks everything has settled into easy recall, a building comes down, a street goes in or out. Portlanders who never thought of leaving home watched as not only the skyline but the mountain line changed on May 18, 1980, when Mt. St. Helens erupted, leaving a flattened shape against the sky and a thin covering of

1

lava dust over the familiar face of the city. The mountain continues to spew, spit, and turn.

Sometimes it blows . . .

Since the initial explosion, which claimed less than 70 lives, residents within watching distance of St. Helens have treated it as another spectacular view—with awe, respect, and pleasure. In spite of the national media which pictured Portland as a disaster area, the quality of life in Portland has improved since the eruption. Neighbors met neighbors as they joined in a hose brigade to clear the sidewalks of ash. Now that the air has cleared, Portland residents are treated to a dual production with each following eruption, as they watch the mountain out the window and on national television simultaneously. Geologists and volcanologists have found utopia within the St. Helens area. Modern technology has made the mountain's activity safe for those who keep a distance.

. . . Sometimes it grows

Since the first edition of this guidebook in 1976, Portland has added a major hotel, a new baseball club, a pedestrian mall, complete with sculpture, and eight major buildings. New parks along the river have grown green grass where industry once deposited its refuse. New restaurants have added new foods to the city; the zoo and the junior symphony have been renamed; and several radio stations have changed tempo from rock to country-western to jazz. Jazz is making a comeback, dancing and roller disco are in. Busses are making another big return, and everyone not riding one is running. Parking lots are being converted to parks, and alfalfa sprouts are taking the place of hamburgers at the corner drive-in. Nothing is the same in Portland. Or is it?

Some geographical limits have remained constant in the city, although Las Vegas bookmakers may give odds on even them, after St. Helens' action. Portland street addresses are divided into five parts: southwest, northwest, southeast, northeast and north. The Willamette River divides east from west; Burnside Street divides NE from SE and NW from SW; and Williams Ave., on the east side of the river, divides N from NE.

Portland's bridges, from north to south, are St. Johns (a suspension bridge considered one of the most beautiful in the U. S.), Five Point One (a railroad bridge 5.1 miles north of Union Station), Fremont (which flies both the state and national flags), Broadway, Steel, Burnside, Morrison, Hawthorne, Marquam, Ross Island, and Sellwood.

Major suburban areas ringing Portland are Beaverton and Lake Oswego (SW) and Gresham, Milwaukie, and Oregon City (SE).

Dunthorpe, an unincorporated area between Portland and Lake Oswego, is probably the most exclusive place to live. Its fine homes are so well hidden behind lush Pacific Northwest greenery you see little of them. In its pre-sewer days, Dunthorpe was known as the "land of septic tanks and social pretentions."

A major seaport, Portland was settled largely by those who arrived by ship. Many of her older streets are named for New England sea captains who brought settlers and cargo to the harbor and then built homes for themselves in the new town. The city still reflects the conservative view brought by the founding easterners who recognized the value of the site near the Willamette's confluence with the Columbia River as a fresh-water haven for traders. Today Portland attracts large freighters through her network of bridges to the heart of downtown, 110 miles from the Pacific Coast.

Portland is the hub of Oregon's far-flung timber and agricultural interests. Ranchers in cowboy boots come from east of the mountains to buy and sell. Portland is also the cultural center of the state, although Salem, 47 miles to the south, is Oregon's capital.

Portland's metropolitan population (1980) totals 1,190,000, with the city accounting for 370,000. The city is located mainly in Multnomah County, but its metropolitan area includes Clackamas and Washington Counties to the south and west and Clark County, Wash., across the Columbia River to the north.

Because of persistent rain in western Oregon, Oregonians are known as webfoots.

Some native webfoots capitalize on their "condition." A popular series of greeting cards and T-shirts proclaims that the state is practically awash and suggests other more desirable places to visit. But the message seems to have a reverse effect, because tourism is one of the state's major industries. Ex-Governor Tom McCall called national attention to Oregon and himself in the mid-70's stumping for the state's environmental purity while hinting at a provincial reticence to receive too many newcomers. This only heightened interest in Oregon, much to the delight of the state officialdom and most Oregonians, who recognize tourism as a desirable part of the economy.

The rain didn't matter when surveyors for a "Quality of Life" study of 243 communities in the U. S. ranked Portland at the top among large cities. Survey categories included health and education, environment, and political, social, and economic conditions.

What most outsiders don't know is that persistent winter moisture is confined to the western side of the Cascade mountains and that eastern Oregon is as dry as the west is wet.

Tri-Met (Mass Transit) Directions—References in succeeding sections to "5th Ave. Mall" or "6th Ave. Mall" indicate on which of the two downtown Portland Mall ★ streets you will find your bus. Symbols (*Snowflake, Fish, etc.*) represent areas within the transit system and tell you at which shelter to wait on the mall. Fareless Square refers to a 340-block area downtown where you can ride free except from 3-7 p.m. weekdays.

Viewpoints

Seattle has its Space Needle, Chicago, its Sears building, but in Portland, the best viewing comes naturally—from one of several hilltops or hillside viewpoints.

Northwest

Pittock Acres Park—3229 NW Pittock Dr. Pittock Acres Park and its Pittock Mansion★ overlook the geography of Portland from 1,000 feet up. In view are four snowcapped Cascade mountain peaks—Hood, Adams, erupting St. Helens, and Rainier—as well as Portland's port and industrial districts, downtown business center, and residential neighborhoods to the east and southwest. Pittock Acres is part of a 5,000-acre 6-park system extending nine miles across Portland's west hills. Part of this system, maintained by the city's park bureau, is Forest Park, ★ said to be the largest wilderness-type park within any city's limits in the U. S. It is laced with hiking trails and dotted with picnic sites.

To get there: By car, travel west on West Burnside to NW Barnes; turn right to NW Pittock Avenue; turn right on Pittock Ave. to park entrance; turn right again and follow signs. By bus—no close service.

Southwest

Washington Park—Among the many vistas and views in Washington Park, the outlook to the east from the International Rose Test Garden ★ is the most sensational, a technicolor tribute to Portland's designation as the City of Roses. Mountains provide the backdrop for riotous color when roses are at the peak of their bloom—June and September.

To get there: Travel west on W. Burnside past 23rd to the Zoo-Rose Garden marker. At Tichner, turn left; turn right on Kingston and follow signs. The parking area for the Rose Gardens is east of the tennis courts. By bus, take #63, which goes directly to the Rose Garden. Board downtown on Morrison Street between 5th and 6th.

Council Crest Park—Highest viewpoint within the city is Council Crest Park, nearly 38 acres of hilltop 1,073 feet above Portland Heights, one of the city's most handsome residential neighborhoods. To the southwest, notice the burgeoning suburban neighborhoods of the Tualatin Valley.

To get there: Travel south on SW Broadway to Broadway Drive, which winds uphill to a spider intersection which includes SW Greenway; turn left on Greenway and follow the signs to the Council Crest viewpoint at the foot of the radio transmission towers on the hilltop. By bus, take #51 on Morrison downtown to Council Crest. Check with driver before you board. All #51s do not go to Council Crest.

Southeast

Mt. Tabor Park—Mt. Tabor, east of SE 60th between Yamhill and Division, is believed to be the only extinct volcano inside a city's limits within the continental United States. An outdoor amphitheater occupies the north end of the crater. You can drive to the crater, but a loop road which goes around the reservoir has been closed to cars. The road is about a third of a mile long, and visitors are free to walk it. The closure is considered to be a temporary measure, so don't be surprised to find it open when you drive to the park.

To get there: From downtown, cross the Morrison Bridge to SE Belmont; continue east to SE 69th; turn right. Follow a winding road to the park. By bus, board #21 going east on SW Yamhill at 10th, Park, or 5th downtown. Get off at east end of Mt. Tabor Park near SE 69th.

Willamette National Cemetery and Mt. Scott—A sweeping view of downtown, the Willamette and Columbia Rivers, and mountains to the north and east is your reward for driving to Willamette National Cemetery, which straddles the Multnomah-Clackamas County line southeast of the city. The cemetery, which some call the Arlington of the West, includes an amphitheater where Memorial Day services are held annually. Nearby are Mt. Scott (elevation 1083 feet) and Top O'Scott Golf Course.

To get there: Take U. S. 30—I-84 east to NE 82nd; travel south on 82nd to SE Flavel; turn left (east) and follow signs to cemetery. By bus, board #14 on 5th Ave. Mall at *Beaver* stops.

Northeast

Rocky Butte (Joseph Wood Hill Park)—The stone viewing platform on top of this Portland hill is a familiar landmark along the route to the airport. Another landmark is an obsolete airplane beacon which still flashes as a reminder of the pre-jet era in flying.

To get there: Drive east on I-84 to the NE 82nd exit; turn right (north) on 82nd; at Fremont, turn right (east), past the gates of a former college and follow Fremont to the park. By bus, take #40 on 6th Ave. Mall at *Snowflake* stops, get off at Fremont, and walk 8 blocks to park.

North

Mocks Crest—Look down on an excellent view of Portland's busy Willamette River harbor, the Port of Portland's dry docks, and the industrial area on Swan Island.

To get there: Take I-5 north to Portland Blvd. exit; turn left (west) on Portland Blvd.; turn right on N. Willamette and follow it to the viewpoint just east of the University of Portland campus. By bus, take #1 on 6th Ave. Mall at *Fish* stops and get off at the east end of the University's campus.

Some Parks and Gardens

Southwest

Washington Park—One of Portland's oldest, it is 145 acres of views, walks, and winding roads and includes the *International Rose Test Gardens, Japanese Garden, Zoo Railway station*, tennis courts, statuary, play equipment, picnic facilities, and groves of tall Douglas firs. Wear walking shoes to tour the park.

The Park Place entrance (end of Park Place near Vista) is marked by a formal garden and the Lewis and Clark column erected for the Lewis and Clark Exposition of 1905.

Not far up the one-way road which begins at the formal garden, you'll see atop a jagged rock one of Portland's landmark pieces of sculpture, a bronze statue of *Sacajawea*, the Indian guide for Lewis and Clark, discoverers of the transcontinental route to Oregon. While on the trail, Sacajawea bore the baby boy seen slung on her back in the sculpture. His father was an expedition interpreter.

Immediately after passing Sacajawea, take a fork to the right up a confusing spiral road that eventually takes you past another piece of fine old Lewis and Clark-inspired statuary, *"The Coming of the White Man,"* which depicts the reaction of two natives to the arrival of Lewis and Clark. Travel down the spiral to a five-point intersection. Take the marked road to the Rose Gardens; parking is provided at the south end. Other parking is accessible only to travelers approaching the gardens from Kingston.

June and September are the best times to view the hundreds of varieties of roses, all labeled. You'll find new ideas for your rose garden or inspiration to plant a new rose garden.

Stroll down through the three terraces of roses to Queen's Walk where plaques set in the walk name Portland Rose Festival Queens as far back as 1907.

Adjoining the garden to the south is *A Shakespeare Garden* planted with flowers and shrubs mentioned in the bard's plays.

To the north is a sunken garden theater where music and theater productions are staged by the Portland Bureau of Parks and Recreation in summer. Call for a brochure on the summer schedule (248-4315). These attractions are free.

To get there by bus, board #63 downtown on Morrison between 5th and 6th.

West of the Rose Garden beyond the tennis courts, the *Japanese Garden* (223-1321 or 223-4070) features five traditional garden forms, a teahouse beside a pond, and much Oriental symbolism. Admission is $2 for adults; $1 for students under 11, seniors, and service personnel; children under 6, free. Special rates for organized groups.

The garden is open during the summer, spring, and fall months but closed from the end of Oct. until April 1. Spring and fall schedule: Sat. and Sun., noon-6 p.m.; Mon.-Fri., 10 a.m.-4 p.m. Summer schedule: Mon.-Sat., 10 a.m.-6 p.m.; Sun., 10 a.m.-8 p.m. On national holidays the garden is open from 10 a.m.-6 p.m. Free shuttlebus service from the parking facilities to the garden is provided on weekends during the spring and fall and every day in the summer. You can arrange for a guide by calling ahead.

Annual memberships in the Japanese Garden Society of Oregon, which has developed the garden, are $15 for families and $5 for senior citizens and students.

Washington Park is the only station stop for the Portland Zoo Railway. During the summer months passengers may board the zoo trains at the Washington Park terminal. Ticket price of $3.25 for adults and $1.75 for seniors and juniors (residents, $2.25 and $1.25) includes zoo admission. Below the terminal is an attractive covered picnic area.

To get there: Take SW Jefferson west from downtown; turn right (north) on SW 18th to Salmon; turn left (west) and continue up the hill, jogging right and then left (west) to Park Place which leads to the entrance. By bus, take #63 on Morrison downtown.

For the intrepid in small cars, try a one-way scenic approach to Washington Park on an unmarked road to the left off W. Burnside, just west of the shopping center at 23rd.

Hoyt Arboretum—4000 SW Fairview Blvd. (228-8732). Pick up a self-guided tour brochure at the Visitor Center before you begin your visit to this wooded showplace, a "zoo" of trees from all over the world. Eight miles of hiking and jogging trails meander through the park, which is adjacent to the Zoo-OMSI—Western Forestry Center complex.★ The Redwood and Oak Self-Guided Tour Trails are each one mile long. Another trail is suitable for visitors in wheelchairs. The arboretum is a bright link in the scenic Wildwood Trail, which starts at the Forestry Center and winds through the Hoyt acreage before continuing on through Forest Park. Free guided nature walks are offered Tues. and Thurs. mornings and afternoons by reservation only; Sat. and Sun. at 2:30 p.m. (no reservation necessary); and Wed. evenings, May-Sept., 6:30 p.m. (no reservations). Participants meet at the picnic shelter.

To get there: Take the Zoo-OMSI exit on U. S. 26 (west). Drive past the Western Forestry Center and up the hill on Knights Boulevard. Turn right on Fairview. By bus, take #63 on Morrison to the Zoo-OMSI-Forestry Center Complex. Cross to the north side of the Western Forestry Center. A trail marker indicates the path to the arboretum.

Northwest

Forest Park—With its 5,000 acres of natural woodland and 30 miles of hiking trails, Forest Park,★ along the northwest side of the Willamette River, is the main link in a chain of parks which form the largest urban wilderness within an American city. Forest's north boundary is on Newberry Road between NW Skyline and St. Helens Road; its southern, at NW 29th and Upshur, where it forms a link with Macleay Park, Hoyt Arboretum, Pittock Mansion and Acres, and manicured Washington Park.

To get there: See instructions below for Wildlife Sanctuary and Macleay.

Pittock Wildlife Sanctuary, Audubon House, and Collins Sanctuary—NW 53rd & Cornell (292-6855). Here, bird-watchers have well over 100 acres of territory to observe that many varieties of birds and more—grouse, pileated woodpeckers, pygmy owls, black-headed and evening grosbeaks, warblers, wrens, bluebirds, and ducks, to name a few. Maintained and managed by the Portland Audubon Society, the wilderness area is accessible by trail from the Pittock Mansion. Raccoons, blacktail deer, and other animals can also be seen. In the spring, visitors with binoculars can view the spectacular sights of the nesting and mating season from the sanctuary headquarters at 5151 NW Cornell or from the trails and pond area of the sanctuary. The Audubon House, which is open to the public certain days (phone for specifics), displays exhibits. No admission charge.

Next to the sanctuary is *Macleay Park,* part of the wilderness network which includes Forest Park. Macleay is only one of the legacies left Portland by one of its most colorful founding fathers, Donald Macleay. This imaginative and innovative Scot was a shipper by trade. Macleay gave the 107 acres of forested land for Macleay Park with the provision that "no wheeled vehicles" be allowed—ever.

To get there: Take W. Burnside west to SW 23rd; turn right on 23rd and travel north to Lovejoy (the streets climb the alphabet on this route so Lovejoy follows Kearney); turn left (west) and continue to Cornell Rd. Follow Cornell to 53rd Drive. Bus #53 puts you near Forest Park Headquarters at NW 29th and Upshur (228-8732) and within hiking distance (4.6 miles) of the sanctuary and Macleay. Get off near NW 29th & Thurman and take steps down from the east end of the Thurman St. viaduct.

Downtown

South Park Blocks—One block east of SW 10th, this strip of green extends from Salmon for six blocks south to and through the Portland State University (PSU) campus all the way to the freeway.

Anchored at the north end by the prestigious Arlington Club, a private men's club, and at the south by PSU, the South Park Blocks (not to be confused with the North Park Blocks on the other side of Burnside) provide an interlude in the downtown scene.

The South Park Blocks have changed dramatically since Portland State University spilled out of the vacated high school where it began and into many buildings both old and new in the surrounding area. Streets that formerly crossed the Park Blocks at their south end were closed to form a stage for the campus with pleasing effects. Viewed from the hills above, Portland State and the South Park Blocks exhibit a green oasis in the busy downtown scene.

A walk in the Park Blocks with its roses, statuary, museums, churches, and university is well worth the time. Downtown office workers brown-bag-it amidst the roses during the summer and fall months. Police sometimes patrol the Park Blocks on horseback.

To get there: Ride Tri-Met in Fareless Square (free except from 3-7 p.m. weekdays) or walk from your downtown location.

O'Bryant Square—Between SW 9th and Park, Washington and Stark, this urban plaza block has a large, contemporary fountain with plenty of refreshing white water. Spacious central gathering area makes O'Bryant an ideal setting for noontime concerts and picnics in good-weather months. Attractive shelters provide protection in the rainy months. An Oregon Historical Society plaque on the Washington Street side gives historical perspective, features bronze engraving of area as it looked in 1850s.

To get there: Ride Tri-Met in Fareless Square or walk west on Washington from Mall.

Waterfront Park—West side of Willamette River between Burnside and Morrison Bridges. Development of a waterside plaza at the foot of Ankeny Street is the culmination of a dream to give Portland's downtown river frontage back to the people by transforming what was a major highway corridor into a recreational showplace. Pedestrian esplanades and open green areas provide river's edge settings for fairs, Rose Festival ship visitation, markets, a Lewis and Clark Botanical Memorial and art, including a large metal screen by Bruce West. Pubs and restaurants are proliferating near the river. A floating dock at the bottom of the seawall at Ankeny Street places you at water level. Note: on the east side of the river is a quiet esplanade which can be reached by a spiral pedestrian ramp near the east end of the Morrison Bridge.

To get there: Ride Tri-Met in Fareless Square (free except from 3-7 p.m. weekdays) or walk 5 blocks east on Oak from the Portland Mall. (If you use Tri-Met, be sure to ask the driver if bus is headed east toward the river.)

Mill Ends Park—For leprechauns and the fanciful, Mill Ends Park, smallest in the world, leads a brave existence in the crosswalk at SW Front and Taylor, a memorial to the late *Oregon Journal* columnist Dick Fagan, who created and tended the tiny patch and wrote about it in his column, "Mill Ends." The park, all of 354 square inches, is an official city park. The Park Bureau has dignified it with a brick-work border.

Southeast

Crystal Springs Rhododendron Garden—SE 28th near SE Woodstock. During April or May, even life-long residents find it hard to be nonchalant about these opulent gardens filled with fat rhododendrons and their relative, the delicate azalea. Catch the azaleas at their peak in April; in May the rhododendrons. The colony of ducks inhabiting the lake adds a touch of magic. More than 2,000 rhododendron plants are maintained by the American Rhododendron Society's Portland Chapter. New residents visit the garden to choose their favorites before shopping at a nursery. This visit can be combined with a walk on the classic Reed College campus just across SE 28th.

To get there: From downtown, travel south to the Ross

Island Bridge, cross it, and get on McLoughlin Blvd. going south. Take the Bybee underpass, then turn east to 28th. Turn left on 28th and continue to the garden. By bus, take #28 (Woodstock) on the 5th Ave. Mall at *Beaver* stops to SE 32nd and Woodstock. Walk four blocks west (ahead) on Woodstock to Eastmoreland Park and entrance to garden.

Westmoreland Park—SE 22nd & Bybee, across McLoughlin Blvd. from the Rhododendron Garden. For spur-of-the-moment recreation, the park, site of Portland's first airport in 1920, now serves as a popular "port" for model plane flying and yachting, fly casting, bowling on the green, bocci ball, softball, baseball, and soccer. The fly casting pool is lighted.

To get there: Follow directions to Rhododendron Garden, turning west at Bybee instead of east. By bus take #28 (Woodstock) and get off on Bybee near the park.

Laurelhurst Park—SE 39th & Oak. An outing designed to cure the "I-can't-stand-the-kids-another-minute" syndrome, winter or summer, is to Laurelhurst Park to feed the ducks. This 33-acre park includes a lake and many playground and recreation facilities. It is part of one of Portland's fine old east side neighborhoods.

To get there: Cross the Burnside Bridge, going east, and follow E. Burnside to SE 39th; drive south one block. By bus, take #20. Board on Yamhill downtown.

Northeast

The Grotto—Off the rush of Sandy Blvd. traffic at 8840 NE Skidmore (254-7371) are 58 acres of peaceful solitude run by the order of Servants to Mary (Servites). Known as the Grotto, or the Sanctuary of Our Sorrowful Mother, this shrine to all mothers includes chapel, wildflower-lined stations of the cross, and the magnificent grotto itself, which is the scene for outdoor masses offered Sundays at noon from May through September. An elevator on the lower levels carries visitors to the heights where the monastery and gardens are located.

To get there: By bus, board #14 on 6th Ave. Mall at *Raindrop* stops and get off at Grotto entrance.

North

Cathedral Park—In its unusual setting under the gothic arches of the St. Johns Bridge, this park is one of Portland's newest waterfront retreats. Boat launching facilities are provided.

To get there: Take St. Helens Road north to the St. Johns Bridge. After crossing, turn right on Syracuse; when you reach Burlington, turn right again and travel to Crawford; take another right and follow Crawford to Pittsburg. Take a left on Pittsburg, which leads into Cathedral Park. By bus, catch #1 (Mocks Crest) or #2 (St. Johns) at *Fish* symbol stops on Mall. Ask driver where to get off within walking distance of park.

Kelley Point Park—In extreme North Portland, at the point where the Columbia River and the Willamette River join, is Kelley Point Park, a creation of the Port of Portland, now maintained by the city. It is named for Hall J. Kelley, a New Englander who made an unsuccessful attempt to colonize the "point" in the 1830s. View passing ocean-going ships here while enjoying the park's vast meadow, many beaches, wooded areas, and good swimming. This is a very popular park on hot summer weekends.

To get there: Take I-5N to North Marine Drive exit; travel west to Suttle Road and follow signs for 4 miles to park. No bus service.

Out of Town

Outside of Portland to the south, but close enough to be considered city retreats are:

Tryon Creek State Park—Between Lewis and Clark College and Lake Oswego (Nature Center, 636-4550). Tryon, the state's first metropolitan state park, is a tribute to the determination of two Lake Oswego women who led a campaign to save the area from residential development. Its 600 acres of wilderness offer natural quiet for hikers, cyclists, horseback riders (no horses for rent), and nature lovers. The first park in Oregon to employ a full-time naturalist, Tryon's nature center is open daily, except Mon. and Tues.; be sure to try its unusual drinking fountain. Tours are conducted at 1 and 3 p.m. on weekends and by request during the week. Phone for up-to-date information. Tryon Creek, home of much wildlife, even beaver, is in the park scene.

To get there: Take SW Macadam south toward Lake Oswego to Riverside Drive; travel on Riverside to SW Terwilliger at the north edge of Lake Oswego; turn right; park is on your left. No close bus service.

Camassia Natural Area—West Linn. Of interest to geologists and naturalists, this area is an excellent record of the Missoula flood at the end of the Ice Age—a flood so vast that it extended all the way from Montana to Oregon. The 22½-acre area is preserved by the Nature Conservancy (228-9561). Call for directions.

Clackamette Park, just off SE McLoughlin, under the bridge at Oregon City. This well-marked park offers picnicking facilities, boat launching, and a beach for swimming. It is located at the confluence of the Willamette and Clackamas Rivers—thus the name.

To get there: Follow SE McLoughlin south to Oregon City (via the Ross Island Bridge if you're downtown). By bus, take #33 or #34 from downtown on 5th Ave. Mall at *Leaf* stops.

Museums and Other VIPS
(Very Important Places)

Three of our VIPs cluster around a single large parking lot on a west hills site which once was the county poor farm and is now known as the *Zoo-OMSI-Forestry Center complex.*

On the hill immediately north of the complex is the Hoyt Arboretum.★

To get there: Drive west on SW Jefferson or SW Clay. Either route leads to SW Canyon Road (U. S. 26). Follow Canyon to the Zoo-OMSI-Forestry Center exit. Route #63 (Zoo/OMSI) goes to the complex via Washington Park.

Oregon Museum of Science and Industry and Harry C. Kendall Planetarium—(248-5900). Hatching chicks that children can handle, live goat kids (also pettable), a walk-in heart, an authentic ship's bridge, an operating beehive, and live reptile exhibits fascinate the youngest members of the family, while electricity, energy, fluid mechanics, space geology, agriculture, and dozens of other displays, many of them viewer-operated, appeal to the scientifically curious of all ages. An excellent *gift shop* sells everything from simulated sea-water crystals to telescopes. Yes, it did carry souvenirs of the eruption of Mt. St. Helens, including a reproduction of the seismograph chart from the morning of May 18, 1980, when the volcano in southern Washington erupted. No other outlet carried the chart because it was from OMSI's own seismograph.

Daily shows are presented in the *Harry C. Kendall*

Planetarium and in an auditorium where the "transparent lady" tells the story of the human body. A new planetarium program is produced every three months with dramatic flair. The facility projects approximately 5,000 stars, planets, sun, and moon.

Admission to OMSI: Adults, $2.50; children (6-12) and senior citizens, $1.50; members free; group rates on request. Membership in OMSI is $27, $15 and $8.50 for families, individuals, and students, respectively. Membership privileges include special rates for OMSI's extensive educational programs and classes for adults and children as well as free admission to the exhibits. OMSI also conducts summer science programs at Camp Hancock in Central Oregon and at a variety of other sites around the state in such fields as astronomy, alpine life systems, rockhounding, coastal life systems, oceanography, archaeology, and paleontology. For additional information call outdoor education (248-5938) or write Camp Registrar, OMSI, 4015 SW Canyon Rd., Portland, 97221.

OMSI is open every day except Christmas.

Hours: daily, 9 a.m.-5 p.m. Planetarium shows daily. Hours and Planetarium schedule are subject to change without notice.

OMSI maintains an intriguing futuristic "annex" at the northern end of the parking lot. *TERA One,* a demonstration solar home built for OMSI by Pacific Power and Light Co., is open free of charge Fri. -Sun. Guided tours are given Fri. and Sat. TERA One is designed to collect, conserve, and reduce the use of all energy normally used in a home and is also a laboratory where new energy-saving ideas are tested.

Washington Park Zoo—(226-1561). The animals at the Washington Park Zoo never take a day off, not even Christmas, when it comes to public appearances, so plan a visit there any time from 10 a.m. to dusk. Of the zoo's more than 400 inhabitants, the elephant herd has been the main attraction since 1962 when Portland's Belle became the first elephant in captivity in the Western Hemisphere in nearly half a century to bear a calf. The baby, Packy, still lives at the zoo, pursuing the record of his father, the late Thonglaw, who sired 15 elephants there. Packy's birthday is a public celebration each April.

Night Country, the stalking grounds for the nocturnal feline exhibits, is equipped with reverse light cycles to enable the public to see cats' "evening" activities during visiting hours. It might sound strange to you, but to a sand cat, a fishing cat, a golden cat, or some of the other prowlers in residence (bats, too), the night lights are all in a day's work. Rugged, naturalistic terrain is simulated in the cat dwellings and repeated outside the entrance to the exhibits so that children can get a feel for the feline world by "stalking" their way in.

The Elephant Overlook is a landscaped, terraced area where visitors can observe the elephants in a large, sand-covered yard which has a shade structure for hot days and an 80,000-gallon pool which can easily accommodate three elephants at a time.

Other special attractions at the zoo include Siberian tigers, lions, snow leopards, red pandas, harbor seals, polar bears, penguins, orangutans, chimps, new and old world monkeys, an insect zoo which hums in summer, a free children's contact zoo and animal nursery, and the Zoo Railway, which travels a winding route to a scenic viewpoint in Washington Park.

A children's theater presents plays and puppet shows on weekends in winter, daily in summer. You can buy unusual gifts in the Elephant's Trunk and eat at the Tiger Terrace Cafe or the Bear Walk Cafe. Guided zoo tours are available seven days a week, with reservations in advance.

Two rate structures apply. Residents (Metropolitan Service District): adults, $1; children (6-11) and seniors, 50¢. Nonresidents: adults, $2; children and seniors, $1. Children under 6 are admitted free.

Family and individual memberships in the Friends of the Washington Park Zoo are available for $25 and $15, respectively. Members receive a discount on zoo admission and a subscription to the WPZ Newsletter.

The Zoo Railway, which travels between the zoo and a quaint canopied station at Washington Park, operates all summer and in winter when weather permits. Regular ticket prices: adults (12 and over), $1.25; children (3-ll) and seniors, 75¢.

Phone the zoo if you're interested in arranging a lively—literally—presentation for your group. The zoo takes small mammals, birds, and reptiles on the road for group programs.

Western Forestry Center—(228-1367). A 70-foot talking tree, a forest fire dramatization, and a simulated paper mill provide a realistic introduction to Oregon's No. 1 industry at the Western Forestry Center, a building as architecturally pleasing as it is interesting.

Outside are a logging locomotive which children can explore

Planned serenity welcomes the four seasons at the Japanese Garden on the lower edge of Washington Park. The garden marks the alliance between Portland and its sister city of Sapporo, Japan.

inside and out and an excellent collection of wood specimens. Visitors can also enjoy a refreshing moment at a fountain by sculptor Tom Hardy.

The $6 million complex replaced a much-loved giant log cabin built for the Lewis and Clark World's Fair held in Northwest Portland in 1905. The old building burned in 1964.

The educational program of the Forestry Center features slide presentations and hands-on activities for groups; summer tours; lectures; classes such as wood carving and landscaping; and guided nature trail walks. (A map for a self-guided walk on the nature trail is available.) Call the center ahead for arrangements. An excellent selection of wood gift items is available at the Forest Store.

Hours are 10 a.m.-5 p.m. 7 days a week. Admission: adults, $1; seniors and students, 75¢; children under 7, with parent, free. Members are admitted free. Annual memberships are $20 for families and $12.50 for individual adults; $7.50, students, teachers.

Northwest

North of the Zoo-OMSI-Forestry Center complex on the other side of West Burnside is the **Pittock Mansion** (248-4469). Fate of this French Renaissance mansion, with its fine marbles, cast bronze, hardwoods, and classic plaster work, was uncertain before it and the 46-acre Pittock Acres Park★ on which it stands were purchased by the City of Portland in 1964. The mansion is now one of Portland's showplace sights because of its fine examples of local craftsmanship and lofty setting (see Viewpoints).

Rooms are decorated as they might have been in the period (1909-1914) when the mansion was built by Henry L. Pittock, the founder of *The Oregonian* newspaper. Greatly enriching the decor are many fine antiques and furnishings which were popular in that era and have been donated to the mansion by long-time Portland residents as well as friends from as far away as New England and California.

Children who visit the Pittock Mansion have to restrain themselves from sliding down the graceful curved bannisters and from turning on Mr. Pittock's private shower, a spectacular example of plumbing "sculpture" which even includes a liver spray.

Displays of collections and curiosities rotate in the exhibit room. At Christmas time the entire mansion is festively decorated, each year by a different ethnic or social group.

Admission is $1.50 for adults, $1 for students, and 50¢ for children with special rates on Fridays for groups of 15 or more (by prior reservation).

Members of the Pittock Mansion Society are admitted free to the mansion. Individual memberships are $7.50 (husband and wife); $5 (single); $1 (students). Address is 3229 NW Pittock Dr., Portland, 97210.

The grounds are open daily without charge. Notice the Gate Lodge which is under restoration. The mansion is open from Labor Day to mid-June Wed.-Sun., 1-5 p.m. Extended summer schedule. Phone for details.

To get there: Follow directions given previously for Pittock Acres Park.

Downtown

Important places to see in the downtown area, moving from south to north are:

Portland Center—a 54-block area south of the Civic Auditorium and SW Market. A city within a city, this glamorous shopping-office-residential complex replaced "Old South Portland," fondly remembered by the city's Jewish and Italian populations as one of their neighborhoods. In the stair-stepped ***Lovejoy Fountain,*** you can watch 2-year-olds and a few 20-year-olds splash on hot days. To the north two blocks is **Pettygrove Park.** The fountain and park honor the two Portlanders who named the city by a flip of a coin.

To get there: Ride on Tri-Met in Fareless Square (free except from 3-7 p.m. weekdays) to 3rd & Clay (Civic Auditorium and Ira C. Keller Fountain). Walk south through the scenic corridor to SW 2nd and Harrison.

Civic Auditorium and Ira C. Keller Fountain (formerly Forecourt)—SW 3rd & Clay, (248-4335, business office; 248-4496, box office).

A delightful contrast: the auditorium, home stage for the glamorous Portland Opera Association and the Oregon Symphony Orchestra, stands window-to-water with Ira's Fountain, an open air stage where real people play in a collection of waterfalls cascading over 4,000 tons of concrete. The fountain, designed by Lawrence Halprin, was dedicated in 1970 to complement the Civic Auditorium and is named in memory of Ira

Photo: Portland Parks

The best barefoot park in Portland is named for the late Ira
C. Keller, chairman of the Portland Development Commission. Wading is encouraged as a collection of waterfalls
cascade over 4,000 tons of concrete opposite the Civic
Auditorium. A perfect stop for a summer's day.

C. Keller, the citizen chairman of the Portland Development Commission, which built it.

Because reveling youth spend as much time in the water as out of it in the summer months, the fountain is patrolled by lifeguards in the summer.

The Civic Auditorium seats 3,000.

Backstage tours of the auditorium can be arranged by calling 248-4335—but normally are not given during performances or on Sat. and Sun. The tours include a discussion of the auditorium's unusual sound system and visit large and small dressing rooms and other elaborate backstage facilities.

To get there: Follow instructions for Portland Center and Lovejoy Fountain.

Benjamin Franklin Museum—Benj. Franklin Plaza, SW 1st & Jefferson (248-1384). This little museum of Franklin artifacts in one of Portland's newer downtown buildings occupies a portion of the Benj. Franklin Federal Savings and Loan Assn.'s Plaza Branch. Principal piece of art is the porcelain sculpture, "Declaration of Independence," depicting Franklin, Thomas Jefferson, and nine others. Three original signatures of Benjamin Franklin are displayed along with authentic reproductions of several Franklin inventions. Your eyes will blink when you view the custom-made carpeting, featuring a medallion similar to the presidential seal.

The red brick Franklin Plaza building was intended to be the headquarters of a wood products company. The recession hit, the company could not afford its new "house," and thrifty Ben took over.

To get there: Walk from downtown or ride Tri-Met.

First National Center—Between SW 3rd & 5th and Jefferson & Columbia (225-2111). For tours (five or more persons), call 10 days in advance (225-2361); no tours on Fri. Despite complaints that "it bisected my view of Mt. Hood," First National Center Tower, Portland's tallest building at 40 stories, has become a downtown mainstay. The center, designed by Charles Luckman Associates, who did the new Madison Square Garden in New York, includes two restaurants, a sandwich and coffee shop and take-out food spot (Tower Tote) on the 28th floor, and The Portfolio, offering a fine view from the 21st, both open to the public, but not for late dining. A collection of over 400 paintings, sculptures, and prints is on view throughout the building.

To get there: Walk from downtown locations or travel by bus in Fareless Square.

City Hall—1220 SW 5th (248-4583 for information). Portland's unpretentious City Hall, filling the block bounded by 4th and 5th and Madison and Jefferson, squats like a brown mushroom between the First National Bank Tower to the south and the Georgia-Pacific building to the north.

After adjusting to its scale in relation to its high-rise neighbors you'll admire its Renaissance lines, detailed columns, and marble circular inserts. Much renovation inside and out in recent years has enhanced its clean lines.

City Hall was born twice. An onion-domed curiosity was planned for the site, but the city fathers decided it was too costly for the times and abandoned it even though it had been completed to the first floor. The present Whidden and Lewis building was completed in 1894 and has been remodeled several times. Before 1929 its inhabitants included 250 stuffed animals in glass display cases.

Suggested visiting days are Wed. and Thurs. when the city council meets. The council of five commissioners deliberates Wed. at 9:30 a.m. and 2 p.m. and Thurs. at 2 p.m. Visitors are encouraged to attend.

A city-county office building is under construction across Madison Street from City Hall. Scheduled for completion in 1982, the new downtown public service building is, as is City Hall, a toned-down version of an earlier plan.

To get there: Ride Tri-Met in Fareless Square (free except from 3-7 p.m. weekdays) or walk from downtown.

Multnomah County Courthouse—Between SW Salmon & Main and 4th & 5th (248-3511). A full judicial smorgasbord from arraignments to trials, from district court to circuit court, from animal court to small claims court is housed in this classic building. The Multnomah County Board of Commissioners and many county services are headquartered here. The building was constructed in 1913 and has been remodeled extensively since—not always for the better.

If you're interested in what trials are "playing," consult a schedule of cases posted in the administrator's office on the second floor of the courthouse—room 236 for district court and 210 for circuit.

The two "showcase" courtrooms in the building are rooms 512 and 544, both good examples of old-fashioned judicial elegance. Notice the portrait of John Marshall above the bench in 512. Wander around the fifth floor and walk in some of the new courtrooms for contrast. Room 526 is a courtroom "in the round."

One floor up, in room 602, the Board of County Commissioners meets Tues. and Thurs. mornings at 9:30 a.m. Citizens are encouraged to attend.

The courthouse is open Mon.-Fri. from 9 a.m.-5 p.m. Visitors are welcome to sit in on most trials and hearings. Special court tours, generally for students only, can be arranged by calling 248-3457.

To get there: Ride Tri-Met in Fareless Square or walk from downtown.

Georgia-Pacific Historical Museum—900 SW 5th (248-7529). It's really a dinner bell, but in logger's jargon it's a "gut hammer" and you can ring it while touring the Georgia-Pacific Historical Museum. Old-time logging days, the story of the modern wood products industry, early saw milling, transportation in the woods, forest conservation, life in the woods, and the advent of plywood manufacturing are depicted in the displays. Exhibits include life-size dioramas of old logging scenes, tools, a logging cart, and other artifacts as well as photographs. A popular feature is an old movie of logging operations in the Oregon woods more than 50 years ago. Another film describes modern reforestation methods. Tours by school or other special interest groups can be arranged by appointment. New exhibits open every three months in the special exhibits room. The museum is located in the parking structure across from the G-P building and is easily reached via a tunnel connecting the two buildings. Admission is free. Hours: 10 a.m.-3 p.m., Tues.-Fri.

To get there: Ride Tri-Met free in Fareless Square (except from 3-7 p.m. weekdays) or walk from downtown.

The Old Church—1422 SW 11th (222-2031). An excellent example of "carpenter gothic," the Old Church, built in 1882-83, was a place of worship until the 1960s when its Baptist congregation moved to a new building. The building was saved by a feverish effort of a few dedicated persons. It is now a historic landmark and is supported by the Old Church Society.

Things you can do at the Old Church, besides just look at it, are: reserve it for your wedding; attend sack-lunch recitals Wednesdays at noon played on the old organ that came around the horn from Boston in 1883; browse in the thrift shop that helps support the church; or attend a political rally or one of the many other public meetings and festivities held there. Phone for special events calendar.

The church is the oldest standing church structure on its original site in Portland. (The oldest surviving protestant church in Oregon, though no longer on its original site, is considered to be St. John's Episcopal Church, now at the foot of SE Spokane at the entrance to Oaks Pioneer Park.) Visit the Old Church and its thrift shop from 11 a.m.-3 p.m.; Tues.-Sat.

To get there: Ride Tri-Met free in Fareless Square (except from 3-7 p.m. weekdays; #57, #59, #60, #21, come closest) or walk from downtown.

Oregon Historical Society—1230 SW Park Ave. (222-1741). Travel back through the long history of the Oregon Territory and before via the exhibits and research library at the Oregon Historical Center, open free to the public 10 a.m.-4:45 p.m. Mon.-Sat.

The Indian life exhibit, the society's most elaborate, is among the long-run displays on the second floor. The main floor is reserved for rotating presentations of current interest and an occasional traveling collection.

Life-size dioramas on the second floor depict the native American way of life on the coast, at the river bank, on the high plateau, and in the desert at the time the first European and American explorers, trappers, and settlers encountered them. A maritime collection features exquisite ship models. A collection of fine wagon miniatures symbolizes the westward movement by land. An original covered wagon, ready to roll, is also part of the long-run exhibits.

The Oregon Historical Society regional research library on the third floor has open stacks for browsing. The society's collection includes rare and general books, manuscripts, maps, microfilm of scores of newspapers, and more than a million photographs. The society publishes an outstanding illustrated journal of western history, the *Oregon Historical Quarterly,* which is mailed to its 7,000 members.

Almost as interesting as the central museum, is the Bybee-Howell House, a renovated farm home which the society maintains on Sauvie Island,★ north of Portland.

Group presentations for children and adults are offered free. To arrange for a program for your group on such subjects as Indian life or pioneer days, call at least three weeks in advance. The society also packages historical presentations, complete with artifacts, for public schools. Historical films and slides are available for a rental charge. *Educator's News,* a bulletin of particular interest to teachers, is issued periodically without charge to those who request it.

Other OHS programs and events include the annual Trappers Rendezvous, a members' tour to interesting destinations around the state, and occasional film series.

Memberships in the society are $10 for individuals and $15 for families, Among the benefits: a subscription to the *Quarterly,* a newsletter, and a discount on publications and items in the gift store. The gift and bookshop offers everything from Portland guidebooks to the Oregon state stone, the thunderegg. Main entrance to the society is on SW Park, just north of Jefferson.

To get there: Ride Tri-Met free in Fareless Square (except from 3-7 p.m. weekdays; #57, #59, #21 come closest) or walk from downtown.

Portland Art Museum—SW Park & Madison in South Park Blocks (226-2811). While best known for its outstanding permanent collection of Northwest Coast Indian Art, the Portland Art Museum merits periodic visitations whether to catch the latest exhibit, to rent a painting, buy an unusual gift, attend a class, or view an offering by the Northwest Film Study Center.★

For the exhibits, guides are available if desired. Other permanent collections include Renaissance, European, African, Asian, and pre-Columbian art, and the largest single collection of works by C. S. Price (though it's seldom all displayed at once). Exhibitions change frequently and include examples of the lively work of the Pacific Northwest's colony of artists. The museum's outdoor sculpture mall is a memorable fresh air experience with its waterworks, intended to drown out street noise, and its huge metal "Split Ring" by Clement Meadmore. A major work in the mall is "Dual Form" by Barbara Hepworth. An indoor sculpture court, featuring outstanding pieces from the museum's collection of 19th and 20th century works, greets the visitor upon first entering the building.

Films, programs, and plays rotate in the museum's attractive Caroline Berg Swann auditorium.

Hours—Gallery: daily and Sun., noon-5 p.m.; Wed. and Fri, noon-10 p.m. Closed Mon. The museum offers a wide selection of gift items, particularly at Christmas time, in a convenient location on the main floor.

Admission contribution: adults, $1; students, 50¢; members, senior citizens, and children, none. Memberships in the Portland Art Association range from $20 ($10 for students) and entitle you to discounts in the gift shop and the monthly bulletin.

The Rental Sales Gallery ★ is located in the lower level of the neighboring Masonic Temple, with the entrance on Madison Street. Hours are Tues.-Sat., noon-5 p.m., and Sun., 2-4 p.m.

The Museum Art School offers college-level courses (a bachelor of fine arts degree) as well as a full array of evening, Saturday, and Sunday classes for adults and children. Call 226-4391.

To get there: Ride Tri-Met free in Fareless Square (except from 3-7 p.m. weekdays; #57, #59, #60, #21 come closest) or walk from downtown.

Central Library (Multnomah County)— SW 10th & Taylor (223-7201). The main building of Multnomah County's excellent public library system occupies a full block facing on SW 10th between Yamhill and Taylor. The Georgian-style structure is one of the finest designs of a noted Portland architect, A. E. Doyle. Passersby may test their knowledge of the names of famous authors and other notable persons which are carved on the exterior and on the benches set in a sidewalk balustrade.

Visitors and residents may use the library's large collections of current and old books, magazines, newspapers, art prints, musical records and tapes, and technical reference material.

The lobby always has an exhibit of literary interest and proudly displays one of the rare elephant folios of John James Audubon's paintings of birds. Free film shows and lectures are regularly scheduled in the library's auditorium. The staff maintains a list of current cultural activities in the Portland area. For visitors to the city, the Central Library can be a place to catch up with hometown papers, to find address directories for Portland and other cities, and to obtain helpful information. (See Walking Tours.)

Use of the material in the building is free to all. To borrow material for outside use, you need a library card, which is issued free at the library to Multnomah County residents. Nonresidents are charged a fee.

The library system also includes bookmobile service and 16 branch libraries. Hours of the Central Library are Mon.-Thurs., 9 a.m.-9 p.m.; Fri. and Sat., 9 a.m.-5:30 p.m. It is closed Sun., but books may be returned to an outside receptacle at the back of the building on SW 11th anytime.

To get there: Ride Tri-Met free in Fareless Square (except 3-7 p.m. weekdays, #21 comes closest) or walk from downtown.

Pioneer Courthouse (and Post Office)—555 SW Yamhill St. (221-3035, post office). Built between 1869 and 1873, the building now known as the Pioneer Courthouse was the first federal office building in the Pacific Northwest and is now the oldest public building in the region. Originally it housed the U. S. District Court and assorted federal offices. After the federal courts were moved to the present Portland Federal Courthouse, on SW Broadway between Main and Madison, in the 1930s, the handsome old building continued in use as a postal station and home for various U. S. government agencies under the name of "The Pioneer Post Office."

An extensive restoration program in the 1970s refurbished the exterior. Its interior was extensively remodeled to provide an elegant Victorian courtroom on the second floor for the 9th Circuit U. S. Court of Appeals, with adjoining offices for judges. Judges of the U. S. Bankruptcy Court occupy chambers and courtrooms on the third floor. The first floor continues to be occupied by a postal station and federal offices. Visitors may wander through the building daily from 8:30 a.m.-5 p.m.

The structure, built on a slight rise facing east toward the Willamette River was thought by some to be much too far from the business district—then some six blocks to the northeast (now Old Town)—when it was first erected, but the city grew in its direction. Today, the Pioneer Courthouse is Portland's central landmark on its full block bounded by SW 5th and 6th and Morrison & Yamhill.

Rutherford B. Hayes, the first incumbent U. S. president to visit Portland, took in the view from the building's cupola in 1880, and its grounds have been the site of many public gatherings and demonstrations. (Also see Walking Tours.)

Someday a long-awaited Pioneer Courthouse Square will probably be developed in the vacant parking lot across from the historic building on 6th. Funding for the public gathering place is uncertain, and the community must still reach agreement on how the square will be enchanced. Plans might include a terraced public forum and open-air market.

To get there: Ride Tri-Met free in Fareless Square (except from 3-7 p.m. weekdays) or walk from downtown.

Old Town and Portland Mall—Formerly "downtown," Old Town★ is generally considered to lie between 1st and 5th on either side of Burnside. Many once dilapidated buildings have been restored to their former elegance, with historical preservation and commercial gain the result. Specialty craft shops, antique shops, book and toy stores, and intimate restaurants abound.

Bridging the gap between Old Town's quaint facades and the electronic, new world of the ***Portland Mall*** is the ***U. S. Bank Plaza*** on SW Oak between 5th and 6th. In a nice touch of design, its triangular plaza points the way across an urban vista to the bank's revered main branch, with its ornate Roman Corinthian columns and bronze front doors, which, unfortunately, can only be seen when the bank is closed (★ Art). Adjoining the temple-like structure to the north is the former Wells Fargo & Co. building, now U. S. Bank office space. Look up and notice the "Wells" inscribed at the top in colorful ornamental work just beneath the balustrade. "Fargo" is similarly inscribed on the north face of the building, which was constructed in 1907 (★ Industrial Tours).

In contrast, the Plaza building across the street includes a spacious contemporary street-level galleria (inside mall) offering restaurant and retail space while floors above it contain the bank offices and operations.

The Portland Mall (★ Transportation, Walking Tours, Art) covers 5th and 6th Avenues between Burnside and Madison. Hundreds of thousands of dollars worth of art, including two large fountains near the Burnside end, are installed on the wide brick sidewalks.

Still on the south side of Burnside, at SW 1st and Ankeny, is the prim ***Skidmore Fountain***★ set in a plaza of rounded cobblestones said to have come to Portland as ballast on ships. It is considered to be the hub of Old Town. Across Burnside are more Old Town and also ***Chinatown,*** which extends as far north as the Steel Bridge.

Portland Police Museum—NW 2nd & Couch, 2nd floor (223-5771). An old-time police precinct station of the roll-top desk era is re-created here. Uniforms and equipment from days long gone, extensive collections of police badges and shoulder patches, arrest dockets, photographs from the era when "police dogs" were really police dogs, and many other articles are included in the rotating exhibits. Old movies, including police training films from the 1920s, are shown. Two retired Portland policemen in old-style uniforms staff the museum with the help of volunteers from the Portland Police Historical Society. In summer Portland police officers patrolling Old Town on foot add to the mood of the area by wearing uniforms of the 1920s. The museum is supported by donations from police officers, and admission is free. It is open afternoons, Tues.-Sat. Groups may schedule tours by calling ahead.

In quarters adjoining the Police Museum is the ***Architectural Preservation Gallery*** (243-1923), founded and managed by the Junior League of Portland. The gallery presents rotating exhibits of Portland's architectural history from the pioneer era to the present day. Exhibits, which change yearly, are planned, researched, and installed by Junior League volunteers with expert help from professionals in the community. Past shows have featured cast-iron architecture, terra cotta ornamentation, and, most recently, Portland amusement park architecture. Whether you seek a nostalgic trip into the city's architectural past or advice on renovating your own historic home, you'll find it here.

A courtyard in between the building housing the two museums (Capt. John Couch Square, formerly the old Phillips Hotel) and another one-time hotel building, Norton House, has been developed to enclose a permanent exhibit of pieces of architectural interest. Both the Phillips and Norton structures house shops, offices and restaurants, and are bridged at the second-story level. Norton House has an elevator. Hours of the architectural gallery are Tues.-Fri., 10 a.m.-3 p.m., and Sat.-Sun., noon-4 p.m. The gallery is closed Mon.

Outside Portland

Fort Vancouver

Fort Vancouver lies across the Columbia River on the Washington State side (use the Interstate Bridge and follow signs). It marks the center of the old Oregon Country and is a National Historic Site.

The replica of the old fort operated by Dr. John McLoughlin,★ physician and chief factor for the Hudson's Bay Company from 1824-1846, represents many years of research (since 1947) by historians, historical architects, and archaeologists to determine how and where the original was built. The reconstruction is on the old site and is part of 165 acres administered by the National Park Service.

Diggings have uncovered one million items and artifacts, including bits of china and earthenware, some of which are on display at the Fort Vancouver Visitor Center and Museum, which is separate from the fort site (but within walking distance).

The fort buildings include replicas of the bastion, bakery, chief factor's house, the 18th century kitchen attached to it, and, under construction, the Indian trade store and blacksmith shop. During the summer, hardtack bread is baked once a week in the huge wood-heated bakery oven, woodworking demonstrations are given occasionally, and fort personnel and auxiliary volunteers wear period costumes.

The fort site and visitor center are open from 9 a.m.-dusk in winter and from 9 a.m.-6:30 p.m., summer. Both facilities are closed all federal holidays but Memorial Day, 4th of July, and Labor Day. The furnished chief factor's house is open for hourly guided tours daily in summer and for limited hours in winter. A slide show is presented in the visitor center on request. For more information call (206) 696-7655.

In addition to the fort and its buildings, you will pass Officer's Row, a line of two-story houses on Evergreen Blvd. These homes represent an attempt by the Veteran's Administration to keep the street intact, yet allow it to pay its own way. The homes are rented. The row dates from the days of Indian wars in the west, and it is believed to be one of three such rows remaining, although 100 were built at various Army posts in the West before the Civil War.

The oldest house on the row, that of U.S. Grant (now a museum), was built in 1849, and the newest is a field officers' home built in 1905. Among those who lived to make their mark in history as former residents were George Custer, Phil Sheridan and the later generals, George Marshall and Douglas MacArthur.

Sauvie Island

Just north of Portland off U.S. 30 lies Sauvie Island floating serenely on the Columbia River. This pastoral farming area, the largest island in the Columbia, draws up its skirts from the dust of industry and seems to incorporate Mt. Hood into its acreage. A haven for farmers, houseboat owners, and those who just like to do it themselves, Sauvie Island provides a pleasant and secluded day trip for visitors. The dike is a natural for bike trips. Sauvie Island was the headquarters for the now extinct Multnomah Indian tribe.

The island remains ideal for cattle, but it also is a good place for picnicking, fishing, and spending a summer's day.

Commanding a wide view of the river is the **Bybee-Howell House**, administered by the Oregon Historical Society. This restored territorial farmhouse dates back before the Civil War. Open to the public, free of charge from June to the end of September, the restoration proves that all pioneers did not huddle in log cabins. Hours are 10 a.m.-5 p.m. daily.

On the grounds to the rear of the house is a pioneer apple orchard, scions of trees from the Oregon country. Next to the barn is the 100-year-old pear tree—not one of the pears is edible, but each is as large as a quart jar.

In the barn is an agricultural museum which can be viewed during the same hours as the house. Though primarily intended for children, it is of interest to all ages as it delineates the four main divisions of farm life and work: (1) clearing the land, (2) planting, (3) harvesting, and (4) distributing.

Visitors are welcome to see the house and barn anytime, but the last Saturday of September should be marked on the calendar for the Historical Society's annual "Wintering-In" party. Take a picnic lunch in the morning and spread your cloth on the wide lawns. Local farmers bring in their harvest bounty to be sold and children delight in age-old games and races.

Cider, made from an old wooden press, proves that the apple trees still fulfill their purpose.

Note: For more historical information about Multnomah County, obtain a copy of *Historical Sites Tour Guide and Map* from the Oregon Historical Society or the county.

Lake Oswego-Oregon City

Macadam Avenue is the easiest route to Lake Oswego and Oregon City, and the old road is shored up by history from start to finish. Passing Johns Landing, the newest park on the Willamette Greenway, you will see what merchants have done with an old mattress factory (The Water Tower★) and are doing to return other industrial buildings as well as the river to the people. Condominiums, restaurants★, offices and a boat launch complete the complex at this point with other shopping areas and restaurants to come.

The watery neighborhoods of houseboats along the Willamette at this point represent only one of several such moorings in the Portland area. This particular group celebrates the Christmas season by lighting all the rooftops, chimneys, and porches, giving the Willamette River a special holiday glow.

You will cross **Military Road** along Macadam, and the name is justified. Lt. Phil Sheridan and his army used the access from the valley to Fort Vancouver during Indian uprisings.

Lake Oswego is a new community but built upon old foundations. Albert Alonzo Durham named the town in 1861 when he settled there with his sawmill on Sucker Creek (polite society now calls it Oswego Creek). Durham had good reason for his sawmill, for the area was heavily forested and the Portland community was awaiting every board and beam he could cut.

Some 150 Chinese settled where the Bay Roc apartments now rise to dig the many canals necessary to float the lumber to Sucker Lake and to the mill. The canals and the lake, now enlarged, comprise some of the most highly taxed land in the state. Once Sucker Lake was enlarged and its name changed to Oswego Lake, the lavish homes began to rise above the shores.

There is an often-told story, probably true many times over, that an excited Easterner bought a home on the lakefront without consulting his wife. He was so taken with the water view, the waterfowl, and the clean atmosphere that he really didn't pay much attention to the house; he knew that all would be forgiven once she looked out the wide front windows. His wife arrived during the periodical lake drainage, and the front windows stared upon a wide panorama of mud, old stumps, and last summer's picnic debris. She was able to enjoy this view for six months until the lake was filled again.

Lake Oswego once tried to become "the Pittsburgh of the West" and indeed did cast the first iron stove in Oregon to be used by the Ladd and Tilton Bank. All that remains of that dream is an old stack of basalt rock and the towering chimney on the river bank at the mouth of Oswego Creek (**George Rogers Park**), a spot so returned to nature that the beavers have come back to rebuild their ancestors' homes. If wilderness is appealing, spend a day at **Tryon Creek State Park**, off Terwilliger Blvd., at the entrance to Lake Oswego. ★

Across Oswego Creek is Portland Blvd., the route to West Linn and Oregon City. West Linn is a sprawling area of farmland and suburban residences, marked by a combination city hall and police station and Publishers Paper Co.

West Linn, or Linn City, as it was once called, is remarkable in that it was purchased from the Indians. History does not tell us what Robert Moore paid for the piece of land across the river from Dr. John McLoughlin's sawmill, but it is clear that he paid for it.

Willamette Falls, a natural drop in the river between the two towns, was brought under control by locks in 1868. Visitors to Publishers Paper Co. are invited to walk through the plant and out under the falls to see the remarkable old locks which control the portage and water flow. For salmon fishermen it is a perfect entrance to the gate of heaven that offers fine Chinook fishing every spring.

Oregon City, first territorial capital, remains a small town, but its accomplishments will always rank it first in the state. In addition to becoming one of the first incorporated cities west of the Missouri, the town is the site of the first Protestant church, Masonic Lodge, and newspaper west of the Missouri. Oregon City saw the first use of water power in the state, was the first settlement to hear a brass band and had the first mint. It was the second Northwest home of Dr. John McLoughlin.

In 1829 he chose a mill site at the falls and started his settlement with the retired trappers and voyageurs of Hudson's Bay Company. In 1842 he gave the city its name. He lived there until his death in 1857.

The *McLoughlin House*, restored (it once slipped to shelter the prostitutes of the city), is open to the public Tues.-Sat., 11 a.m.-4 p.m. in winter and 10 a.m.-5 p.m. in summer. It is open Sun. from noon-4 p.m., winter; noon-5 p.m., summer. It is closed Mon. Admission is $1 for adults, 25ᶜ for persons 18 and younger. To make special arrangements for group tours, call 656-5146.

The house is located on the "third" level of Oregon City and can be reached by driving to the top of the hill or by parking on the lower level and riding the city's public elevator (the only one in North America they claim) which connects the downtown business section with the upper streets.

Next door to the McLoughlin house is the home of *Dr. Forbes Barclay*, Hudson's Bay surgeon at Ft. Vancouver, who resigned and followed McLoughlin to Oregon City. Step in during business hours of the Tri-City Chamber of Commerce, which occupies the house.

To reach Lake Oswego and Oregon City by bus take #36 or #37 from downtown Portland at *Leaf* stops on 5th Ave. Mall.

Visitors' Information

Maps and printed brochures are plentiful at the **Greater Portland Convention and Visitors' Association, Inc.** (GPCVA), at the southwest corner of SW Front and Salmon (26 SW Salmon, Portland, 97204). Phone: 222-2223. Hours: Mon.-Fri., 8:30 a.m.-5 p.m. The GPCVA's visitor's information service, occupying street-level space in the Willamette Center complex, offers a Portland tour map and guide which describes 50 downtown sights and more than 30 other places of interest in the outlying area. It is free. Other information covers restaurants, motels, hotels, and scenic tours as well as an up-to-date calendar of Portland events.

Among the most popular free maps at the GPCVA office are the Oregon parks, state highway, and Portland city maps. A TraveInfo kiosk is maintained in front of the GPCVA, especially to serve visitors at times when the office is closed.

For a more complete array of information and maps pertaining to tourism statewide, visit the **Oregon Hospitality and Visitor Association**, Suite 305, 610 SW Broadway, 97205, between Morrison and Yamhill (227-1263).

Economic and statistical information about Portland area business and industry is available at the **Portland Chamber of Commerce** on the Portland Mall at SW 5th and Taylor (228-9411).

Tri-Met buses travel parts of many of Portland's most scenic drive routes, including the drive to the top of Council Crest. Call Tri-Met (233-3511) or visit its Customer Assistance office at 522 SW Yamhill for help in planning a tour by bus.

Neighborhoods

While taking scenic drives, walks, or bicycle tours, be aware of Portland's many neighborhoods, some of which took root as small river towns or streetcar line terminals. Landmark buildings are especially noticeable in areas like St. Johns, Albina (now the King, Boise, Eliot neighborhoods), Lents, Sellwood, and Linnton, which once were separate towns. The old city hall in St. Johns is a classic landmark and now houses Portland's north police precinct. These signs of the past strengthen neighborhood awareness while the city government encourages neighborhood activism through its Office of Neighborhood Associations. (See phone list under Neighborhood Assns.)

Neighborhood Association Boundaries

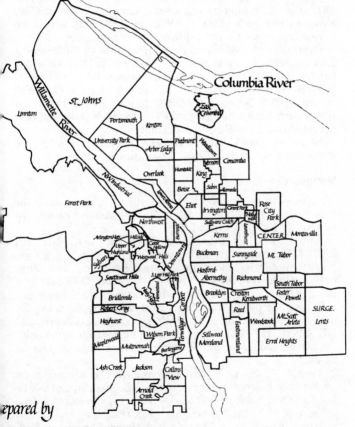

Columbia River

Willamette River

Linnton

St Johns

Portsmouth   Kenton

University Park

Arbor Lodge   Piedmont   Woodlawn

East Columbia

Overlook   Humboldt   Vernon   Concordia

NW Industrial   Boise   King   Alameda

Forest Park   Eliot   Sabin

Irvington   Grant Park   Rose City Park

Northwest   Sullivans Gulch   Hollywood   Montavilla

Arlington Hts   Hillside   Kerns   CENTER

Upper Highland   Goose Hollow   Buckman   Sunnyside   Mt. Tabor   Laurelhurst

Westover Hills   Downtown

Sylvan   Hosford-Abernethy   Richmond   South Tabor

Southwest Hills   S. Lair Hill Park   Brooklyn   Creston Kenilworth   Foster Powell

Bridlemile   Hamilton   Homestead   Read   Woodstock   Mt. Scott Arleta   S.U.R.G.E.

Robert Gray   Eastmoreland   Lents

Hayhurst   Wilson Park   Sellwood Moreland   Errol Heights

Maplewood   Multnomah   Burlingame

Ash Creek   Jackson   Collins View

Arnold Creek

Corbett

Terwilliger

Prepared by

Office of Neighborhood Associations   Phone 248-4519

Robert Gray

Neighborhood Haunts

Every neighborhood has a favorite local tavern, restaurant, ice creamery, gathering place or landmark—and they're not all in the Yellow Pages. Here are a few we've heard about:

North

Albina—When the Portland Trail Blazers won the National Basketball Assn. world championship on a June Sunday in 1977, the celebration moved directly from the Memorial Coliseum to **Geneva's**, 4228 N. Williams (282-6363), a favorite Albina night-spot for food, drinks, and comaraderie.

Overlook—**The Alibi**, 4024 N. Interstate (287-5335) is a long-established restaurant and lounge in the Overlook neighborhood and lives up to its advertisement as a "special place to rendezvous." In the same neighborhood is **Overlook House**, 3839 N. Melrose (282-2053), former home of the Raven (Creamery) family, deeded to the city by the Ravens and now operated as a Park Bureau community house.

St. Johns—**Dad's**, 8608 N. Lombard (286-5512), is a favorite gathering place in the heart of downtown St. Johns.

Northeast

Eliot—One neighborhood rendezvous here, particularly for young persons and the elderly, is **Matt Dishman Community Center**, 77 NE Knott (282-1460).

King—**King Neighborhood Facility**, 4815 NE 7th (288-0371), adjoins Martin Luther King School and is a community center for meetings, classes, programs, and other events. **Oscar and Milton's**, 5700 NE Union (287-6347), is a popular lounge and restaurant which attracts a loyal clientele, reflecting the population of this integrated neighborhood. So does the congregation of **St. Andrew's Catholic Church**, 806 NE Alberta (281-4429), a vital ethnic magnet for community festivities and services. Worship services include one in Spanish.

Vernon—"Let's go Ribbin' at **Boss's Deli**" is a line from an ad for this favorite eatery at 1438 NE Alberta (281-9691). Boss's serves hamburgers, black-eyed peas, and sweet potato pie as well as its famous beef and pork ribs.

Woodlawn—Warren Chung's **Woodlawn Pharmacy**, 6728

NE Woodlawn (289-3312), is a neighborhood fixture where customers pay their water and phone bills and buy pet and animal supplies as well as sundries and prescriptions. If you happen to be racing a horse at nearby Portland Meadows, Chung stocks the latest in horse remedies for your thoroughbred.

Beaumont and vicinity—Neighbors meet while lunching or dining at *Hamburger Patti's* at 43rd & Fremont (287-3655); and shopping at the *Wilshire Pharmacy*, 4060 NE 42nd (288-1366). Ice cream is made and served at *Roses*, 4444 NE Fremont (282-4615), while a few blocks east at *Stanich Ten Till One Tavern*, 4915 NE Fremont (281-2322), the town's biggest and best hamburgers, or so some believe, are being served to a clientele heavily populated with sports enthusiasts.

Irvington—Rivaling the posh downtown banquet facilities for some of the best annual luncheon and dinner business in town is *Westminster Presbyterian Church*, 1624 NE Hancock (287-1289), where a caterer and volunteers from the congregation cook and serve marvelous meals for moderate prices as a church fund-raiser. Nearby at 1631 NE Broadway, children of Irvington and the city at large find just the right atmosphere for book browsing at the *Children's Place* (★see Shopping), where there's almost always someone reading in the tub. For sandwiches, Irvington neighbors like the *Taste Tickler*, 1704 NE 14th (282-3681).

Kerns—If you visit this neighborhood, you should go away with a souvenir—a fresh baked one from *Couch Street Crumpets*, 713 NE Couch (238-5765). These crumpets travel, so look for them in your favorite grocery or deli.

Hollywood—It's *Pal's Shanty*, 4630 NE Sandy (288-9732), for clam buckets and gourmet sandwiches at reasonable prices and *Paulsen's Pharmacy*, 4246 NE Sandy (287-1163), for an ice cream soda while you wait for your prescription.

Gateway and Vicinity—Neighbors in the Madison High School area are particular about their chicken salad, and they know it's good at *Holland Gateway Restaurant*, 10805 NE Halsey (253-0079). They're still chuckling about the time the Northeast Portlander asked a Holland waitress whether the chicken in the salad was "real" or "molded." The indignant waitress replied, "We boil our breasts every day!" *Glenhaven Park* adjoining the high school is the neighborhood rendezvous for sports fitness enthusiasts.

Southeast

Inner Southeast (Warehouse District)—The patrons of the *Produce Row Cafe*, 204 SE Oak (232-8355), probably don't live in the neighborhood, but this restaurant-tavern, known for its reasonably priced sandwiches and wide selection of beers and ales, has all the qualities of an indigenous neighborhood haunt.

Buckman—Among the bright signs of rejuvenation in this inviting old east side neighborhood is attractive *St. Francis Park* with its Bruce West fountain (★Art). The park adjoins *St. Francis of Assisi Catholic Church*, 330 SE 11th, which mothered the park.

Sandwiches and soup are favorite menu items at the *East Bank Saloon*, 727 SE Grand (231-1659).

Laurelhurst—Roller skating around the spacious grounds of *Laurelhurst Park* has become almost as popular as feeding the ducks in the lake there. Look for a skate rental van on weekends. Laurelhurst neighbors are likely to meet at the *Easy Shop Sentry*, 3136 NE Glisan (just over the boundary in northeast).

Sunnyside-Richmond—Politicians and one-time athletes are said to frequent *Nick's Coney Island*, 3746 SE Hawthorne (235-4024). But you don't have to be an aging "jock" to chomp into Nick's specialty. This restaurant welcomes minors 'til 9 p.m. Portland's former mayor, Neil Goldschmidt, is one of the restaurant's celebrity habitués. A few blocks east, a neighborhood candy shop does a thriving mail-order business. It's *Ed Curry Candies*, 4317 SE Hawthorne (236-8131). Mint sticks are a specialty. If you don't get to *Buttertoe's* early for lunch or dinner, you'll probably have to wait in line—but it's worth it. Children enjoy the menu at this quaint spot at 3244 SE Belmont (239-9205).

Mt. Scott—Take a turn around the roller rink at *Mt. Scott Community Center*, 5530 SE 72nd, and find a friend.

Mt. Tabor—Mt. Tabor area residents claim one of the city's few remaining drugstore soda fountains and lunch counters at *Seaton Pharmacy*, 5939 SE Belmont (232-6171).

Hosford-Abernethy—Visitors from other neighborhoods invade the *Wooden Spoons*, 2525 SE Clinton (232-6282), for breakfast, lunch, and dinner.

Sellwood—Still like the small town it once was, Sellwood, which has been rejuvenated into a mall of antique shops and other quaint spots, also shelters *The Strudel House*, 1605 SE Bybee (232-7711), excellent for sandwiches, luncheons, dinners, and, of course, strudels. For more pastries and many other delectables, it's **Papa Haydn's**, 5829 SE Milwaukie (232-9440).

Eastmoreland—It's definitely **Davidson's** for ice cream and snacks in this Reed College neighborhood. You'll find Davidson's at 4633 SE Woodstock (774-7742). **Otto's Delicatessen**, 4138 SE Woodstock (771-3785), is another neighborhood favorite.

Milwaukie

Outside Portland in the suburban community of Milwaukie, **Pal's Shanty**, 11056 SE Main (653-2044) is a favorite place to eat and relax.

Southwest

Corbett-Terwilliger—Neighborhood needs are shared by many haunts in this charming old area where an arts and crafts colony, a blue collar community, and a new shopping-condominium complex (Johns Landing) all live compatibly. **Porcelli's** Grocery at 6500 SW Virginia (246-4814) is as good a place for a visit as a loaf of bread; across the intersection at **Trinity United Presbyterian Church**, elderly neighbors gather regularly for coffee and blood pressure checks (not necessarily in that order); popular jaunt in the Terwilliger neighborhood is a hiking trail from the end of Iowa St. (behind the **Nature's Food and Tool Store**, 5909 SW Corbett) to Terwilliger; and **Billy Bang's Pub** in the Water Tower at 5331 SW Macadam (227-4663) is one of many convivial spots in Johns Landing favored by the young sophisticates of the neighborhood and the city. At the north end of the area in the Lair Hill Park neighborhood is the **Children's Museum**, 3037 SW 2nd (248-4587).

Goose Hollow—This old Portland neighborhood gave its name to the **Goose Hollow Inn**, 1927 SW Jefferson (228-7010), which draws a large clientele from city hall, the courthouse, and the press (see Restaurants).

Hillsdale—Southwest Hills residents usually find a friend at **Lynch's Market**, 6344 SW Capitol Hwy. (244-3110); at **Haffners Delicatessen**, 1517 SW Sunset (246-8549), where giant sandwiches are sold in half sizes; or at **Shoji's**, 6366 SW Capitol Hwy. (245-3216), where Japanese dishes are cooked at the table.

Multnomah—Once a rural village connected to Portland by the Oregon Electric Line, this area has retained some of that small town flavor as well as the *Fat City Cafe*, 7820 SW Capitol Hwy. (245-5457), where neighbors meet over coffee and Fat City's famous cinnamon rolls.

Portland Heights—Inconspicuous as it is, *"The Fountain,"* a nondescript bubbler where Broadway Drive, Vista Avenue, and Patton Road come together, is universally accepted by residents of these green hills as a landmark and meeting place. Close by on Patton is *Strohecker's★*, where notices for lost and found kittens, baby-sitters and sales are posted for community exposure. Sooner or later, the entire community gets to Stro's to grocery shop. At the bottom of the hill, at 23rd and Burnside, Portland Heights residents follow the aroma of fresh-brewed coffee to the lunch counter at the *Town Pharmacy*, 2334 W. Burnside (226-6211).

Oregon City

Oregon's geological formation is causing havoc in old Oregon City, where parking is difficult simply because the giant cliffs of rock prohibit growth on the first level. But a stop on the lower level is worthwhile to visit several shops, the *Clackamas County Courthouse* (which holds steadfast to the original plat of San Francisco), and lunch or supper at *The Chopping Block*, 716-B Main St. (655-3354).

Downtown, Old Town

One of the few remaining neighborhood retreats indigenous to downtown is the *Golden Dragon Cafe*, 324 SW 3rd (223-9669), which was established more than half a century ago when Chinatown occupied much of what is now downtown. That there is so little remaining of that Chinese neighborhood is difficult to believe because in the 1890s, Portland's Chinatown numbered 10,000 or 48 percent of the population and was crowded into an area bounded by Front, 3rd, Salmon, and Ash. Now, what remains of Chinatown is in Old Town, where two Chinese groceries, *Tuck Lung* (223-1090) at the southeast corner of NW 4th and Davis, and *Fong Chong* (223-1777), at NW 4th and Everett, thrive. Tuck Lung serves lunch and dinner. *Erickson's Cafe* at NW 3rd and Burnside, once known as a working men's bar, could be considered native to Old Town but is definitely out of step today, with the rejuvenation process catering to tourists rather than Skid Road inhabitants.

In the heart of today's downtown, where the neighborhood feeling is being encouraged by the city in the hope that more people will make their homes there, gathering places are as wholesome as the *Multnomah County Library* and the *YWCA*, 1111 SW 10th (223-6281), and as alluring as *Jake's* (see Restaurants) on a weekend night when singles congregate there. *Chuck's* (also see Restaurants) is another such hangout, as are the *Brasserie Montmartre*, 626 SW Park (224-5552), *Paddy's*, 65 SW Yamhill (224-5626), where the hors d'oeuvres are the talk of the town, and *Key Largo*, 31 NW 1st (223-9919).

The bureaucrats like to eat Eggs O'Connor at *O'Connor's*, 529 SW 4th (228-0854). A renaissance in shake-making is occurring at the *Bijou Cafe*, SW 3rd and Oak (222-3187), where downtowners flock for lunch. For downtown picnicking, O'Bryant Square, the South Park Blocks, the Plaza Blocks, Ira's Fountain, Pettygrove Park, and Lovejoy Fountain are favorites. In the Portland Center, *La Fontana*, 1975 SW 1st (222-1417), is convenient. Delicatessens and sidewalk food in the downtown core are plentiful, but one of the best buys is at the *Downtown Deli*, 345 SW Yamhill (227-0202).

Northwest

With a long history of organized neighborhood activity and many successful restorations occurring there, the northwest area hosts more popular haunts than can be mentioned here. Among them, the long-established, respectable *Henry Thiele's* at NW 23rd and Burnside (223-2060) commands a steady clientele, especially for its German pancakes, as do the *Foothill Broiler* (see Restaurants) and the *Lovejoy Tavern*, 2074 NW Lovejoy (227-4270), each with its own style of hamburger cookery. Other popular eateries are *Northwest Breadline*, 2301 NW Kearney (222-2666), *Wheel of Fortune*, 1201 NW 21st (228-7528), noted for its soups and bread, and *Eat Your Heart Out*, 831 NW 23rd, primarily a caterer but unbeatable for salads and hot dishes served at lunchtime. The late-night crowd meets at the *Long Goodbye* at 300 NW 10th (228-1008) and at the *Earth Tavern* (see Entertainment).

The spacious auditorium at the *Northwest Service Center* on NW Everett between 18th and 19th (formerly a Christian Science church) is used for a variety of entertainments and community events. On Wednesday and Friday nights the floor below reverberates with the sounds of "BINGO."

At the *Old Portland Post Office Cafe*, NW Broadway and

Glisan (224-6808), neighbors, friends, and employees of the area dominated by the main post office gather for "hush puppies" with their coffee. These deep-fried cornmeal fritters, flavored with onion and herbs, are best eaten with molasses or honey.

Guided Tours

Port of Portland

The story goes that sea captains sailed to the fresh-water Port of Portland to rid their encrusted ships' bottoms of the barnacles that slowed them down.

While barnacles can't survive fresh water, it isn't the reason that today Portland harbor is among the West Coast's largest.

The many facilities which the port offers shippers are the magnet, and the casual visitor or the resident can see many of these by courtesy of the port, which offers tours on a regular basis in the summer.

You'll see: the big ships which bring the world to Portland from such far-off places as Japan, Italy, and Germany and which take away Oregon's main agricultural bounty—lumber and wheat—as well as products from other parts of the country; and five marine terminals, two of them near downtown. The port's berths total 29.

While efficiency and containerism have taken some of the romance out of a visit to a large port, you can still see general cargo loaded and get close to the sights and sounds of shipping.

The two downtown terminals are on NW Front, north of the Fremont Bridge. For safety reasons, they are closed to pedestrian traffic.

In the "good weather months," as the port puts it, a free guided tour leaves the Sheraton Motor Inn at 1 p.m. every Tues. and Wed. and the Hilton Hotel at 2 p.m. every Wed. and Thurs. Phone 231-5000 for required reservations.

For other months of the year, group tours may be arranged by calling the same number. These tours may be scheduled Mon.-Fri. Groups must provide their own transportation. The tours are all guided by port personnel and are free.

For a do-it-yourself tour, recommended by the port, travel north on I-5 to the Marine Drive West exit. Follow the signs and stop at the check-in gate, where you will be directed to the observation tower and administration building of Terminal 6, the port's newest terminal and the most modern container facility in the Pacific Northwest. There three 50-ton Hitachi cranes handle large truck-size steel containers of goods. In this same area are the **Rivergate Industrial District**, a former swampland which is being filled by port dredgings, and Kelley Point Park.★

Terminal 4 in St. Johns is the most diversified facility, handling autos, lumber and logs, steel, containers, and bulks.

Terminal 5 is home of the fastest grain elevator in the lower Columbia-Willamette region.

Terminal 3 doesn't exist. A small municipal dock in St. Johns was designated No. 3 when that community was annexed into Portland in 1915. The dock was torn down when the St. Johns Bridge was built.

At Swan Island is the **Portland Ship Repair Yard**, located on a 125-acre tract of land at the northern tip of the island in the center of the Willamette River harbor. The yard includes four floating drydocks. The shipyard was acquired by the port following World War II. During the war years, about one ship a week was produced there. A new drydock, the largest floating drydock on the West Coast, became operational January, 1979. Swan Island is reached via the I-5 freeway by taking the Swan Island exit. Take #71 bus right to the drydock. From downtown, catch a #2 on the 6th Ave. Mall at *Fish* stops and transfer to #71 north of Going at Bess Kaiser Hospital. The #71 stop is across the street.

Sometimes, from a vantage point at **Henry P. McCarthy Park** on Swan Island, you can see the sternwheeler *Portland,* the only steam-powered sternwheel towboat in the world. The 219-foot boat, which is often at work on the river, gives vital leverage when moving ships against the Willamette River current. It is equipped with seven rudders. The port maintains the steamer not only because she is useful but as a tribute to an era when the Willamette and Columbia Rivers were crowded with sternwheelers hauling cargo into the Columbia Basin and carrying passengers to seaside resorts.

The park is located between the Ports O'Call building and the Freightliner corporate headquarters building.

Portland International Airport

Daily one-hour tours are conducted at Portland International Airport, also operated by the Port of Portland. For tour reservations call 231-5000, ext. 422. A slide presentation and walking tour are featured; group arrangements can be made—for third graders and up.

To get there: Take I-84 to NE 82nd, travel north on 82nd and follow the signs to the airport. By bus take #14 on 6th Ave. Mall at *Raindrop* stops to NE Sandy and 82nd. Transfer to a #72 which goes directly to the airport.

The Port of Portland also operates Portland-Hillsboro Airport and Portland-Troutdale Airport.

Airplane rides can be arranged by calling Aurora Aviation in Aurora (222-1754); Hillsboro Aviation at Portland-Hillsboro Airport (648-6631); Western Skyways, Inc., at Troutdale (665-1181).

Gray Line Tours

Tours to Mt. Hood, the Columbia River Gorge, and the Oregon Coast as well as city tours are offered by the Gray Line (226-6755).

By bus, sightseers may choose a trip to Mt. Hood via the gorge, a visit to Timberline Lodge, and an all-day trip to the coast, among others.

Winter and summer schedules differ, so it's important to obtain the latest Gray Line flyer or to phone.

Boat Tours

Tours aboard the *Columbia Sightseer* are sometimes offered in the spring and fall in the Portland area. These package tours are advertised. For more information call the Port of Cascade Locks (1-374-8474). Both the *Columbia Sightseer* and the *Cruise-Ader Princess* from Yachts-O-Fun Cruises (285-6665) are available for charters (the *Sightseer*, only in the spring and fall because in the summer months it keeps a regular sightseeing schedule in the Columbia Gorge—see Getting Away from it All).

Portland Walking Tours

Portland Walking Tours, operated by a group of vivacious women who have done their historical and architectural homework, offers four 2-hour tours for groups of 10 or more.

On each of the tours the guides discuss history, city planning, art and architectural styles, inner-city problems and solutions, and significant buildings, both old and new. Cost is $3 per person.

The four choices are "Old Portland," which features the terra cotta and cast-iron detail on historic buildings, the Waterfront Park, the Architectural Preservation Gallery, craft and boutique shops; "City Walk," covering the central downtown core, Pioneer Courthouse, Portland Mall, Willamette Center, and City Hall; "City Walk South," including the urban renewal area south of downtown, the Halprin fountains, parks, gardens, and Portland State University; and "Northwest Portland," showing renovation of Victorian houses and several churches, including Trinity Episcopal, where the tour begins and ends.

For more information, call or write Portland Walking Tours, P.O. Box 4322, Portland, 97208 (223-1017).

Portland Walking Tours also provides guides on bus tours of the city, Columbia Gorge, Mt. Hood Loop, and the Oregon Coast. Bus and walk combinations to see special places like the Grotto, Pittock Mansion, Forestry Center (admission charges, if any, to be paid by the group) can be arranged. The fee for this service varies with the time required, starting with a minimum of $30 per guide.

During the summer months, the *Urban Tour Group*, which conducts walking tours for Portland school children the rest of the year, opens its program to the public, scheduling group tours of Old Town, downtown, and the Portland Mall. For additional information, call 232-7241 or 228-1505 (adult tours).

Note: *Circling the City*, "a guide to the accessibility of public places in and near Portland, Oregon," compiled and published by *The Junior League of Portland* (297-6364), is an excellent resource for handicapped and elderly sightseers.

Industrial Tours

Oregon business and industry offer tours of their operations, some to groups only and some to groups and individuals.

Blitz-Weinhard Co.—1133 W. Burnside (222-4351). The complete brewing process from hops to bottle is covered in this one-hour tour of the oldest brewery west of the Mississippi River. The tour includes a slide show at the beginning and refreshments—beer, if you're over 21, pop if you're not—in the brewery's attractive hospitality room. Tours Mon.-Fri. at 1, 2:30, and 4 p.m. No need to call ahead unless for a group of more than 10. Group tours for adults at night must be arranged for 6 months in advance.

ESCO Corp.—2141 NW 25th (228-2141, ext. 371). Tours of the ESCO foundry operation are limited to groups of high school age and older. A slide presentation is also given. Arrangements must be made in advance.

First National Bank—1300 SW 5th (225-2361). A general banking tour is available to groups no smaller than five or larger than 15. Tour includes a trip to the observation area on the 29th floor of Portland's tallest building. In addition, First National offers tours of its art collection of over 400 pieces. Call at least a week in advance to arrange for either tour.

Goodwill Industries—1831 SE 6th (238-6133). This interesting tour visits the facilities where disabled persons rehabilitate your old castoffs. Tours are given anytime before 2 p.m. daily and there is no age limitation. Visitors see shoes being sorted, furniture reconditioning, the cleaning and laundry operation, the print shop, and the assembly and packaging division which does subcontract work for Northwest industries—everything from testing beachballs to packaging chocolate-scented toys.

Hoody Corp.—5555 SW 107th, Beaverton (646-0555). See Hoody peanut butter, jam, mustard, and vinegar in the making on this tour designed for groups of second-grade age and older. You'll also learn that Hoody produces for a number of other familiar labels. Peanuts are screened, cleaned, and squashed on tour. Visitors receive a bag of peanuts as a souvenir. Groups are limited in size to 15 and must start the tour before 2:30 p.m. Call in January for reservations for this popular tour. All available tour times for the entire year are booked the first month.

Ice Cream Saloon—3815 SW Murray Rd., Beaverton, at Tualatin Valley Highway (643-1881). A dish of the ice cream you've seen in the making is the finale for this tour, limited to school and youth groups. Phone ahead. Tour days are Tues., Wed., Thurs. Ice Cream Saloon is also a restaurant serving lunch and dinner. It is closed Mon.

KATU (Channel 2)—2153 NE Sandy (231-4222, tours; 231-4610, *A.M. Northwest* tickets). For a tour of this ABC network station, call at least 2 weeks in advance for a reservation. In addition to the tour, KATU also offers tickets to *A.M. Northwest*, with Jim Bosley and Margie Boule. Call a week ahead for tickets to the Mon.-Fri. 9 a.m. live telecast featuring local and national personalities on a variety of topics.

KBPS (1450 radio)—546 NE 12th, in the Benson High School auditorium (234-5469). Call ahead to arrange for a tour of the Portland Public Schools station.

McDonald's Hamburgers—9475 SW Beaverton-Hillsdale Highway, Beaverton (646-1816). This is one of 14 McDonald's restaurants in the Portland area. If another is closer to you, chances are it gives tours, too. One of the most popular youth group tours, this one inspects every square inch of the McDonald's operation. At the end, the store supplies each visitor with a hamburger and a shake or soft drink—free. Hats are also provided. The Beaverton McDonald's gives one tour a week, so call at least a month ahead for a reservation.

Memorial Coliseum—1401 N. Wheeler (235-8771). While known best as the home of the Trail Blazers (National Basketball Assn.), the big glass box on the east side near the Broadway Bridge is in almost constant use providing space and seating for everything from ice shows to boat shows. Seating capacity is 13,000 (9,000 permanent seats). Group tours only are given by appointment.

Nabisco, Inc.—100 NE Columbia Blvd. (285-2571, ext. 16). Nabisco's famous Oreo cookies and Premium crackers are made from the raw ingredients and packaged at this plant, which offers tours by appointment Tues. and Thurs. at 1:15 p.m. Tours are limited to groups (sixth grade and up) of 25 or less. Nabisco asks that you confirm your request to tour by letter. Tours are offered between Oct. and May only and are usually booked for the year by October.

Oak Knoll Winery, Inc.—Burkhalter Rd., Route 4, Box 186, Hillsboro (648-8198). Visitors are invited to take a self-guided tour through the winery and grounds to see how wine is made. After the visit, those 21 years or older are invited to the tasting room. The winery is open from 2-6 p.m. Thurs., Fri. and Sun. and from 11 a.m.-6 p.m. Sat. Groups must call ahead.

Oregon Humane Society—1067 NE Columbia Blvd. (285-0643). As popular a part of the tour here as the dogs and cats is a visit to the barnyard to feed the farm animals and poultry which the society has accepted from persons who could no longer keep them. The farm animals are not readopted as are the dogs and cats but are kept in the barnyard to give urban children the experience of seeing, touching, and feeding them. Visitors are invited to come with stale bread and vegetables for the barnyard pets. Gifts of dog biscuits and cat food are also welcomed. Also on the itinerary is a visit to the pet cemetery, the only one in the Portland area. Flowers and wreaths are regularly delivered to many of the graves which have been purchased for beloved pets. Children get a chance to hold and pet the puppies while on tour. The society offers tours for groups of 10 to 60—and asks that you call for an appointment two weeks ahead. Programs on pet care and responsible ownership are presented in the society's education auditorium as part of the tour. Groups under 10 are welcome to visit from 9 a.m.-5:45 p.m. Mon.-Sat. and 9 a.m.-4:45 p.m. Sun.

Oregon Journal and Oregonian—1320 SW Broadway (221-8336). A press run of the *Oregon Journal* at the Oregonian Publishing Co.'s offset plant at SW 16th and Taylor is part of this tour for high school and college students 9th grade or older. After the press run, the group provides its own transportation to the two newspapers' offices at 1320 SW Broadway for tours of both newsrooms and display advertising, classified, and other departments. The tour, which starts at 1 p.m., lasts 2-2½ hours and is limited to groups of 10-15. Call for an appointment at least one month ahead for the Tues. or Thurs. tour.

Pendleton Woolen Mills—(226-4801, ext 378). See fine woolen sportswear produced from raw wool on tours of these two Portland-area facilities of this famous old Oregon company. No appointments necessary unless for a large group. Children under 12 must be accompanied by parents.

Washougal Weaving Plant, No. 2, 17th St., Washougal, Wash. One-hour tours at 10 a.m. and 1:30 p.m. Mon.-Fri. view the complete process which the cleaned wool undergoes—dyeing, spinning, carding, and weaving into the finished fabric. When the fabric leaves this plant, it's on bolts, ready for the store or garment factory.

Milwaukie Garment Factory, 10505 SE 17th, Milwaukie. Complete construction of a man's shirt, from cutting to boxing, is viewed by tours at 10 a.m. and 1 p.m. Tours last 45 minutes.

All of the Pendleton tours are limited to 25. Large groups who wish to make appointments for Pendleton tours should call at least two weeks ahead. The famous Pendleton blankets are made at the company's Pendleton, Ore., facility.

Portland Air Base—5501 NE Cornfoot Rd. (288-5611, ext. 306). Aero-space education tours for high school age youth must be booked far in advance. This excellent tour visits the shops and maintenance area at the base and explores educational opportunities of an air career.

Portland Fire Bureau—55 SW Ash (232-8135). Television's crises are daily routine for the men at the Central Fire Station, and they're happy to tell visitors all about it. An elaborately outfitted emergency vehicle leaves children wide-eyed. Call ahead for a date and time.

Post Office—Main office, 715 NW Hoyt (221-2363). This 1½-hour tour, for fourth-grade age and up, visits workroom floors where mail is sorted both mechanically and by hand as well as other parts of the postal operation. You'll see why it's important to zip-code your mail when you watch the "zip mail translator" in action. Call ahead for a reservation, but avoid the end or beginning of each month, the busiest days at the post office. If you're looking for a postal tour for younger children, try calling one of the branches.

Publishers Paper—419 Main St., Oregon City (656-5211). Newsprint for the daily papers is made here as well as paper toweling. Wood goes in and paper comes out. You see it all on tours Wed. at 2 p.m. The tours accept walk-ins but call ahead if you're arranging for a group. Minimum age for the tour is 12.

Reynold's Metals Co.—Sun Dial Rd., Troutdale (248-1111). At Reynold's Troutdale Reduction Plant you can see aluminum oxide reduced into primary aluminum through an electrolytic process. The molten aluminum is then cast into various ingot sizes. Call ahead to arrange for group tours of the plant during the work week. No one under 12.

Rose's Bake Shop—35 NW 20th Pl. (227-4875). Tours of this very special bakery operation can be arranged for groups by calling two weeks ahead. The shop is known for its spec-tacular chocolate cakes, giant-sized cinnamon buns, and braided breads.

Trojan Nuclear Plant—Rainier, Ore. (1-556-4741; from Portland: 226-8510). Trojan Visitors Center at Oregon's first nuclear generating plant features exhibits which explain the story of nuclear energy. Visitors may also see the Ecosphere, a multi-dimensional film which looks at man and his relationship to natural energies. At conclusion of the tour, test your nuclear knowledge at a bank of computers. Special guided tours for groups may be made by calling ahead. Trojan is on U. S. 30, 42 miles north and west of Portland. Landmark is its 499-ft. cool-ing tower. Continuous tours are given 5 days a week, Wed.-Sun., in fall and winter, and seven days a week Mar.-Aug. Tour is not recommended for children under 5. Hours of the center are 9:30 a.m.-5 p.m., Mon.-Sat., and noon-6 p.m., Sun. They are extended slightly during the summer months. Adults visiting Trojan must carry identification, such as a driver's license; children must be accompanied by a group leader or parent.

U.S. National Bank★—Main Branch, 321 SW 6th (225-5156). Main branch tour, lasting one hour, shows visitors the elegant Romanesque building with shiny marble columns

and coffered ceiling displaying "U. S." eagles in the frieze
work; the revered board of directors' room; the international
banking section; and the world behind the teller's window. The
building is maintained exactly as it was when it was new. The
first half was built in 1917; the second in 1924. Architect was
A. E. Doyle, who also designed the Central Library. Phone
ahead. Group tours only.

Waterway Terminals Co.— 3838 NW Front (226-6901).
Call ahead for Mon.-Fri. tours of this public warehouse and
marine terminal, where Northwest products are prepared for
shipment and loaded. The one-hour tour visits the company's
21-acre warehouse and views some of its fleet of 120 lift trucks
in action. Children must be 12 or older.

Indian guide Sacajawea, who led Lewis and Clark expedition to Oregon, points the way for contemporary explorers
to Washington Park in this bronze by Alice cooper.

Photo: Greater Portland Convention and Visitors' Assn.

RESTAURANTS

From champagne to cola;
hamburgers to hollandaise

THE ABILITY to recall a taste sensation," writes native Portlander James Beard, "is a God-given talent."

This international master of the palate, who honed his taste buds as a child in Portland's liveliest kitchens and finest restaurants, cutting his teeth on Edwardian pound cake at the Benson Hotel and paupiettes of sole sprinkled with tiny Olympia oysters at Henry Thiele's, now lives in New York City.

But like all Portland residents, his heart remains where his stomach was fed best, in Portland—gateway to the lush Willamette Valley and its bountiful produce, doorway to the Columbia River where the chinook and silver salmon run, and setting for the finest sea-fresh delicacies prepared and served anywhere on earth.

In Portland many become experts in taste sensation.

Doug Baker, columnist for the *Oregon Journal,* writes lovingly of his own River Place where the reward for cutting up an old alder tree is a steelhead, caught that misty morning by his wife, a good bottle of wine chilled at riverbank, and a mellow slab of well-aged cheese. (More of Doug's impressions appear in *River Place, One Man's Search for Serenity,* Timber Press, 1980.)

From pert to imperious, Portland's restaurant business continues to grow abundantly and imaginatively, tempting the most indifferent diner. Although the city does not claim a "restaurant row," residents have learned to look to its side streets as well as some unlikely areas for imaginative dining.

Even before the flowers began to bloom along downtown Portland's new Transit Mall, a bright new crop of unique eateries blossomed. Regulars to the Southwest streets have their favorite hot pretzel vendor or hot dog stand, and new window signs every day call mall munchers in to investigate yet another fast sandwich outlet. Many are excellent, and the products they offer draw nearly as much comment as the new mall sculpture.

Portland claims two virtuosi in the restaurant business, and it would be as difficult to favor one over the other as it is to choose Haydn before Beethoven.

John Rian is a sophisticated conservative, who quietly opens his finest eating establishment on Thanksgiving to seat only the Skid Road homeless. He orchestrates his dining spots with the surprising twists of a true Haydn: fish fried according to an old English family recipe, salads with the bite of romaine, unusual sandwich ingredients tucked into pocket bread, and fresh Dungeness crab when all other kitchens have run dry.

Horst Mager, on the other hand, casts his Beethoven spell grandly over each of his eating places, giving each an opulent theme—one totally different from the other, from furnishings to herbs and sauces. This energetic Germanic chef has become a household name after presiding daily over a televised stove where he whacked, whisked, and slipped wondrous combinations out of the pan and onto a plate in living color.

Both have played a major part in the inspiration of finer eating in the Portland area.

While this list is by no means complete, it holds most of the best meals offered in the Portland area.

Abernethy's—1239 SW Broadway (228-3455) snuggles up to the side of the Oregon Historical Society with its doors facing the Oregonian-Oregon Journal building. Although the food is good, the ambience is at the tables which draw from a great cross section of Portland's famous and infamous. Look for a well-known priest sitting back to back with the city's leading newspaper reporters, historians waiting for a table while the town's dowagers sip a noon glass of sherry. Sandwiches, casseroles. Open Mon.-Sat., 11 a.m.-2:30 a.m.; Sun. 5 p.m.-2:30 a.m. Liquor. Credit cards. Moderate.

Abou Karim—221 SW Pine (223-5058) serves an outstanding lunch and light meals from 11 a.m. to 7 p.m. Mon.-Fri. in the newly remodeled Porter Hotel. The catchy menu is Lebanese and is converting most office workers in the downtown area. Moderate.

Ainsworth's—6443 SW Beaverton Hillsdale Hwy. (297-1889). Abernethy's (named for an Oregon territorial governor) and Ainsworth's both offer the same considerate and intelligent service coupled with innovative menus. Look for the halibut florentine at Ainsworth's—a tribute to the sea captain who brought more than his ship to early Portland. Mon.-Sat. 11 a.m.-2:30 a.m., Sun. 5 p.m.-2:30 a.m. Liquor and wine. Moderate.

Aldo's Trattoria—824 SW 1st (241-2550). Sit out in the back patio if you need a quiet talk, but the Italian food is outstanding here, including Veal Picatina, fettucini and an Italian spinach and cheese pie. Wide variety of Italian wines. Lush but comfortable atmosphere. Lunch and dinner. Liquor. Closed Sunday. Credit cards. Reservations. Moderate to expensive.

Austin's Place—8209 SE 13th (232-4364) is just up the narrow staircase across from the Sellwood Boy's Club. Stop by during an afternoon of antiquing in Sellwood's unique second-hand district, to enjoy Austin's own cream of broccoli soup (the mainstay) or the soup of the day along with a sweet (cheesecake) prepared in the home of a master baker. Closed Sun. and Mon. Wine. No credit cards. Inexpensive.

Bart's Wharf and Marina—3829 NE Marine Dr. (288-6161). Closed Mon. The rest of the week you can pick out your own fresh Maine lobster from the tank which greets you at the door. Seafood is the specialty, and the view (if you can get a table by the window) is of the Columbia River, sailboats, houseboats, and the jets landing at the airport. Complete bar. Reservations suggested. Lunches and dinners. Credit cards. Expensive.

Belinda's—8324 SE 17th (232-6606) grows its own fresh herbs out back and features delightful French dining. The house paté serves the table plus some to be taken home. Salads are blended with fresh herbs and fresh Wisconsin roquefort. Entrees include veal, beef, and fresh seafood. The wine list is probably the finest in the state. Dinners Tues.-Sat. Reservations suggested. Credit cards. Moderate to expensive.

Benihana of Tokyo—315 SW 4th (226-4754). If you don't want to share your Japanese-modern meal with strangers, take 6 or 8 friends along, although the food is well worth the lack of privacy. An ideal spot for children who can't sit still at a meal. The swinging cleavers will hold them spellbound or terrified, depending upon their temperament. Bar. Reservations required. Lunch and dinner. Moderate. Credit cards.

Brasserie Montmartre—626 SW Park (224-5552). The decor sets the mood for dining here. You'll think you have stepped into a 1930 black and white musical. Dinner and luncheon served in the French style to live music. Parking is validated, but distant. Hors d'oeuvres and pastries served all hours. Wine and liquor with a large bar. Reservations suggested. Credit cards. Expensive.

Bush Garden—900 SW Morrison (226-7181). Traditional Japanese food; wear clean socks—you must remove your shoes. Reservations advised. Cocktails. Credit cards. Moderate.

Captain's Corner—1201 SW 12th (224-9877). Owner-host Barney Giansante makes this one of the most popular lunch spots in town for businessmen. Dinners are also excellent. Don't expect a view; there are no windows. Best for adults because there will be a wait. Reservations. Closed Sun. Liquor. Credit cards. Moderate.

Carnival—2805 SW Sam Jackson Park Rd. (227-4244). Hamburgers and hot dogs done on the charcoal broiler. On a hot summer night you can dine by the waterfall outside. Excellent for children with its cafeteria-style do-it-yourself service. Homemade pies, cookies, and ice cream come last in the line-up. Lunch and supper. Closed Sun. No liquor. No credit cards. Inexpensive.

Caro-Amico Pizzeria—3605 SW Barbur Blvd. (223-6895). The godfather of all Portland pizzerias. There may be some heated arguments in the kitchen but it's all in the family and you'll still get fine pizza as well as spaghetti and ravioli. Children welcome. Cocktails. No credit cards. Moderate.

Chez Moustache—224 Hwy. 99E, Aurora (1-678-1866). Former White House chef stirs up miracles in this tiny Willamette Valley historic town Tues.-Sat. The prices are moderate and the entrees, at the chef's whim, are superlative. Reservations are a must. Plan ahead for a special experience. Wine. Moderate.

Chow's—329 SW 2nd, Lake Oswego (636-0331). When the owner reads the Chinese newspaper in the rear booth with his tea, you know you've found the right neighborhood restaurant. Most regulars order lunch or dinner from the Chinese menu, but hamburgers are available. Food to go. Beer. Credit cards. Moderate.

Chuck's—823 SW Front (226-0256). Steak, seafood, hamburgers, and sandwiches served with some unusual side orders and coffees in this dinner house. Parking can be difficult in this area, but the meals served here are worth the extra steps. Liquor. Credit cards. No reservations. Moderate to expensive.

Cisco and Pancho's—107 NW 5th (223-5048). This is a Mexican restaurant the children will like. Adults come for the Margueritas. Californian-style Mexican food is served for lunch Mon.-Fri., and dinner Sun.-Thurs. Wine, beer, and cactus. Moderate.

Couch Street Fish House—105 NW 3rd (223-6173) is open for dinners only and is, without doubt, one of the finest Oregon spots for elegant dining and seafood. Master chef Horst Mager proves himself especially able as he supervises the careful preparation of a wide variety of fresh-daily seafood. Fresh Maine lobsters are standard, but look for the unusual as in the delicate bits of sole gently simmered and turned between two tablespoons in a fine wine sauce, then lightly covered with an ethereal shrimp sauce. Liquor. Reservations. Credit cards. Expensive.

Dan & Louis' Oyster Bar—208 SW Ankeny (227-5906). An institution in Portland. Dine on oyster stew or clam chowder from 11 a.m.-1 a.m. 7 days a week. Take the children, they will love the decor. No liquor. No reservations. Credit cards. Inexpensive.

Dandelion Pub—31 NW 23rd Pl. (223-0099). Hearty sandwiches with beer or wine. No children. Closed Sun. No credit cards. Inexpensive.

Dave's Delicatessen—445 SW Yamhill (222-5461). New accommodations for this kosher-clean eatery. Dave has moved his food, lox, stock, and bagel, and continues to serve followers from 6 a.m.-7 p.m. Mon.-Sat. Take out service. No credit cards. Inexpensive.

Delevans—1425 NE Glisan (224-5597) offers it all: light meals, full course meals, serviche, carpaccio, prosciutto and oysters on the half shell. There's a piano in the bar on the main floor and no pipes or cigars upstairs in the dining room, please. The building is an old firehouse and the kitchen responds to a four-alarm menu with orders ranging from Italian sausage to huevos rancheros. It all meshes elegantly much to the delight of its many devotees who have discovered that you can have your cake and eat it too at Delevans. Open Mon.-Sat. 11:30 a.m. to 2 a.m. Credit cards. Liquor and wine. Moderate to expensive.

Delphina's—2112 NW Kearney (221-1195). Makes all its own pasta and sells it to other restaurants, but you might as well get it fresh here. Pizza on the menu as well. Open seven nights a week for dinner, lunches Mon.-Fri. Wine. Inexpensive to moderate.

Digger O'Dell's—532 SE Grand (238-6996). Two young Portland businessmen are renovating east side buildings to provide low income housing. They also provide a sense of humor with the inclusion of this seafood and oyster bar in a refurbished mortuary on the main level of the Barber Block. Seafood with a creole flair is the lure here and one of the premier guests was Rosalynn Carter during her Portland visit. Elegantly served dishes by bright waiters are making this a landmark once again. Lunch Mon.-Fri., dinner every night. Liquor and wine. Credit cards. Moderate to expensive.

Don Elton—340 N. State St. Alley, Lake Oswego (636-3702). One of a kind. Owner D.E. Foss has decorated freely, and each room is filled with his eclectic tastes as is his menu. A favorite with Lake Oswego matrons who wait for dessert and the special chocolate cake. Sandwiches, fried chicken, seafood. Closed Sun. Wine. No credit cards. Moderate.

Eat Your Heart Out—831 NW 23rd (222-6111). This is a catering service with kindness. Open at 7 a.m. for fresh brioche, they also serve lunch not only in Portland but at the old post office on the coast at Gearhart. Everyone has a favorite, but the full course menu varies daily. Call the manager, Sandy, if you can't wait for another serving of fresh tomatoes tossed with black olives and fetta cheese or your current favorite. No liquor. No credit cards. Moderate.

Elephant and Castle—201 SW Washington (222-5698). Traditional English pub atmosphere complete with fish and chips and dart board. No credit cards. Inexpensive.

Farrell's Ice Cream Parlour restaurants serve no alcohol and do not take credit cards, but you will find plenty of entertainment to go along with hamburgers, hot dogs, and ice cream. Great for children. Portland is the home of this fast-growing chain which exploits the all-American American. Visit them for lunch or supper at:
Washington Square (639-1883)
1600 NE 122nd (255-5776)
4955 SW 76th (292-9103)
1613 NE Weidler (281-1271)

Foothill Broiler—33 NW 23rd Pl. (223-0287). Hamburgers, hot soup, and homemade pies with orders to go. If you take in your own pie pan, the owners will bake you a wild blackberry pie for your next dinner. Good for lunch or early supper. Closed Sun. Take the children as they are. No credit cards. No liquor. Inexpensive.

Forest Inn at Aldercreek—(phone 668-6079 toll-free from Portland). Portland diners travel just through Sandy toward Mt. Hood on U.S. 26 to enjoy the sumptuous menu offered at this old favorite. Entrees include stuffed abalone steak, fillet of Columbia River salmon, steaks, veal Cordon Bleu, and tornedos Rossini. Reservations are a must for dinners served seven days a week; open at 5:30 weekdays and 4 p.m. on Sun. Wine, liquor. Credit cards. Moderate to expensive.

4 & 20 Blackbirds—455 SW 2nd, Lake Oswego (635-4312) specializes in quiche, salads, and home made breads. The only constant selection on the daily menu is its famous tomato tart. Open from 9:30 a.m. to 3 p.m., this former Ward's catalog ordering site, converted with a flair, draws a large crowd daily to see what's new on the menu. Wine. No credit cards. Closed Sunday. Moderate.

Gazebo—4 SW Mt. Jefferson Terr., Lake Oswego (635-2506). Wine served to guitar accompaniment on weekend evenings. Treat yourself to a tree-house perch with a view of all the mountains. Lunches and dinners Tues.-Sat., Sun. brunch. Wine. Credit cards. Moderate.

Genoa—2832 SE Belmont (238-1464) has a recipe for tomato soup which begins "Start with a lot of onions," which should give you an idea of the originality of the northern Italian menu. Do not take children, since this is leisurely dining for a few. Reservations are a must. Open Tues.-Sat. for dinners only. Wine. No credit cards. Moderate.

Goose Hollow Inn—1927 SW Jefferson (228-7010) is probably the most crusading tavern in the city. When the bartenders aren't raising funds for a worthy cause or holding "smokeless Mondays," they are thinking up something else, much to the delight of the regulars and drop-ins who enjoy the sandwiches here. Inexpensive.

Granberg's—811 SW 6th (241-8242) is the poor man's view restaurant on the 12th floor of the Executive Building. Open 7 a.m. to 4 p.m. Monday through Friday for breakfast, soups, sandwiches, and desserts cafeteria style. The charm of the place is its quiet atmosphere with a view of downtown landscapes through floor to ceiling windows. At the south end there's even a set of sofas for a few minutes of quiet sitting. No liquor. Inexpensive.

Grandma's Table—12255 SW Denney Rd., Beaverton (644-2372) lets today's grandmother keep her date for bridge and still take her youngsters to dinner farm-family style with chicken and dumplings, barbecued ribs, spaghetti, and steaks. Soups come by the tureen and salads by the large bowl at this ideal spot for families with varying appetites. Brunch is served Sun. from 9 a.m. to noon, lunches and dinners, Mon.-Sat. Liquor. Reservations. Credit cards. Moderate.

Harris Wine Cellars, Ltd.—2300 NW Thurman (223-2222). The late Bert Harris brought wine and a little culture to Portland some 20 years ago and his students still practice his art. A new generation has discovered the new shop which includes a comfortable spot for sandwiches washed down with fine vintages. A good place to sit, sip, talk, and select a few bottles for the cellar at home. Closed Sun. Inexpensive.

Helvetia Tavern—on Helvetia Rd., 2 miles off U.S. 26 going west, is drawing some unlikely customers as the word spreads that they serve a meal-sized hamburger with a difference. Good stopping place on the way home from the beach. Beer. No credit cards. Inexpensive.

Hilaire's Restaurant—622 SW Washington (223-5192) is close to becoming a landmark in Portland. Serving once again from the Washington St. entrance, after losing a lease on the other corner, Larry Hilaire keeps businessmen happy at lunch and couples well fed during an early evening downtown. Fresh crab and quiche are just two of the specialties. Liquor. Credit cards. Moderate.

Horatio's—4850 SW Macadam (242-1460) offers old English pub dining right on the Willamette River. The British flag flies over everything here and the house specialty is Steak Horatio, top sirloin medallions covered with crab and surrounded by asparagus spears. The overstuffed chairs make this comfortable and the personal service guarantees that this is one slip on the Willamette due to stay. Liquor. Credit cards. Moderate to expensive.

Huber's—320 SW Stark (228-5686). If you want to eat in "old" Portland atmosphere, this is the one. For lunch or supper, Huber's reputation has long been based upon turkey and cole slaw as well as prime rib. Closed Sun. Liquor. Credit cards. Moderate.

Ice Cream Saloon—3815 SW Murray Rd. in the K-Mart Shopping Center (643-1881). Makes its own ice cream on the spot as well as excellent sandwiches. Extra activities for active children. Lunch and dinner. No liquor. No credit cards. Closed Mon. Inexpensive.

Indigine—3725 SE Division (238-1470) is a sleeper in the

Portland restaurant business, and those who support this small spot like to keep the address a secret. Reservations are a must for dinners served Fri. and Sat. at 6 and 8:30 p.m. and Sun. brunches from 8 a.m.-2 p.m. Such care is taken with each meal that even the cinnamon rolls don't go into the oven until the customer is seated. No liquor. No credit cards. Moderate.

Jade West—122 SW Harrison (226-1128). Across from the Civic Auditorium with complimentary bus service for its pre-performance customers. Cantonese dining 7 days a week for lunch and dinner. Liquor. Credit cards. Moderate to expensive.

Jake's Famous Crawfish—401 SW 12th (226-1419). In Portland since 1892 with several managements although the magnificent bar and fine service are still intact. Seafood is the specialty. Liquor. Credit cards. Moderate.

Jasmine Tree—401 SW Harrison (223-7956). From the outside this looks like a typical neighborhood Chinese restaurant—but consider the neighborhood which encompasses all the newest high-rise apartments on the west side. Residents keep a former Trader Vic chef busy at his new post filling orders for Malaysian, Polynesian, and Indonesian lunches and dinners—each plate cooked to order. The menu also includes American food, Margaritas, and Mai Tais. Liquor. Credit cards. Moderate.

Joe's Warehouse Restaurant and Loading Dock Bar—12300 SE Mallard Way, Milwaukie (659-2640). A couple of slightly crazy Portland businessmen have underwritten this restaurant which stars Joe Colistro, long-time barber at Portland's Aero Club, and his pasta. The restaurant is located in the center of Omark Industrial Park with the menu also including seafood and steaks. This is all traditional enough, but diners are seated amid packing crates or urged to pull a stool up to a full size Freightliner truck, complete with air horn, which serves as a bar. Between the barber, the truck, and the food, this establishment offers everything. Open weekdays for lunch, with a delightful outside patio, Sat. and Sun. for dinner. Credit cards. Moderate.

John's Meatmarket—115 NW 22nd (223-2119). Good steak and soup with an intimate bar. Not for children. Open 7 days a week for dinner. Liquor. Credit cards. Moderate to expensive.

L'Auberge—2180 W. Burnside (223-3302). Open Tues.-Sat. for dinner. French cooking with menu adjusted to fresh market buys of the day. Wine. Credit cards. Moderate.

L'Escargot Restaurant—1987 NW Kearney (223-6964).

Reservations must be made here, since the seating is limited. But there's no limit to the imagination in this kitchen which may, at the chef's whim, offer two styles of French onion soup as an appetizer. Don't ask for your salad; a delightfully herbed blend of fresh greens will arrive after the main course. Lunches Mon.-Fri., dinners, Mon.-Sat. Liquor, wine. Credit cards. Moderate to expensive.

L'Omelette—815 SW Alder (248-9661). Rated by many as one of the best in the city for lunch or dinner. Comfortable atmosphere in the Mager manner. Reservations a must, even for lunch. Closed Sun. Liquor. Credit cards. Moderate to expensive.

London Grill—309 SW Broadway (228-9611). In the basement of the Benson Hotel. Open 7 days a week, breakfast through dinner with a Sunday champagne brunch. Excellent service and beautiful decor. Moderate to expensive. Liquor. Credit cards.

Marketplace—4F SW Monroe Parkway, Lake Oswego (635-3456). Lunches and dinners with a wide menu. Elegant, but suitable for children during early hours. Fine soups, steaks, and seafood. Liquor. Credit cards. Moderate to expensive.

Mazzi's—5833 SW Macadam (227-3382). Italian Sicilian food 7 days a week. This Portland branch is an offshoot of the original Eugene spot which later spread to Corvallis. Discerning college students keep both alive and the word has spread to Macadam. Pizza with a difference, excellent canneloni. Beer and wine. Inexpensive to moderate.

McCormick & Schmick's—2358 SW 1st at Oak (224-7522). This kissing cousin to Jake's offers a Bentley to chauffeur diners from one colorful restaurant to the other. Lunch and dinner include alder smoked fish, pastas, duck, and veal. House specialties on the appetizer list are fried calamari (squid) and fried mozzarella marinara. The French onion soup is superb. Liquor. Credit cards. Moderate to expensive.

Monte Carlo—1016 SE Belmont (235-9171). Seven days a week from 11 a.m.-2 a.m. The Italian businessmen still meet for lunch here, so it has to maintain its standards. Take the children for pizza. Dancing after 9 p.m. Full Italian menu. Liquor. Credit cards. Moderate.

Nendel's Inn—9900 SW Canyon Rd. (297-2551). This began as a "home fried chicken" family restaurant, and its owners must have pulled the right side of the wishbone. The restaurant, part of the luxury motel, continues to serve fine chicken as well as an excellent family menu. Sunday brunch. Liquor. Credit cards. Moderate.

Northwest Breadline Restaurant & Delicatessen—NW 23rd & Kearney (227-7478) is one of the brightest examples of youthful ingenuity. Not only do they run a fine deli (wines, kosher meats, English teas, and homemade desserts), but they serve a great hamburger alongside a slice of fresh fruit in the adjoining restaurant and, in addition, keep the nearby hospital patients supplied with good milkshakes and extra tidbits. Inexpensive.

Norton House—53 SW 1st (223-0743). Lunch and dinner daily with opera on Sunday have made this attractive addition to Old Town a regular for Portlanders. Fine weather friends enjoy a very private garden area in the summer. Limited, but choice, menu. Liquor. Credit cards. Moderate to expensive.

O'Connor's—529 SW 4th (228-0854) is a working man's bar which is attracting the 3-piece suit advertising crowd. The hamburgers are outstanding. Beer. No credit cards. Inexpensive.

Odyssey—State St., Lake Oswego (636-6359). Popular Portland chef Horst Mager is serving everything up in Mediterranean style at his establishment open on the lakefront. Boat moorage is just off the bar, where live music is offered nightly. Dinners from 5 p.m., Sunday brunch, music, and bar service until midnight weekdays and 2 a.m. Fri. & Sat. Liquor. Credit cards. Moderate to expensive.

Old Country Kitchen—10519 SE Stark (252-4171). If you are heading back from a day at Mt. Hood, take on the 72 oz. steak. If you can eat it all, it's yours for nothing. Good place for children and family dinners. Credit cards. Liquor. Reservations suggested on weekends. Moderate.

Old Spaghetti Factory—126 SW 2nd (222-5375). Spaghetti for everyone, served everywhere, even aboard an old street car, and no one cares if the children drop some pasta on the floor. Open for lunch and dinner. Liquor. No credit cards. Inexpensive.

Old Town Pizza Company—226 NW Davis (223-4447) serves pizza with a difference every day except Leonardo da Vinci's birthday. Diners are asked to design their own concoction, and it is served atop a thick, but light, yeast base. Wine and beer. No credit cards. Inexpensive.

Organ Grinder—5015 SE 82nd (771-1178). Open 7 days a week, from noon on Sun., 4 p.m. daily. Rube Goldberg would be proud of this multi-greeting of pipe organs, drums, and bubble machines which go into action as the pizza cooks. Kids love it, and the noise and commotion drown out the cries and whines of those who don't. Front row seats in the balcony give the best view of the magnificent music machine, but the bubbles drop front, right, and left, just behind the organist. No reservations. Beer and wine. No credit cards. Inexpensive.

Pancake House—8600 SW Barbur Blvd. (246-9007). Check first on this one, since the owners often take a month's vacation at a time. For this they are forgiven, since they offer some of the finest pancakes in town. No liquor. No credit cards. Inexpensive.

Paola's Pizza Barn—U.S. 26, Sandy (668-8058). Stop after a day of skiing on Mt. Hood to enjoy pizza in front of a roaring fire. Soft drinks and beer are served in canning jars, so don't bother to dress for this relaxed atmosphere. No credit cards. No reservations. Inexpensive.

Park Place—SW Front and Morrison (221-1271). The restaurant at Riverside West offers continental dining with a varied menu, well served in attractive surroundings. Lunch and dinner. Credit cards. Liquor and wine. Moderate to expensive.

Pizza Quarry—1229 SW 11th (222-2227). Pizza for lunch and pizza for dinner. For those who want a plate, there's a liberal assortment of the traditional ravioli and lasagne. And for those of age, jazz is alive in the bar. Liquor. Moderate.

Plainfield's Place—901 NW 21st (223-2995). Continental cuisine in a French country atmosphere. Lunch and dinner. Beer and wine. Moderate.

Portfolio—1300 SW 5th (224-4166) is yet another aerie for a luncheon glimpse of city. Located in the First National Bank Building, this restaurant keeps banker's hours except on Friday when cocktails are served until 10 p.m. Liquor. Credit cards. Moderate.

Rafters at Sellwood (The)—220 SE Spokane (238-7067) has one of the largest bars in the city and is a good meeting place for singles. Lunches, dinners, cocktails, and dancing are featured, and the menu includes steak and the chef's special seafood. The vegetables are especially well prepared. This restaurant faces the Willamette River, but planners have chosen an excellent view of the parking lot with the river peeking through the headlights. Not for children. Reservations suggested for those who are hungry. Credit cards. Moderate.

Rheinlander—5035 NE Sandy Blvd. (288-5503). Horst Mager's oldest restaurant in the city continues to purvey plain hokum and fancy German food. Steer the children away from the bottle of non-alcoholic wine; it is expensive. Otherwise moderate prices and overwhelming portions in the German tradition. All this is accompanied by an accordionist, a few yodels, and lots of fun. Reservations should be made. Liquor. Credit cards. Moderate.

Rian's Breadbasket—in the Standard Plaza (223-6111). Open Mon.-Fri. for lunch. Sandwiches, soup, and tamale pie are the favorites. Beer and wine. No credit cards. No reservations. Inexpensive.

Rian's Eating Establishment—through the wrought-iron gates between Park and Broadway in Morgan's Alley (222-9996). The dark-suit member of John Rian's restaurant successes. Closed Sun. Lunches and dinners served by some of the city's most charming young people. Look for quiche, onion soup, excellent steaks, and plenty of fresh Dungeness crab. Rian's ingenuity with food is matched only by his method for keeping his ferns fresh and green (one to show, one to go, and an even bigger one coming in on the next truck). Liquor. Credit cards. Moderate to expensive.

Rian's Fish and Ale House—66210 SW Beaverton-Hillsdale Hwy. (292-0191). The elder brother of this group, featuring an old Rian family recipe for deep-fried fish and chips. The menu has been broadened to include sandwiches and other seafood. Wine and ale. Credit cards. Moderate.

Rian's Sandwich Express—located in Morgan's Alley, Rian has a knack for tucking the best into small spaces. Check the Survival Kit for children's and picnic lunches. Unusual sandwiches, plenty of good coffee and blueberry muffins supreme. No liquor. No credit cards. Inexpensive.

Ricardo's—16035 SW Boones Ferry Rd., Lake Grove (636-4104) started as Richard's but is now flying the flag of Italy. Specialties include veal and stuffed sole. Lunch and dinner. Wine and beer. Moderate.

Ringside—2165 W. Burnside (223-1513). For steak before or after the game at the Civic Stadium or any evening when beef is on your mind. Liquor. Credit cards. Moderate.

Rose's—315 NW 23rd (227-5181). Nonkosher delicatessen with large dining area open 7 days a week, featuring cakes a foot high, lox and cream cheese on rye and blintzes. Good for the entire family. Liquor. No reservations so you may have a wait during lunch and dinner hours. No credit cards. Inexpensive.

Rusty Pelican—4630 SW Macadam (222-4630). A la carte seafood and steak served dockside on the Willamette River. The lunch trade might be up due to waitresses who serve in Danskins and little else, but the view and food are in keeping with its southern relative in Newport Beach, California. Lunch and dinner. No reservations. Liquor. Credit cards. Moderate to expensive.

Salty's—Foot of SE Marion (239-8900). In more formal terms this is known as Salty Pickeral and Angus MacHereford's, but by either name it serves seafood and steak on the east side of the Willamette River just south of the Sellwood Bridge. Some of the best hors d'oeuvres in the city are served at the giant bar which offers an excellent view of the river in the evening. The food is good, plentiful, and reasonably priced. Lunch and dinner. Liquor. Credit cards. Moderate.

Señor Korte—SW 3rd and Stark (223-7582). There's a definite New Mexico feeling here, complete with muraled walls, streamers of chili peppers and leather and cotton wood chairs. A limited menu delivers some new twists for northerners, a choice of chicken or beef and a special pork dish. Owner Beverly Strong has even developed a knack for sopaipillas, served piping hot with honey. Sangria, beer. Credit cards. Moderate to expensive.

Sherwood Peddlar—21105 SW Pacific Hwy. (625-5505) serves farm cooking at Six Corners. The menu includes chicken fried steak, home made pies, and Verboort sausage dishes. Liquor. Inexpensive to moderate.

Silver Garden—210 SE Ash (233-9333) serves continental dinner 7 days a week just off produce row. The decor includes a recycled vista dome railway car which serves several tables. Imagine yourself traveling through any city. Liquor. Moderate to expensive.

Skyline—1313 NW Skyline Blvd. (292-6727). It took him awhile, but James Beard has put his blessing on this renowned hamburger stop. Open Fri. and Sat. until midnight. Closed Sun. No liquor. No credit cards. Inexpensive.

Stephen's Wine Cellar and Quichery—852 SW 21st (222-1799) offers a country atmosphere in a renovated house near Civic Stadium. Quiche, frittata, and wine. Moderate.

Stock Pot—8200 SW Scholls Ferry Rd. (643-5451). Fine restaurant at golf course. Liquor. Credit cards. Moderate.

Sweet Tibby Dunbar—718 NE 12th (232-1801). Open 7 days a week, Sat. and Sun. for dinner only. Most romantic atmosphere in the city, and features only fresh fish on its menu, which includes steak and other specialties. The reservation policy saves tables for one third of the house only, so prepare to wait in the English pub bar. It's well worth it for a special night out, but not with the children. Liquor. Credit cards. Expensive.

Sylvia's Italian Restaurant—5155 NE Sandy Blvd. (288-6828). Sylvia Posedel has delighted Portland for years both on stage and at the stove where she wields an exuberant hand over the tomato and garlic. For those who believe a good meal means "Italian," this is the spot. Open 7 days a week. Liquor. Credit cards. Reservations.

Taco House No. 1—3255 NE 82nd (252-1695) and ***No. 2*** 3550 SE Powell Blvd. (234-6401). Mexican food for the Gringo taste. The long lines waiting (no reservations) prove that these restaurants have come up with the right ingredients. Dinners only. Beer. No credit cards. Inexpensive.

Tebo's Famous Hamburgers—19120 SE McLoughlin Blvd. (655-6333). Long and excellent reputation for charcoal grilled-to-order cafeteria-style food. Pick up your tray and watch the cooks go into action. The hamburger will be done just as you've passed the salad and pie section. Lunches and dinners. Other branches located at: King City, SW Pacific Hwy. & Durham Rd. (620-0225) and 1230 NE Cleveland, Gresham (667-1650). No liquor. No credit cards. Inexpensive.

Thunderbird Downtown—1225 N. Thunderbird Way (just across from the Memorial Coliseum) (235-6611) and ***Thunderbird at Jantzen Beach***, 1401 N. Hayden Island Dr. (283-2111). Both are open for dinners 7 days a week, and it depends upon which river you want to see or where you are to determine your choice. Both offer dressy dining, the Downtown on the Willamette, the Jantzen Beach overlooking the Columbia River. Both have full bar service. Both accept credit cards. Children do not belong in either, except for lunch. Expensive.

Tivoli Gardens—SW 1st at Columbia (222-4894) is Horst Mager's newest venture abroad. Look for Scandinavian food served with the Mager flair. Children welcome. Liquor. Credit cards. Moderate to expensive.

Trader Vic's—309 SW Broadway (228-9611), in the Benson Hotel. The place to fill up on such tidbits as barbecued spareribs (a former governor's wife holds the consumption record), crab Rangoon, and other exotic combinations. At lunch or dinner order the Bongo Bongo soup, an original with this South Sea island chain. Closed Sun. Liquor. Credit cards. Moderate to expensive.

Trees—Hilton Hotel, 921 SW 6th (226-1611). The spot to order thin pancakes rolled in lots of melted butter and served with hot maple syrup and crisp bacon or strawberries. Even the friendly waitresses will agree this is the best choice, although the menu is large. Children eat at half price when accompanied by mother and father. Liquor. Credit cards. Moderate.

Tuck Lung—NW 4th & Davis (223-7475). This started out as a Chinese grocery and grew like Topsy Lee. When the business moved across the street from its former location, its owners saved the Japanese cherry trees. Good lunch, dinner spot. Alcohol. Credit cards. Moderate.

2601 Vaughn—2601 NW Vaughn (222-2601) caught the eye of Portland's resident curmudgeon Doug Baker who calls it "Oregon's best venture into la nouvelle cuisine." Baker lauds the duck with figs and raspberries, but less venturesome diners will find other entrees on the menu to please their tastes. Fresh foods and bright waiters are featured along with light dining and desserts in the bar. Dinners Mon.-Sat. Sunday brunch at 10 a.m. Liquor. Reservations suggested. Moderate to expensive.

Uncle Chen's—529 SW 3rd (248-1199). Imperial Chinese cuisine from 6 provinces of China complete with waiters to lead you through the Asian continental fare. This is not a fried shrimp-fortune cookie variety restaurant, but some youngsters may enjoy it. Large bar. Lunch and dinner Mon.-Fri. Credit cards. Moderate to expensive.

Veritable Quandary—1220 SW 1st (227-7342). Special shrimp salad served up to a classical music accompaniment. Tempting sandwiches. Open for lunches and dinners. No liquor. No credit cards. Take-out service. Inexpensive.

Victoria's Nephew—212 SW Stark (223-7299). Sandwiches and homemade breads and soups. Open 7:30 a.m.-4 p.m. Closed Sat. and Sun. High tea served. No liquor. No credit cards.

Victoria Station—6500 SW Macadam (245-2241). Lunches and dinners featuring a frosty salad bar and prime rib all served in a boxcar setting. Reservations. Credit cards. Liquor.

Wong's, Johnny—7601 SW Barbur Blvd. (245-2479). Owner-host Johnny Wong is so congenial that he has businessmen driving out for lunch at his large restaurant on the edge of the city. In addition to the regular menu, appreciative customers may request special dishes. Liquor. Credit cards. Moderate.

Yaw's Top Notch—2001 NE 40th (281-1233). The original high school hangout in the city. Hamburgers are loaded with pickles, relish, juice, and sophomore sensitivity. Good spot for lunch or light supper. No credit cards. Inexpensive.

Ye Olde Towne Crier—4515 SE 41st (774-1822). Open 7 days for lunch and dinner served in comfortable "early grandmother" period. Liquor. Credit cards. Moderate.

Zapatas—2719 SW Kelly (222-6677). Spanish spoken in kitchen. If your tongue is tender, bring your own taco sauce. Wide menu. Beer and wine. Open 7 days a week. Credit cards. Inexpensive to moderate.

Zen—910 SW Salmon (222-3056). Japanese full-course dinners in addition to a la carte. Open for lunch and dinner. Liquor. Credit cards. Moderate.

(For a list of some favorite neighborhood restaurants, see Sightseeing.)

SHOPPING
A Guide to Buying

SHOPPING is a fine art, honed to the last checkbook decimal and shaved to the tune of an exhausted partner's final plea. Portland is rich in shopping experiences and environments.

Its residents maintain the shrewd New England attitude of their forbears. They look for the best buy, regardless of where a store is located. Generally, one good store will draw others into its area; however, some remain smugly isolated, alone in their exceptional quality.

In this section you'll find individual services, regardless of location, a listing of shopping centers or areas, and finally thrift-minded shopping and out-back ventures.

Stores sometimes resemble the circuit rider; just as they begin to spread a particular gospel, they move on. So check, by telephoning, before you head into the hinterlands.

Antiques

Is it an antique, is it junque, or is it just secondhand? Only the dealer knows for sure, so be sure of your dealer. Some reliable sources include:

Cast Iron and Cast-offs, 14941 S. Henrici Rd., Oregon City (656-0193). Warm yourself by one of the great variety of woodburning stoves for sale. During sunnier days you will see the best collection of carousel horses anywhere. Even their oddments are endearing.

Cathy's Antique Shop, 2425 NW Lovejoy (223-1767). Excellent collection of fine glassware and china.

China Gate Antiques, 1024 SW Alder St. (222-2541). Some excellent jade pieces and some old furniture.

Eclectic Art—Arthur W. Erickson, 610 SW Alder (227-4710). Has the best collection of Indian baskets in the city.

Evilo Eaton Antiques, 7825 SE 13th (235-6414). Respected name in the business. English pieces and fine jewelry as well as doll house memorabilia are included in her specialties.

Gallery Mongeon, 115 SW Ash (223-9093). Estate appraisers bring in many fine pieces including silver, glass, and furniture.

Marneff Antiques, 6515 N. Interstate Ave. (289-2645). Museum quality for some things; leave your children elsewhere.

Root, George Jr., 2381 NW Flanders (223-7834). Call before on this one also. Fine collection of brass and furniture.

Second Hand Rose, 2168 W. Burnside (227-5282). Begins to to lead us into the funquey junque, but there are some definite buys scattered about.

Sellwood Peddler, 8535 SE 13th (235-0946), tucked clear at the end of the Sellwood "antique row," offers a wondrous collection of sentimentalia as well as some sound advice on what each is worth and where to eat lunch that day.

The Antique Finder, 7843 SW Capitol Hwy. (245-7382). Primitive, American and European furniture, glass.

Bakeries

Bagel Ladies, 4118 NE Fremont (282-8627). Open Tues.-Sun. to prepare fresh bagels for Sunday brunch (9 a.m.-1 p.m. on Sunday). Lox and cream cheese sold, too. Also at 4830 SW Scholls Ferry Rd. (292-9750).

Beaverton Bakery, 12375 SW Broadway, Beaverton (646-7136). Customers come from miles to buy donuts, special breads, pastries, and pies from this bakery which is so successful that it delivers by the oven load to some grocers, including Strohecker's on Portland Heights.

Helen Bernhard Bakery, 1717 NE Broadway (287-1251). An institution in Portland. Most weddings don't feel blessed unless the cake comes from this establishment.

Ikeda Pastry Shop, 6330 SW Capitol Hwy. (244-7473). Customers argue over whether the cake donut or the raised donut is better. Everyone agrees on the black bread and the pink champagne cake.

Le Panier, 71 SW 2nd (241-3524), imported both its ovens and its two bakers from France to prepare French bread daily. Tuck a long loaf into your bag, and your local accent will rise with every slice.

Middle East Bakeries, Inc., 8005 SE Stark (252-3006). Makes the unleavened Middle and Far East pocket breads which have become so popular this bakery has some local imitators. It's a special treat to get it right out of the oven on Stark Street.

Murray's Bakery (at West Linn Thriftway, 5639 NE Hood, West Linn (655-7575). Bill Murray and his wife bake daily except Sunday to the delight of three generations in the West Linn area who say it isn't a birthday without Murray's chocolate cream cheese torte. Fresh maple bars and cinnamon rolls feed most of the nearby high school as well as shoppers in Thriftway where the owners have set up a free coffee outlet to complement this time-honored baker.

Rose's, 35 NW 20th Pl. (227-4875). Home of the giant cinnamon roll and twelve million calories, every one of them worth it. Yes, this is the Grandma Rose of national fame and these are her original recipes.

Three Lions' Bakery, 1133 SW Morrison (224-9039). The brioche wears the crown, but customers rarely leave without some pastries, strudel, cookies, or classic chocolate bread. Special order desserts are part of the oven plan for Mon.-Sat.

Books

Annie Bloom's Books, 7829 SW Capitol Hwy. (246-0053). Books and cards in Multnomah Village.

B. Dalton Bookseller, five branches in the Portland area—Lloyd Center (288-6343), Mall 205 (255-5650), Washington Square (620-3007), downtown at 530 SW 5th (222-3851), Vancouver Mall (206-256-7526). Dalton carries the largest inventory of new titles and classics in the state and proves itself doubly literate by knowing where to find its own stock.

Book Cellar (The), 7 Village Shopping Center, Lake Oswego (636-7403). Shhh! The owner is probably reading. Widely diversified stock, good stopping place for a special gift. Special orders placed willingly.

Book Vault (The), 3125 SW Cedar Hills Blvd. at Beaverton Mall (646-0396). The shop is narrow but the selection is wide—both paperbacks and hardbound.

Brian Thomas Books, Galleria, 921 SW Morrison (222-2934). Marvelous selection of Oregon books; paperbacks for children and adults at this shop, which is becoming an institution for those who read.

Catbird Seat (The), 1231 SW Washington (222-5817), promises selections for the "omnivorous reader" and carries through with shopping hours seven days a week.

Children's Place, 1631 NE Broadway (284-8294). Books and records for the young.

Children's Book Store, 425 SW 2nd, Lake Oswego (636-5438). Even the librarians check the stock here. Will gladly order special books for children and has a paperback book club to encourage young readers: buy 12, get one free.

Gill, J. K., Co., 408 SW 5th (224-2805). Branches at Eastport Plaza, Jantzen Beach Center, Lloyd Center, Washington Square, and Gresham Village. This store, one of the "pioneer" firms in Portland, now has included office furniture, games, stationery, and art supplies in its inventory. Autograph parties often.

Goatsbeard Bookshop, 8828 SW Hall Blvd. (643-4121). Near Washington Square. Personal service is a shop policy.

Graham's Book & Stationery Stores, 460 SW 2nd, Lake Oswego (636-5676); 181 SE Main, Milwaukie (654-7706). Offers a fine selection of classics in paperback form, making it simpler to lure the children through Orwell or O. Henry as well as early shipment of best sellers. Unusual stationery, huge card selection, gifts, and office supplies.

Green Dolphin Bookshop, 215 SW Ankeny (224-3060). Outstanding assortment of old and rare books, particularly well shelved. Owner has sense of humor.

House of Titles, Water Tower, 5331 SW Macadam (228-0290). Best sellers but better yet good specialty sections including music, outdoors, science, and young readers.

Katharine McCanna Book Counselor, P.O. Box 13534 (234-7664). The lady to call when you know what you want but can't find it. She and Edith Bristol, both retired from local bookstores, represent nearly a century of involvement in literature. The two not only can get it, they've read it.

Lewis and Clark College Bookstore, SW Palatine Hill Rd. (244-6161) makes up in quality what it lacks in quantity. In addition to open stacks of liberal arts books suggested by professors, this store offers an outstanding selection of books in the fine art fields as well as the best books just off the press (the buyer has an uncanny ability to purchase before a book is reviewed). Practical student selection of windbreakers, backpacks, and other gift items. Closed Sat. and Sun.

Looking Glass Book Store, 421 SW Taylor (227-4760). For paperbacks.

North Willamette Book Co., 707 Main St., Oregon City (656-6626). Fastest growing bookstore in the area, due to the owner's idiosyncrasies: sidewalk sales on special editions, even if it rains; 10 percent off if customers show their precinct cards during election years. In addition, a wide variety of local publications, books for young people and the latest best sellers.

Nor' Wester Bookshop, 220 NW Davis, (228-2747). There's a fountain courtyard signaling the unusual for this shop which offers specialty books (literature, poetry, nature, and music) as well as cards and maps.

Old Oregon Book Store, 112 SW 2nd (227-2742). Rare books, especially dealing with the Oregon country.

Oregon Historical Society, 1230 SW Park (222-1741). Like all projects undertaken by the society, this is a bookstore with a difference. Large selection of regional publications (members receive 10 percent off), and in addition, the public may purchase back copies of the society's Quarterly or have prints made of rare old photographs, using the library on the 3rd floor. Closed Sunday.

Portland State University Book Store, SW 6th & Hall (226-2631). Not just for the intelligentsia. Wide inventory.

Powell Books, 1005 W. Burnside (228-4651), is the largest outlet for new and used books in the state. The shop promised 195,000 titles in all fields—and it is telling the truth.

Skidmore Village Children's Books, 50 SW 3rd (222-5076). Probably the largest inventory of children's books in the state. Will place special orders.

Walden Books, Jantzen Beach Mall (289-3319).

A Woman's Place Bookstore, 2349 SE Ankeny (236-3609).

Children's Clothing

Without doubt, the finest and most extensive shop for children is:

Youngland, 30 NW 23 Pl. (227-1414) which outfits children from the bib stage to the junior prom. This store has gained a West Coast reputation for its boys' sport coats, beautifully tailored and proportioned. Everything, including these famous coats, goes on sale twice a year. Anyone not afraid of a determined horde of mothers should make the sale a must.

Cooking Supplies

Greb's Kitchen Kupboard, 5027 NE 42nd (284-7023). Specializes in hard-to-find kitchen tools.

Kitchen Kaboodle, 8788 SW Hall Blvd. (643-5491); 606 SW Washington (248-9158). Generally has a chef at work to prove the value of its stock.

The Kobos Co., The Water Tower, 1553 SW Macadam (222-5226). Freshly ground coffees and many teas, spices, and herbs plus a multitude of cooking aids from small accessories to imported food processors.

Lakeside Drugs, 464 SW 1st, Lake Oswego (636-4593). Almost half of this large pharmacy is given to baskets, French cookware, and unusual crockery to perk up your interest in cooking.

Copies

J.Y. Hollingsworth, 104 SW 2nd (223-8181). Instant copying service and the home of Portland calligraphers at Christmas time. These gentlemen are most helpful when it comes time to reproduce a homemade card.

Print-Right, 1975 SW 1st (226-3648). One of a chain of do-it-yourself and quick-print centers, this outlet in Portland Center is unusually accommodating.

Copy Print Center, 1222 SW Morrison (222-4913). Not to be confused with its mini-relative on Alder. The larger shop specializes in quick-printing and latest copying service. Prices are competitive.

Fabrics

Calico Corners, 8526 SW Terwilliger Blvd. (244-6700). Everything for upholstery, draperies, bedspreads, and your imagination. This special spot sells designer seconds and factory close-outs all of the finest quality at 50 percent discount. In addition, helpful clerks will recommend upholsterers or seamstresses to the perplexed shopper. Open 7 days a week.

Daisy Kingdom Wholesale Fabrics and Trims, Inc., 217 NW Davis (222-9033). Fabrics with a flair, trimmings beyond your imagination.

June's Fabric Shop, 429 SW 1st, Lake Oswego (636-5505). Probably the widest selection in the greater Portland area at retail prices. This is a spot where you can find outing flannel in June and dotted swiss in December.

Sarah Jane's, 15450 SW Boones Ferry Rd. (636-7130). Offers a complete wardrobe coordination service in addition to classes for the would-be fine seamstress. Sarah provides the energy, Jane the know-how, as these two women serve up Saturday brunch before class or weeknight gourmet box lunches before evening sessions. Open 6 days a week, 10 a.m.-5:30, the shop carries a wide variety of imported fabrics including Horikoshi, Yves Gonnet, Mettler, Harris tweeds, Tootal, and Moygashel. All interpretations are free. Call or write to be included on the mailing list for sales and special classes.

Fine Arts, Graphic Arts, Crafts

Artist's Materials

Art Media Inc., 820 SW 10th (223-3724). Complete stock of tools, materials, and accessories for the fine and graphic artist, professional or student. Specializing in calligraphic supplies, fine papers, and knowledgeable service.

Art Circle, 3rd floor of the Galleria, SW 10th and Morrison (222-2970), outgrew its old facility in a short time and doubled its inventory, proving that Portland is a renaissance city. Everything for the serious artist.

Reed College Book Store, 3203 SE Woodstock Blvd (774-2826). Treasure trove for serious calligraphers. The college was the classroom for Professor Lloyd Reynolds, "the father of 20th century calligraphy." It rises to the occasion.

Other Outlets

Gill, J.K. Co., 408 SW 5th (224-2803). Entire basement level has art materials, including engineering supplies at one end and handmade paper at the other with craft items in between.

Howell's Creative Craft Center, 630 NW 10th (227-3125). Craft supplies by the binful at "Northwest's largest craft supply house." Long-time Portlanders remember when this shop was on an upper floor of a creaky downtown building. It's easier to find the abundant supply of decorative materials now.

Macramé

Let's Knot, 702 5th, Oregon City (655-2385). Has a very
unobtrusive sign, since it is an old residential area of the city
and is the home of Connie Nicoud. Her main floor rooms are
filled with baskets of tempting beads of all types and string
of every possible weight and color.

Knitting

Oregon Worsted Co., 8300 SW McLoughlin Blvd. (236-
2128), offers the state's widest selection of yarns, some spun
at the mill here and some imported. Oregon knitters and
needlepointers look to the mill ends bins where 4-ply wools
and synthetics can be purchased for low and even lower
prices, depending upon the machine's mistakes. Also
fabrics, sewing, and knitting accessories. Craft classes on
premises.

Westover Wools, 2336 NW Everett (223-7845). Look for
Icelandic wool as well as other fine yarns for knitting. Instructions are given by Prudence Jones and her presiding
wool experts.

Needlepoint

Flying Colours, 1016 SW Morrison (222-2673). Absolutely no
one in the city carries a better selection of English yarns,
canvasses, or original needlepoint designs than this sharp-
eyed shop.

In Stitches, 515 SW Broadway (226-0814), has a wide variety of needlepoint and stitchery materials, including yarns
and canvas; also counted thread materials and Paternayan
yarns.

Yarn Barn, 4805 SW 77th (292-8355), in Fred Meyers-
Raleigh Hills shopping center, specializes in personal instruction and carries needlepoint and stitchery materials.

Spinning and Weaving

Arachne Webworks, 2930 NW Thurman (227-0134). Indigo
as well as other hard to find dyes and wool.

Wildflower Fibres, 211 NW Davis St. (222-4044). Looms,
wool, and specialty yarns as well as many wood and china
bits for macrame or weaving. Second location at 1018 SW
Salmon (243-2590). Stocks fine yarns in wool, linen, and cotton.

Robin and Russ, McMinnville (1-472-5760). Draws the serious spinners just south of Portland for a wide assortment of wheels, looms, wool carders, and other weaving accessories.

If all you lack is the inspiration, drive to the **Pioneer Craft School** at the Damascus barn (658-2704), Damascus, about 15 minutes from 82nd Ave., to see classes in progress. Two dozen different spinning wheels are chattering in a great circle while the looms, both traditional and Navajo, clack away in another room. The barn also offers classes in quilting and is an inspiration in itself should you be tempted to tear down an old building of your own. The shop sells swifts and other spinning and weaving accessories as well as some fine handmade items. Open weekdays until 4 p.m.

Fish and Seafood

To live less than two hours from the ocean and not know where to find fresh fish is ridiculous. But if you have no time to cross the mountains, several stores will do it for you on a daily basis. Incidentally, never look for sole two days after a storm at sea. The sole is a shy fish and will not rise in rolling waters.

Plancich Fish Co., 300 NW 13th (227-6416). The last of the colorful fish markets; located in the warehouse district. Just pull over the train tracks and park between the boxcars.

Tony's Fish Market, 14th & Washington, Oregon City (656-7512). This market is so particular that the owners have their own crab pots. Like Frank Buck, they "bring them back alive."

Florists

We're not called the City of Roses for nothing. Some specialty shops go a scent further.

Flowers by Dorcas, 617 SW Washington (227-6454). Complete turnover of merchandise with every season. Specialties include imported silk flowers, imaginative dried arrangements year-round, and special gift items for children. Don't miss the annual open house with punch and cookies just before Christmas.

Plant Kingdom, 6550 SW Scholls Ferry Rd. (245-4415) and 1320 SW 2nd (222-1007), offers constant greenery for in-

door plant lovers along with the containers and baskets to
hold them.

Tommy Luke Downtown Shop, 625 SW Morrison (228-
3131). Owner Charles Kofler has made the pages of
House Beautiful with his Victorian floral arrangements for
old Portland homes.

Uptown Flowers Tommy Luke, 2405 W. Burnside (227-3134)
shows a full selection of flowers and plants as well as imported gifts such as brass, porcelain, candles, and other gift
items.

Wildwood Weeds, 2036 W. Burnside (228-0325). Great varieties of indoor plants. Proprietor is happy to advise you on
your sick ones at home as well as to sell you new ones.

Gifts and Import Shops

Anyone, and usually his mother, can operate a gift or import
shop. But some do it with flair, such as the woman who had just
finished decorating a birthday cake for her grandson behind
her shop. A customer dropped by as she added the last slap of
icing, and it was love at first sight when he saw the cake. Of
course she sold it to him and then rushed out to a nearby supermarket to buy another for the grandson. That's what gives a
gift shop owner élan.

Others equally unpredictable and interesting, include:

Add-On, 6362 SW Capitol Hwy. (245-6541), where among
other treasures shoppers can view recent works by Pacific
Coast artists.

Ames, Elsie, Gifts, 12300 SW Bull Mountain Rd., Tigard (639-
1802). Open just before Easter and Christmas with ap-
propriate and special decorations.

Calendar (The), Johns Landing (227-5855). Christmas year-
round and a lively stock of miniatures.

Carl Starker Shop, 5220 SE Hall, Milwaukie (654-6361). A
literal pioneer in the area with an eye and a shelf for
anything interesting.

Carriage House Boutique, 629 SW Washington (227-3077).
Hand-blown eggs with a porcelain quality. They will mount
your child's picture on the egg; handsome patchwork skirts
and other extra-ordinaire.

Cloudtree & Sun, Inc., 55 N. Roberts, Gresham (666-8495),
located in a restored hardware store—the antiques here are
just for admiration. But visit them for fine linens, kitchen

pieces, baskets, and toys all beautifully giftwrapped on request.

Designs of Scandinavia, 2173 NE Broadway (288-3045), is the spot for a heavy woolen sweater, brightly patterned, or wooden art from the Scandinavian countries.

Hawaiian Shop, East, 12102 NE Glisan (254-7750); Galleria, 921 SW Morrison (223-8815); and West, 11345 SW Canyon Rd., Beaverton (643-2102). Tired of seeing the baby done up in pink and blue? This is the place for jazzy colors for the toddler. Also other island accents equally at home on the mainland.

H-K Limited, 622 SW Alder (248-1015). Look for the unusual and fanciful and reasonable prices here as well as a complete array of contemporary bright plastic ware and cottage pottery. H-K also has outlets at Eastport Plaza, Jantzen Beach, Lloyd Center, and Washington Square.

Import Plaza, 1 NW Couch (227-4040), is the granddaddy of all import shops in the city. The main branch stretches just off Portland's harbor, and the blackboard at the door tells shoppers what to expect on the next tide. Smaller versions of the same shop are at the Galleria, Jantzen Beach Center, Lloyd Center, and Washington Square.

Kathleen Connolly, Irish Shop, 725 SW 10th (228-4482). St. Patrick's Day may come and go, but Kathleen Connolly has kept the shamrock in Portland for decades. Go for fine woolens and linens by the yard, tea towels, and table linens.

Kathleen Rockwell, 803 SW Morrison (223-6235). Fine antiques, porcelain eggs, and exquisite dolls.

La Paloma, 6316 SW Capitol Highway (246-3417), carries an inventory representing all of Latin America. Look for designer dresses from Mexico, cotton casuals for men and women, and small gift items.

Made in Oregon, Portland International Airport (282-7827), the Galleria (241-3630), Washington Square (620-4670), and the Lloyd Center (281-3328). Ready for immediate export are all of the state's finest products—from chocolates to knitwear, woolens to wood, and, of course, publications telling all about Oregon.

Old Homestead Market & Gallery, 4121 SE Woodstock Blvd. (774-1691). This old house is loaded with gift selections. One room features Christmas every day of the year, and the gallery has one of the largest inventories of its kind in the state.

Orientale Motif Shop, 725 NW 23rd (223-4978), offers some unbelievable treasures from China. Be sure to check out the back room, which is like a short stop at a Chinatown 5 & 10.

Paper Parlour Ltd., 921 SW Morrison at the Galleria (221-0700). Pick a paper present and wrapping all in one at this unique shop, which features the most unusual selection of paper fun in the area including stationery, prints, and most unusual invitations and cards.

Pier One Imports, with three outlets, is yet another docking point for import shipments. Better check each store out, since no two ships carry the same merchandise. Visit them at 14410 SE Stark (255-4828), 9307 SW Beaverton Hillsdale Hwy. (292-0105), and 5331 SW Macadam (248-0359).

Quintana's Indian Arts and Crafts, 139 NE 2nd (223-1729), holds some fine Indian craft work in addition to Japanese-made tomahawks.

Realites Ltd., 8756 SW Hall Blvd. (641-3210). Antique baskets, contemporary giftware. Very small, very expensive, and worth the visit.

Red Wagon Store, 19730 NE Sandy Blvd. (666-4561). Freshly ground coffees, rare teas, and the perfect pots and cups to serve them in.

Simpatico, Morgans Alley (223-1734). Bright imports from Mexico.

Tickled Pink, 4905 SW Scholls Ferry Rd. (297-4102). Fran Frane has added her school teacher's touch to this gift shop which features Lalique on the school desks; also flowers and consignment antiques.

Gourmet Shops

An over-used word if ever there was one, but the enticing odors wafting from these doorways would probably draw you to them if we did not:

Anderson's Delicatessen, 9575 SW Beaverton Hwy., Beaverton (643-5415). Owner Verne Anderson built a following with his wines, cheeses, and special salads, and new owners Christian and Teri Joly continue to live up to it. The shop has added a professional chef and a catering director as well as a full line of East Indian and Pakistani foods. Fresh lox and some 15 salads made daily are still offered along with a full line of cheeses and imported meats and a complete wine selection.

Anzen Oriental Foods and Imports, 736 NE Union (233-5111). Everything, including fresh vegetables, for the wok.

Better Book & Beef, 600 NW 23rd (227-2299). Amiable young proprietor of this combination Christian book and meat market offers competitive prices—sometimes lower—for quality Midwestern beef. Flank steaks are exceptional. Deliveries for a minimum.

Harris Wine Cellars Ltd., 2300 NW Thurman (223-2222). The late Bert Harris taught many Portland businessmen the right way to smell a cork. Now the shop has expanded to cheese and wine and sandwiches.

Oriental Foods and Gifts, 9970 SW Bertha Beaverton Hwy. The ultimate in Oriental offerings including Asian magazines, records, chopsticks by the hundred pack, fresh vegetables, strained poi in the dairy counter, seaweed, Teriyaki beef, rice by the 50-pound bag, clothes, china, and fried bean curd.

Pieri's Delicacies Inc., 3824 SE Powell Blvd. (232-7003). Memorize this telephone number, and call ahead for the finest pizza ever assembled to be taken home and baked in your own oven. While you wait for the final touches, browse through marzipan and dried mushrooms, wine, and cheese.

Strohecker's Inc., 2855 SW Patton Rd. (223-7391). Far more than a delicatessen. It is the last of the neighborhood grocery stores—but what a neighborhood. Here you can find strawberries, out of season, and many other foods to tickle a tired palate. Liquor store on premises.

Tuck Lung Co., NW 4th & Davis (223-1090). The next time you return from the grocery store and your husband says, brightly, "did you have a nice time, dear?" make sure that you have been to Tuck Lung and for once you can say "yes." Sit down for a cup of tea and an excellent Chinese lunch before or after you shop in this unique combination restaurant-grocery.

Kennels

Since some accommodations do not welcome Fido, this seems like a promising spot to include kennel boarding services. Two of the best:

The Charlton Kennels, Sauvie Island (621-3675), also trains gun dogs and those for field trials. In addition, the Charltons will give boarders extra love and attention as well as a good run in the open fields. Dogs once boarded there will return to jump from the car and run in eagerly. Call ahead several weeks for reservation, if possible.

Forest Glen Kennels, Rt. 1 Box 442, Beaverton (649-4962), is most often recommended by west side veterinarians, so call several weeks ahead for reservations. The kennels, up under the fir trees, are scrupulously tended and so are the animals. Just 4.2 miles from the Progress turn-off on Scholls Ferry Rd.

Purr-Tender Lodge, 6590 SW Oleson Rd. (244-2667) is for cats only, which cat lovers can appreciate if they have ever taken kitty through the lobby of any general admission kennel.

Jewelers

Contemporary Crafts Gallery, 3934 SW Corbett (223-2654), sells the works of most of Oregon's finest jewelry artists. All one of a kind, some with precious stones. Reasonably priced and constantly changing merchandise.

Jerome Margulis, Broadway and Yamhill SW (227-1153), offers rare jewels, precious gems, estate jewelry, styling, and repair and the supervision of Mr. Margulis himself, representing a half-century of experience.

Stewart Jones, 2340 NW Westover (223-0136), jewelry designer and manufacturer.

Zell Bros. Jewelers, 800 SW Morrison (227-8471) and Washington Square in Tigard (620-3610). Both stores do custom work and repair in addition to carrying a fine selection of jewelry.

Men's Specialty Shops

All of the following men's stores suit Portland especially well:

Albert Ltd., 900 SW 5th (224-2020). Began in Seattle, but we will forgive them since they stock such smashing tartan trousers.

Estes, 2364 W. Burnside (227-0275), is not complete without a word with owner Este Morrison. An avid golfer, he has designed his own "wet suit" and can run through the hazards and handicaps of any West Coast golf course. Custom tailoring.

John Helmer, 969 SW Broadway (223-4976) can wear a hat like
no one else in town, and he also sells them. His assortment
includes Irish and Greek fisherman hats, derbies, top hats,
silk opera hats, driving caps, Western hats, and Irish caps.
Sizes are from 6½ to 8. Also a complete haberdashery with
branches elsewhere.

Klopfenstein's, corner SW 6th & Alder (226-4701). Very complete men's haberdashery.

M and HH Sichel, 519 SW 6th (223-1800). Solid conservatism in
the best English tradition.

Norm Thompson, 1805 NW Thurman (221-0764). Low on
decor, high on the unusual. Look for shearling jackets and
Irish tweeds.

Richard Ltd., 725 SW Alder St. (227-6601), offers a snappy
well-turned collar for men and women in the conservative
line, including tweeds, cashmeres, and British imports.

Nurseries

George L. Routledge Co., 1852 SE Hawthorne Blvd., (232-
7111). The place to go with garden questions. Mr. R. has all
the answers.

Gerber Gardens, 15780 SW Boones Ferry Rd., Lake Oswego
(636-5565). This garden center plants hanging herb baskets
which flower into beautiful meals. Come summer, when the
fields are yielding the best produce, Gerber's cannily gathers
just the best and displays freshly washed carrots in a granite
bowl, just-picked blackberries, and pickling cucumbers
wood-crated by size.

Herbs Etc., 528 SW 2nd, Lake Oswego, (636-4372). More than
300 different types of herbs—good for cooking and what ails
you. Owners prove themselves unique by growing their own
plants in the backyard, which means that everything will
transplant well to a Northwest garden. Advice and unique
planting ideas given gladly.

Kasch's Garden Center and Nursery, 8135 SE McLoughlin
Blvd. (231-7711); 3250 SW Cedar Hills Blvd., Beaverton
(644-1640). More than 200 varieties of rhododendrons, large
supply of young trees. If you can't find what you want, they
will get it for you if it's growing anywhere.

Oregon Grape, foot of Dollar St., Willamette (656-7199), open
from early spring through early fall. The place to buy native
shrubs and wildflowers well started and potted. Also Burpee

seeds and some unusual hanging baskets. (See Back Bargains section.)

Wishing Well Farm and Garden Center, 19080 Pacific Hwy., West Linn (636-7744). Home gardeners count on them for good seed potatoes, Oregon Giant green bean seeds, and other hard-to-find garden starts—all hidden behind a verdant front of annuals and shrubs.

Pets and Pet Supplies

Boyd's Pet Shop, 5540 E. Burnside (232-6830). When the birds say, "Hello, creature," you know you are in the minority. This shop has a wide majority of pets, all kinds, tropical fish, and superior advice for fin and four-footed owners.

Gentle Bird Ranch, Gresham, phone for directions (663-4694). Owner Goldie Gentle (it's his name, not necessarily the bird's disposition) raises a voluminous stock for bird lovers. Look for more than a dozen pheasant varieties, 30 types of pigeons, doves, unusual chickens, quail, partridge, turkeys, ducks, and geese as well as household birds. Visitors are welcome, and the Gentles will order special varieties.

Holland Feed, Pet and Garden Supply, 12250 SW Broadway, Beaverton (644-3400). Take all your problems here: the broody hen, the uncomfortable rabbit, bedding plants which refuse to settle down. Family-owned and operated, this shop has the advantage of three generations of knowledge on the premises. Excellent place to buy chicks, ducklings, and goslings and also to buy small bags of cedar shavings for the single hamster owner.

Pharmacies

Irving Street Pharmacy, 638 NW 23rd (223-6297). Keeps its prices down by doing a high volume business. And it isn't hard to find out why once you've met owner Milt Olshen, a Portland landmark in himself. He opens his store every day to dispense drugs and philosophy.

Medic Pharmacy, Inc., 1016 SW Clay (222-9611). Open Mon.- Fri.; offers economy in prescriptions also.

In after-hours emergencies, pharmacies of some hospitals will fill your prescription. Call the pharmacy of the hospital nearest you to check.

Records

CrystalShip, SW 10th & Morrison (222-4935) has the largest selection of records and tapes in the city. "Why I even heard opera!" one matron exclaimed. The store has tapes and records well filed and marked. Chances are if you can't find it here, it hasn't been recorded. This shop is open until midnight 7 days a week.

Django Records, 1111 SW Stark St. (227-4381), run by a jazz writer and teacher, is the city's largest and best used record store, including classical, rock, jazz, and country western. Records bought and sold.

Everybody's Record Co., 8660 SW Canyon Rd. (297-4141) or 7901 SE Stark (255-4141).

Music Millennium, 3158 E. Burnside (236-1724) and 636 NW 21st (248-0163); wide variety of records and tapes.

Long Hair Music, SW 2nd & Stark (224-8542).

Music on Records, 1033 SW Morrison (227-1311). Classical selections and hard-to-find recordings.

Shoes with a Difference

Achilles Heel, 1000 SW Jefferson (248-9910). Especially accommodating about fitting the agile foot in the namebrand athletic shoe and roller skate. The price is competitive, but shoppers do receive a great plastic bag, good for needlepoint or wet bathing suits long after the shoes are outgrown.

Athletes Foot, Washington Square (639-8328). Nothing is catching here but the peer group pressure which brings the family in for the right stripe or color combination in athletic shoes.

Birkenstock Footprints, 730 SW 11th (227-4202) and 225 NW Miller, Gresham (667-1436), both build their inventory around the "must have" sandals. Custom moccasins, natural fiber socks, and repairs.

Cobbler's Bench, 816 SW 10th (222-2577). Frye boots, Birkenstock sandals, and rubber moccasins.

Danner Boots, 5188 SE International Way, Milwaukie, in Omark Industrial Park (653-2920). This Portland manufacturer of work, hiking, hunting, and casual boots since 1936 offers custom fitting for men and women. The brand is found at other outlets, but hikers with foot problems might want to go to the source.

Multnomah Leather Shop, 315 SW Pine (227-4887). The only place in town for custom-made clogs with closed heels. Also other leather items.

Nordstrom, 701 SW Broadway (224-6666), also at Lloyd Center and Washington Square, has the largest selection of shoes for adults and children in the city. Those with odd shoe sizes are most apt to fit in here.

Sports and Recreation

Barbless Hook, 23 NW 23rd (248-9651). Fly-fishing purists shop at this second-floor location in the Uptown Shopping Center.

Caplan Sport Shop, 521 SW 4th (226-6467). Larger than two basketball courts and meets price competition from every source.

Howell's Uptown Sport Centre, 21 NW 23rd Pl. (227-7910). Skiing, tennis, hiking clothes and equipment.

Larry's Sport Center, Oregon City Shopping Center, Oregon City (656-0321). Hunters' and fishermen's paradise (licenses available here). Also plenty of baseball, basketball, and football equipment for students.

Mountain Shop of Portland, 628 NE Broadway (288-6768). The original store with three outlying branches. This Portland store has a midnight ski equipment sale each February where your discount depends on what you're wearing and your arrival time. The later (or earlier in a.m.) you arrive, the greater the discounts, which top at 30 percent. Cloud Cap Chalet, 625 SW 12th (227-0579); Mountain Shop Progress, 8836 SW Hall Blvd. (641-1991).

Oregon Athletic Equipment, 1338 NE Sandy Blvd. (234-7346). Team uniforms a specialty.

Oregon Mountain Community, 60 NW Davis (227-1038). In new spacious quarters adjoining Import Plaza, this favorite haunt of mountaineers and outdoor enthusiasts has plenty of display room for its colorful dome tents, arctic sleeping bags, ski gear, and a large array of clothing which is as popular with the non-mountaineer types as with the purists. Closed Sun.

Osborn & Ulland, 1302 Lloyd Center (288-7396). Skiing, hiking, and mountaineering equipment.

Recreation Outfitters Inc., 38 SW Village Lane, Lake Oswego (636-8866) and NW 185th & Sunset Hwy., Beaverton

(645-2711). Name the sport, they've got the shoes. Also standard equipment, clothing, and some unusual accessories.
Very knowledgeable staff is understanding to untutored
mothers.

REI Co-op, 1798 Jantzen Beach Center (283-1300). This is an
outlet for the large REI Co-op store and mail-order house in
Seattle.

Scott's Mountain Sports, 106 Tigard Plaza (620-5033). Mountain tents, ski and backpacking gear.

Ski Chalet, 4800 SW 76th, in Raleigh Hills Fred Meyer
Shopping Center (297-1891). Large inventory of quality
equipment. Open Sun. during ski season.

Ullr Ski Shop, Ltd., in the Water Tower at 5331 SW Macadam
(225-0040) and Lake Oswego at 569 SW 1st (636-8557).

Stationers with Style

Helen M. Clark Co., 811 SW Broadway (222-5666). Small but
select and very friendly.

Zell Bros. Jewelers, 800 SW Morrison (227-8471). A most traditional stationery department on the 2nd floor, including
engraved monogrammed notepaper and hard-to-find
heavyweight blank place cards.

Tailors

Bee Tailors and Cleaners, 1222 SW Salmon St. (227-1144).
Eventually gets most of the alterations in town anyway so
you might as well meet Heinz, the magician, who can make a
pair of pants fit right just by looking at them.

Toys and Hobbies

Callin's Novelties, the House of Magic, 412 SW 4th
(223-4821). Where you take a bored boy on a rainy day. In
addition to the Atlantic City poo-poo cushions and the joy
buzzers, look for magic tricks (which employees will
demonstrate) and small party favors. Tell them the theme,
and they will dig in the deepest boxes, cheerfully. The help
will steer children from the center aisle, which contains
some off-color items for boys who never grew up.

Finnegan's, 922 SW Yamhill (221-0306), carries everything you've ever dreamed of, whether you're a child or child at heart. Look for wonderful stuffed animals, kites, models, games, puzzles, imaginative greeting cards, and wrap. There's something for every child, at every price in this shop.

Hobbyland, 4503 N. Interstate Ave. (287-4090). Trains, planes, race cars, and all types of model kits. Repairs, too.

King Norman's Kingdom of Toys, Washington Square (620-3700). A child's paradise, King Norman offers weekly specials which are below discount house prices and are offered on his best toys.

Mrs. Tiggy-Winkles, Water Tower Building, Johns Landing (227-7084). Some say, the best teddy bears in town. Toys, children's clothing, handcrafted items.

Tony's Crafts and Hobbies, Inc., 4454 NE Cully (288-4004). Elaborate electric train display in window gives some indication of the inventory inside. Exotic imports in trains, other models, are worth a stop. Repairs. Second location at Jantzen Beach Center.

Toyland, 1305 Lloyd Center (284-6414). Still ranks high in its assortment of toys. Model train buffs will like the display. Also toy soldiers and dolls.

Women's Apparel

Fifth Avenue Shop, 711 SW 10th Ave. (223-8127). Very old-Portland.

I. Magnin, 930 SW 6th Ave. (226-7811) is I. Magnin with possibly the prettiest women's restroom in town.

Lance Apparel, 709 Main, Oregon City (656-3582). Don't overlook this fine women's shop; small-town they are not. In addition to lingerie, coats, and a wide selection of blouses and sweaters, you will find designer fashions and German knits, all sold by friendly, helpful women who care enough to take an extra tuck in the back room while you wait. Regular sales bring savings up to 50 percent.

Mercantile, 724 SW 9th (227-6820) and 23rd and W. Burnside (227-7882), has developed a well-established clientele in Portland since its first shop opened on W. Burnside more than 20 years ago. Look for conservative tweeds, cashmeres, and an occasional avant garde touch for women.

M. Willock, 3rd floor, the Galleria, 921 SW Morrison

(226-3405). One-of-a-kind designer fashions make this an exclusive shop. Owner Maxine Willock also takes pride in the
fact that hers is the only store other than Nieman-Marcus
carrying Ib Jorgensen fashions. Also moderately-priced
lines unique to Oregon.

Nordstrom's, 701 SW Broadway (224-6666), Lloyd Center, and
Washington Square, carries the usual throughout the store
and the unusual in the Collector's Corner. Clerks are very
helpful in telephoning to other branches to find the correct
size.

Norm Thompson, 1805 NW Thurman (221-0764) has built its
reputation on English shearling coats, Irish woolens, and
safari pants.

Traveler's Choice, 459 SW 2nd, Lake Oswego (636-3310).
Specializes in packables, including several well-known imported knit and woolen labels.

Shopping Centers and Special Spots

When Portland was just a day or so younger and all her
shops lay cozied up to the Pioneer Courthouse lawns, it was not
an unusual sight to see Tommy Luke, himself, step out of his
flower shop to hand a passerby the first bunch of spring violets.

Aaron Frank was a common sight striding the aisles of his
downtown department store, and as time goes on his legend
grows with every credit-card-carrying generation.

One of the city's most unique refunds, credited to Aaron
Frank, is the return of the 20-year-old toilet seat.

"It cracked clear through," claimed the indignant customer,
who took the wooden oval right back to the store's owner, "and
it had a lifetime guarantee."

She turned it in for a new model. And the same fair treatment has come to be expected from most of Portland's merchants, even though the downtown area has duplicated its image all around the city's edge in the form of shopping centers.

Downtown Portland yet remains the most colorful shopping
area with its continually developing alleys, renovated shopping
areas, and the time-mellowed department and specialty shops
which the alert eye can spot tucked between the fast-rising new
buildings.

Counting downtown Portland as a shopping center, which it
has become since so many merchants allow free parking with a
stamp of a sales slip, the Portland area claims 19 centralized

areas for shopping. Some seem to be stretching the word a bit, by including a strip of stores strung along a parking lot.

Downtown

Puzzled visitors may well ask "down from what?—but all small communities have a downtown area, and Portland in spite of her current size remains a small town girl at heart. While three major stores maintain headquarters in the southwest part of the city, they also draw customers to outlying shopping centers. The charm of the city's downtown is in its old buildings, festooned with architectural whipped cream and the lace of Victorian fire escapes. The drawing card lies in the many small shops which sparkle along Broadway, Sixth, Fifth and then glimmer continually from SW Jefferson north to Old Town at NW Everett, from SW 12th clear down to the waterfront. Some are old friends, some are pert, new, sassy, and bound to last. With additional parking facilities and park-and-shop stamps for customers, the downtown area is a pleasant and practical way to spend a Saturday shopping as the surbanites pour into the outlying area stores swelling the "free" parking to mile-wide perimeters.

City Center parking lots throughout the downtown area allow free parking after customers have tickets validated by participating stores. The newest of these lots, Morrison Park West, SW 10th and Morrison, and Morrison Park East, at SW 4th and Morrison, have multi-level parking facilities as well as shopping and eating spots on the street level. Theoretically it would be possible to park, shop, validate, and never leave the square, although most downtown shoppers have more than one spot to stop. Tri-Met's Fareless Square ★ enlarges the "free" zone, giving shoppers an extra lift, except between 3 and 7 p.m. weekdays so long as they remain within its confines.

Frederick & Nelson, 521 SW 5th (228-8111) bought out Portland pioneer Lipman's but wisely retained the same telephone number at the main store as well as one of the finest *watch repair services* in town. The downtown address has nine floors of merchandise for women, men, children, and the home. Eating establishments on the premises including a pub atmosphere in the basement.

Meier and Frank, 621 SW 5th (227-4400). Ten floors (not counting the basement and sub-basement levels) of general merchandise. Famous for its Friday Surprise sales. Look in its bargain basement for seconds. Waitresses at the tearoom (10th floor) have been serving luncheons on white linen cloths with silver settings since the store's beginning.

Nordstrom, 701 SW Broadway (224-6666). Portland's flashiest new store with emphasis on women but with special departments for men and children. Nordstrom's also carries the widest assortment of shoes in the state, happily for the hard-to-fit. Other branches at the Lloyd Center and Washington Square.

Penney, J.C., 638 SW 5th (221-6520). This is one of the smaller outlets for this national chain and suits the urban worker nicely. Larger Penney's stores are found at Lloyd Center, Washington Square, and at the Oregon City Shopping Center.

Quick Turns Down Narrow Streets

The Galleria—921 SW Morrison. Enterprising businessmen who refused to let an old Portland landmark die are happy with the resurrection of the old Olds, Wortman & King Building, which now holds many specialty shops within its ornate arms. Stop here for Brian Thomas Books, CrystalShip Records, *Barney Bagel and Suzy Cream Cheese* restaurant (224-3312) on the main floor, as well as some of the best ice cream in the city at *Gelati Roberto Ice Cream* (224-4234). Several restaurants are also located here.

Morgan's Alley—Enter through the grilled doorway at 515 SW Broadway or turn down the brick steps to Rian's Eating Establishment off Alder St. Either way you will run into a subterranean honeycomb of fine specialty shops and restaurants. Spend a rainy day, as well as the money intended for it, here.

Old Town—Reaching from SW Ankeny to NW Everett Sts. along 2nd Ave. Old Town is a monumental effort to restore Portland's old iron-front buildings and other early structures. (See Walking Tours).

Uptown Shopping Center—One of those "strips along a parking lot," but has spread well. This area, located at W. Burnside & 23rd, includes three specialty women's wear shops, a good men's store, children's wear, Uptown Hardware, which is more than tacks and nails, Uptown Variety, and on and on. This one grew like Topsy, park your car and walk it. Several restaurants will sustain your tour.

Outlying Shopping Centers

The Lloyd Center—NE 10th & Weidler. At last count this center contained more than 140 stores and a covered ice arena. Free parking for 8,000 cars. Shoppers will find enclosed pedestrian malls, landscaped with trees, flowers, and fountains. The largest store in the development is Meier and Frank, followed by Penney's and J.J. Newberry Co. Other large stores include H-K Ltd., F.W. Woolworth, Nordstrom, Frederick's, Klopfenstein's, and Roos/Atkins.

Jantzen Beach Center—Just south of the Interstate Bridge. Fast growing and fun for children, since developers have retained the original amusement park features. Carousel rides are a quarter, and the old automatic fortune teller still plies her cards for a dime. Frederick & Nelson is the largest store in the center, which includes many small specialty shops.

Washington Square—9585 SW Washington Square Rd., off Oregon 219. Newest of the centers. Completely enclosed and built around California-style concourses planted with trees and flowers, the multitude of department stores and small shops have no doors but open onto temperature-controlled walkways.

The Water Tower—5331 SW Macadam. First in a series of Willamette riverside enterprises which abut the newest greenway on the water's edge. The building itself was once a mattress factory, and architects left the old hardwood floors and other structural devices when they added more than 40 specialty shops at interesting angles. The Water Tower also houses six restaurants. Look here for the *Honey Cured Ham Co.* (243-1181); ham sliced, glazed, and ready to serve.

Thrifty Places to Shop

Once-a-Year Sales

Ascension Attic Treasure Sale, 1823 SW Spring (227-7806). Held every May. The ladies of the chapel do a fine job of assembling antiques and lesser objects from Portland's older homes.

Bybee-Howell House Wintering-In, Sauvie Island. Sale held by the Oregon Historical Society the last Saturday in September.

Catlin-Gabel Rummage Sale is such a Portland institution that the date is set a year in advance. The sale runs three days at the Memorial Coliseum. One year the offerings included an entire room of used bicycles. Call the school (297-1894) or watch the newspapers for the dates.

Oregon Episcopal Schools' Country Fair. Last Saturday in April on the school grounds at 6300 SW Nichol Rd. Children can ride the carnival midway attractions while you shop the rummage and antique sale. Book buyers bring their own empty cartons to carry away the vast selection of used books and records.

Schnee Voegli sponsors an annual buy-and-sell sale at the Mountain Shop, 628 NE Broadway, the first three weeks in October. It's the place to go to recycle your children's ski gear and replace it with larger sizes.

Also noteworthy are the sales held by Temple Beth Israel (222-1069) and Trinity Episcopal Church (222-9811). Call for the dates or watch the newspapers for announcements.

Charity Thrift Shops

Assistance League Thrift Shop, 735 NW 23rd (227-7093).

Bargain Tree (Junior League), 837 SW 3rd (227-7413)

Christie's Attic Thrift Shop, 7907 SE 13th (236-0222)

Council Thrift Shop, 300 SW Stark (227-2877)

Goodwill Industries of Oregon, 1831 SE 6th (238-6165).

Nearly New Shop (Portland Chapter of Hadassah) 3415 SE Hawthorne Blvd. (235-8053)

Old Church, The Church Mouse Thrift Shop, 1422 SW 11th (222-2031)

Parry Center Thrift Shop, 709 NW 23rd (227-6201)

St. Vincent de Paul, 2740 SE Powell Blvd. (234-0594)

Salvation Army, 200 SE Union (235-7806)

William Temple House (Episcopal Laymen's Mission Society), 706 NW 23rd (222-3328)

Young Women's Christian Assn., Y's Buys Shop, 1127 SW Morrison (222-2669)

Portland Super Shopper by Connie and Terry Hofferber is a new book for thrifty shoppers that details the location and available goods for sale at sharply reduced prices at more than 250 factory outlets, sample shops, thrift stores, and many others. The book is available wherever books are sold.

Back Road Bargains

The family who picks together, stays together—at least for another winter. For who can say which box of strawberries was his and which jar of grape juice was hers, when everyone works the row? And somehow the squabbles in the pumpkin patch are remembered fondly by the time the east winter wind whistles down the Gorge.

Preserving the produce you find can be very simple with the use of a freezer, canning kettle, jars, and Ziploc bags.

Green peppers go for less than supermarket prices in the U-pick fields. With half an hour out of a summer's day you can snub the produce section when the price soars to 89 cents a pound the following winter.

Peppers lend themselves beautifully to freezing. Rinse off the outsides, top them, and pull out the seeds. Stack the peppers, just like cups, in Ziploc bags, zip up and toss in the freezer. To stuff them later, fill while still frozen. They will maintain their shape. Take a few more minutes and dice up the tops, sans stems, for seasoning and color in other dishes. If you find a good buy on *red peppers*, you can confuse the crowds by freezing these to use as pimento.

Raspberries, the envy of southern California residents, can be frozen in Ziploc bags. Just rinse and drop them in gently; sprinkle a little sugar over the top (or not) and freeze. Serve them while still touched by frost, and they will maintain their firmness.

Blueberries will freeze in a large Ziploc bag. Fill the bag to the top, then as you need the berries, give the bag a slight tap on the drainboard and the berries will come loose just as they did from the bush. Drop them into muffin or pancake batter in their frozen state—it makes no difference.

Corn is so simple to freeze you will be sorry if you don't do it. Drop the ears into boiling water for a minute (the corn will turn a brighter yellow). Remove to cold water. Get out your angel food cake pan and a sharp knife. Poke the stem of the corn cob into the funnel part of the pan and scrape away. The corn will fall all around you, hopefully into the pan. This is a good project to do before you mop the floor, however. Empty the cut corn into a large Ziploc bag and freeze it en masse. To prepare, just smash the bag against the drainboard and drop what you need into a little boiling water.

Mushrooms will freeze well if you saute them a minute in

butter. The oil seems to keep them from going "leathery." However, one thrifty housewife says she freezes hers dirt and all and then cleans them up as she needs them. She has her own theory about dirt as a preservative. Do bag them up, though, regardless of your method.

Blackberry juice is time consuming, but delicious when mixed half and half with frozen lemonade. Since blackberries are free for the picking in many parts of the state, it all depends upon what you think your time is worth. (Do not pick close to a busy highway. Studies show that lead content may be dangerous.)

After you have put up your share of jelly, bring the rest of the washed berries up to a simmer in a little water (very little). Drop them into a heavy sieve and grind away. There is a special conical sieve sold with its own wooden pestle and stand which is perfect for drawing out juices and very few seeds. It also works well for fast jelly, although purists will say the jelly will not be "clear," but who can taste "clear" anyway? Fill fruit jars with heated juice and drop into boiling water bath in the canning kettle for 10 minutes to seal.

Squash, potatoes, and **dry onions** need little care. Find a cool place and store them in baskets which let them breathe.

Apples can be canned as sauce or in pieces for pies, but one of the quickest methods for pies is to freeze them up in the Ziploc bags. They will turn a bit brown as you slice them but after you have baked them in an pie, with cinnamon and sugar, no one will know. Toss them into the pie pan in their frozen state and reserve what won't fit for another batch of pastry.

Stop Here for Bargains

Early in April, when the soil is beginning to warm, take a drive to the old town of Willamette (actually part of West Linn, but they prefer not to talk about it). Turn toward the Tualatin River on Dollar Street and just before the road bends at the river is **Leitz's Oregon Grape,** a greenhouse and garden supply shop in the backyard of Steve and CZ's home (656-7199).

It's here you will find your own trilliums and lambs tongue, already potted, for a wildflower garden. The enthusiastic couple also carry Burpee Seeds as well as shrubs, bedding plants, vegetables (many of them well established in plant form) and some hanging baskets which put Victoria, B.C., to shame. Since Steve Leitz stocks many of the nurseries in the area, you can save by buying directly from him 7 days a week, 9 a.m.-6 p.m., spring and summer.

Come June, keep a couple of flat boxes and brown paper bags in your car. Otherwise you may find youself looking wistfully over a fence as someone else gathers the fruits of the field.

Oregon strawberries begin in June with the Marshalls, known throughout the state for their ability to produce the best jam. They have a short but sweet season. The Portland area growing season runs through October when you will find squash, pumpkins, potatoes, and nuts. Naturally, the more labor you provide, the more you will save.

On the road to Carver is a sign for filberts: picked and U-pick. If nothing else, one U-pick season will help you to appreciate the high price of labor.

One word of caution: some transitory vegetable stands, including those by the "truckload" can be factory seconds for the vegetable market. A dead give-away is a large sign reading "oranges." Science has yet to introduce the orange tree to Oregon orchards. With this sort of operation, you pay your money and hope.

You will find oranges, early on in the season, at the *Faist Fruit Stand,* between Oregon City and Canby on 99E. The honest ladies who run this fresh air market will tell you flatly that it is too early for Oregon produce, and they open Memorial Day and close Halloween. This stand sells some of the plumpest blueberries in the state, as well as cantaloupes with great taste. As the summer progresses, all the out-of-state produce is replaced by local produce of the finest quality. It pays to make this a regular stop. Summer telephone, 266-9425.

Territorial settlers found Oregon City an ideal place to gather in the crops from the Tualitan Plains. They still do at the *Oregon City Saturday Market.* Street shops are open every Saturday selling woodworking and quilting in the winter, fresh produce and plants in the summer, and wildflower honey in the fall. It's not unusual to find a Dixieland band striking up at the foot of the falls. The territory still thrives on Saturday in Oregon City.

Blueberries are an Oregon delight, and some Oregonians seem to have a better knack than others for growing them. For berries so plump that one is a mouthful, visit the gardens of *James Hough* (625-7823) just out of Wilsonville. Call first to be sure the berries are ripe and, most importantly, for directions. Plan on a country road drive.

Richard Burdon and his family have blueberries from the 4th of July on at 5851 SW Kahle Rd., Wilsonville (682-1247). The Burdons will pick or you may pick until early September, since they have such a wide variety of berries. Also plan to stop here for grape cuttings, whether you're planning a vineyard or just want a few to come up over the back porch. Burdon's Landscape Nursery supplies a wide variety of grape cuttings as well.

Cross the Willamette River on the Canby Ferry—it's free—to find *Weber's* corn patch. It must be the river silt, but the corn grows as high as a dinosaur's eye, and it is easy to become lost in the stalks. One veteran picker noted that it is easier to walk in with the basket and pick your way out. Corn should be processed immediately for the best results, so this should be a pick-and-prepare day.

The *Stafford area,* south of Lake Oswego, is abundant with U-Pick fields. One of the largest belongs to the *Wilhelm* family (638-5387) and includes raspberries and strawberries. If you time it just right and have the stamina, you can pick both in one day.

Farmer Lee is what his employees call him, and his berries are some of the best. Take a left at the Tualitan exit off I-5 and follow his berry field signs for strawberries, raspberries, marionberries (a perfect cross between the tiny wild and domesticated blackberry) and boysenberries. Open from 8 a.m.-8 p.m., the crew will pick flats to order. For directions for a ready-picked flat, call 638-4200 to reach *Lee Berry Farms.*

Typical of the backroad U-pick gardens is the *Weed Patch.* Don't expect much undergrowth, it's owned by the Weed family and offers some of the plumpest raspberries around. Like many of their type they have no telephone at the field and no address, just a lush field of berries to be picked. Look for the sign at the corner of Stafford and Rosemont Roads out of Lake Oswego. Take your own boxes and something to drink. Have the children use a nearby restroom first. The price and quality are well worth the trip.

Just about the time you think you've picked enough raspberries, *Spada U-Pick Farm* at NE 156th and Sandy offers a good second crop of garden peas ready for the freezer. This large farm complex offers a variety of vegetables and fruits and is open from 9 a.m.-7 p.m. Call 253-2313 for what's on the vine.

Fiala's on Johnson Road, just off Stafford Road, does a brisk business in broccoli and beans. Incidentally, you can get there from here. Stafford will connect with the Canby Ferry.

If you must go through doors to purchase fruits and vegetables, a rural atmosphere continues at the **Big E Market** in Gladstone, where strawberries can be as big as half dollars and the prices are a little less. They also have the best geraniums in town.

Rather out of the way, but worth knowing about, is **McCormack's** in Woodburn (1-981-1863). Fussy housewives telephone orders for broccoli, among other vegetables, and McCormack's picks to order by the hour to insure freshness. Take the Woodburn exit on the I-5 freeway heading south. McCormack's is at the exit going south just at the curve of the road.

As long as you've driven to Woodburn, you might take another quarter tank of gasoline and push on to Salem to visit the **West Mushroom Farm,** 255 50th NE (1-581-2471). The plant's salesroom is open Monday through Friday, and you can buy five-pound crates of freshly picked mushrooms for less than supermarket specials.

Check valley fruit stands for peaches, an item rarely found "up north" out of the orchard basin. Brooks prunes are a treat worth taking home and can be found fresh off Salem trees.

From mid-July on, take the Champoeg exit from I-5, turn right 1½ miles following the signs for Casale's. The monstrous aluminum barn sits smack in the midst of lush fields of produce just the way grandpa used to grow it. Make **Joe Casale and Son** a must for broccoli, pickling cukes and dill, cabbage, carrots, squash, and tomatoes. You can pick it yourself or have it picked, and the quality is exceptional.

Out beyond the St. John's Bridge lies Sauvie Island, ★ and in late October it means just one thing: the **Pumpkin Patch.** Everyone becomes a child again when he sees acres of roly-poly pumpkins lying in the muddy reaches. Wear your boots and take the children. At these prices everyone can have a jack-o'-lantern. After the pumpkins have been gathered in, check out the barn for every sort of squash imaginable, including some crosses unheard of, and potatoes by the 50-pound bag. Potatoes come in gunny sacks, which later become fine far-West costumes, and carrots come by the 25-pound bag. If that amount tends to over-kill your creative ability, take a friend along. Old timers say that carrots, as well as other root vegetables, will keep well if buried in a foot of straw. Honey comes by the gallon jar; decant your own and save even more. At these prices it's worth being a pioneer again.

WALKING TOURS
Seeing Things & Places In-Depth

IF YOU want to get a substantive, historic profile of your city on location, a guided walking tour, such as those given by Portland Walking Tours or the Urban Tour Group,★is the best way. Short of that, we recommend five do-it-yourself tours.

Park Blocks-PSU-Portland Center

Portland's revered old *South Park Blocks,* the *Portland State University Campus* and *Portland Center* with its steel and glass high rises and contemporary "walk-in" fountains offer many contrasts on two suggested tours originating in the vicinity of SW Clay and Park. (More details about some of the sights noted are found in Sightseeing and Art.)

Tour #1

Head south through the South Park Blocks into the Portland State University campus. As you enter, notice old Lincoln High School on your left at Market Street. The building is now an elegantly refurbished PSU performing arts hall. Inside *Lincoln Hall,* in addition to the main auditorium are the Studio Theater and a small auditorium (room 75) where PSU film series are presented. The PSU Players perform in Lincoln Hall as do local and visiting music and dance groups.

In the north corridor of Lincoln on the main floor is Manuel Izquierdo's *"Campana,"* a metal sculpture placed in memory of a PSU faculty member.

Continuing south, you might see a chess match in progress at a permanent board on a sturdy pedestal facing Mill.

As you pass *Cramer Hall,* view Frederic Littman's

99

"Farewell to Orpheus," a graceful nymph placed above a reflecting pool facing Montgomery Street.

The next building on your left is *Smith Memorial Center,* which houses the *White Art Gallery* and the *PSU Box Office* (room 120), where you can find out what's playing at Lincoln Hall and about other campus events. Phone is 229-4440.

Still favoring the east side of the Park Blocks, pause at *Neuberger Hall* (between Harrison and Hall), to see one of the campus showpieces—sculptured bronze panels by Tom Hardy depicting flora and fauna of Oregon. Opposite Neuberger Hall on the west side of the Park Blocks are the PSU Branford Millar Library and, on Hall, the Health and Physical Education building with its 1,880-seat gymnasium. In the Park Blocks, between the two buildings, is a Don Wilson sculpture, "Holon," a tribute to the late Gordon Hearn, founding dean of PSU's School of Social Work.

Continue your walk past *Shattuck Hall,* another old Portland school building, and through a playground where you will be tempted to climb up the "Lincoln Log" structure leading to the top of a slide. At SW Jackson turn left (east) and proceed east across Park and Broadway. As you walk, look to the southwest at Piggot's Castle on the hillside. The residence was built in 1892 by an eccentric and is being restored. At SW 6th turn left (north) and walk two blocks. Turn right (east) at SW Hall, but as you do, look north to locate the *Portland State Bookstore* and *Sam's Hofbrau,* a good sandwich spot. On SW Hall, you'll pass the *5th Avenue Cinema* on the south side of the street. Cross SW 5th and SW 4th and enter a brick plaza leading into Portland Center. ★ Walk straight ahead past an orange tile "smokestack," clever camouflage for a Pacific Northwest Bell air intake shaft. Pacific Northwest Bell won a Portland Beautification Assn. Award for its 4th Ave. Plaza because it so skillfully conceals an underground parking structure.

You are now near the top level of the *Lovejoy Fountain* ★ and can descend its concrete steps via the water or skirt the edges. From the base of the Lovejoy, you can walk the mall to the south to see the *Lee Kelly Sculpture Park* (★ Art), which lies between the American Plaza apartments and the Red Lion Motor Inn, and then return to tour the attractive avenue of shops and services east of the Lovejoy.

Follow the mall north across Harrison to *Pettygrove Park*, between SW 1st & 4th and Market & Harrison. Walk on to Market via the *200 Market Building.* Look on its west wall for a

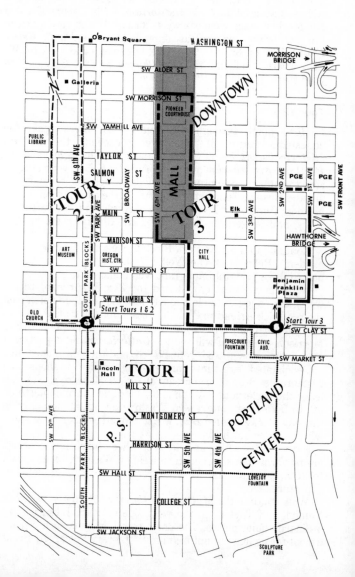

decorative yellow folded aluminum sculpture, 60 feet wide, by a Vancouver, B.C., artist, Douglas Senft. Across Market you will see the rear of the *Civic Auditorium.* ★ Place yourself at 2nd and Market, walk one block west, turn north and pass between the auditorium and the cascading falls of the *Ira C. Keller Fountain* ★ on 3rd. At Clay turn left (west) and walk to SW 11th where you'll find the *Old Church.* ★ Take Clay east to your starting point at Park Avenue.

Tour #2

Head north through the South Park Blocks past the equestrian statue of Theodore Roosevelt, the *Oregon Historical Center* ★ at SW Jefferson (on your right), and the *Portland Art Museum* and *Sculpture Mall* ★ on your left. Be sure to enter the Sculpture Mall, which is between the museum and the Masonic Temple to the north. In the park in front of the Masonic Temple is a bronze statue of Abraham Lincoln. Tulips, roses, and joggers bloom in the Park Blocks in spring and summer.

Continue to the next Park Block to view the delicate bronze maiden, "Rebecca at The Well," in the Shemanski Fountain, named for a grateful immigrant who donated it.

At Salmon Street (you'll find the *Zen Restaurant* to the west), take a jog to the left to SW 9th and continue north past the red brick Arlington Club (last stand for the male establishment in Portland). Cross SW Taylor and continue north to SW Morrison where you will see the *Galleria,* an old department store which was gutted, refurbished, and then developed, like an enchanted egg, into an alluring array of shops and restaurants. Stop for ice cream at *Gelati Roberto's.* You can leave the Galleria at SW 9th and Alder and continue north on 9th to *O'Bryant Square* ★ at Washington Street, stopping on the way at *The Brown Bag,* ★ 620 SW 9th, either for a sandwich to go or lunch there.

After seeing O'Bryant Square, where lunchtime concerts are performed in summer, turn west on Washington and walk to 10th, your avenue for your return trip to your point of departure.

Walk south to the *Multnomah County Library* ★, between Yamhill and Taylor, on the west side of 10th. Libraries are ordinarily quiet places. The downtown library is such a place except for its huge sculpture/mural, "Library Piece," by Brent

Jenkins, a triumphant hanging on the third-floor landing. This piece in wood, clay, and plastic celebrates the knowledge and information the library houses. Also in the third floor are two paintings by C.S. Price and a study sculpture of horses by Tom Hardy.

After leaving the library, cross to the east side of 10th and walk south past a variety of small shops and businesses. Look for the *YWCA,* which you will pass before reaching Clay. At Clay, turn left (east) and walk to SW Park.

Downtown

Tour #3

Buildings and sights north of the Civic Auditorium may be taken in either on an extension of the Park Blocks-PSU-Portland Center tour or on a tour beginning at SW 2nd and Clay. Walk north on 2nd one block and turn right (east) on Columbia. Walk to the *Benj. Franklin Plaza* and *Museum.* ★ Museum entrance is at 1300 SW 1st. Continue north on 1st, passing the *Veritable Quandary Restaurant* ★ (east side) and Hawthorne Bridge, until you reach the polished granite *Willamette Center,* the sprawling headquarters of Portland General Electric Co., at 1st and Salmon. Explore the center, which is architecturally interesting because of its glass and steel "spaceframe," an elevated walkway joining the three-building complex. Escalators up to the spaceframe are at the northeast corner of 2nd and Salmon and the southeast corner of 1st and Salmon. Retail and retaurant space is provided on the ground level. At the northeast corner of 1st and Salmon is the Willamette Center Activities Rink, a covered arena where downtowners gather for roller skating, a concert, or a quiet picnic. At 26 SW Salmon is the *Greater Portland Convention and Visitor's Assn.,* ★ where you'll find brochures, maps, and information for travelers.

Continuing your tour, proceed west on Salmon. At SW 4th, look (or detour) south to the *First National Bank Tower* ★, Portland's tallest building, and *City Hall* ★, First National's diminutive but vital neighbor to the north. *Terry D. Schrunk Plaza,* a memorial to a long-time Portland mayor, is across the street from City Hall (you're looking at the rear entrance). Between you and Schrunk Square, where there is a replica of the Liberty Bell, are *Chapman Square* ★, a throwback to the old

Photo: Julie Goodnight

An older Portland gets a new image on the reflecting face
of the Orbanco building along the city's southwest mall.

days, where there are benches marked "women and children only" and a women's restroom, and *Lownsdale Square* ★ (directly south of you), paired with Chapman as the men's park. Here is the Spanish-American War Memorial defended by "Howitzers used in defense of Fort Sumter 1861." You might see men playing chess in the park. Yes, the restroom here was marked "Men"—until a malcontent tossed a bomb inside it in 1980 and destroyed it. Between the two old parks, bisecting Main St., is the *Elk Fountain* ★.

At the southwest corner of 4th and Salmon is the *Multnomah County Courthouse* ★. Continue west and at 5th and Salmon look for the reflections of the city—as they would appear on softly rippled water—on a new downtown building—the *Orbanco Building,* first major structure to be built on the Portland Mall. (See also Art in Public Places.) Head north on the 5th Avenue Mall. Between Salmon and Taylor, on the west side of 5th is the *Georgia-Pacific Building* with its redwood and bronze sculpture "Perpetuity." Continue north on the Mall. You are in the heart of Downtown Portland, within view of *Meier and Frank* and *Frederick & Nelson,* two large department stores. (At Broadway and Morrison, is *Nordstrom's,* another major store.) On 5th at Yamhill is the rear entrance to the *Pioneer Courthouse* ★, (on the west side of the street).

Enter the courthouse any weekday between 8:30 a.m. and 5 p.m. and wander about the building, which has been remodeled to the last Victorian detail—in keeping with its status as the oldest public building in the region. In the modernization, the iron cage elevator, with "U.S." medallions emblazoned in gold at waist level, was updated to incorporate the cage. Ride it to the second floor to see the elegant courtroom used by the 9th Circuit U.S. Court of Appeals (you might have to ask to have the door unlocked) and to the third floor to see plainer but still exquisite U.S. Bankruptcy Courtrooms.

If you want to imagine what the city was like 100 years ago, ask the main floor guard to unlock the door to the cupola. There at the top of a fairly steep stairway, is a series of photos, owned by the Oregon Historical Society, which were taken in 1877 from that spot.

The Pioneer Courthouse is a downtown landmark which many take for granted, and some overlook. It will be deservedly enhanced if a proposal to build a public square across the street (6th) from it is realized.

Leave the courthouse via the post office portion and exit through the front entrance on 6th. You are now on the 6th Ave. Mall. Walk south, past the front of the Georgia-Pacific Building with its marble fountain.★ At Madison, turn east, passing the Standard Plaza and *Rian's Breadbasket* on your left and looking ahead to the front of City Hall on your right. Turn south on 5th, and wander into City Hall (City Council sessions are Wed. morning and afternoon and Thurs. afternoon). Continue south on 5th until you reach Clay. Walk east to your starting point. (Remember, you are in Tri-Met's Fareless Square so if you want to skip some of the suggested sights, board a bus headed in the right direction during free hours.)

At 5th and Clay consider walking two blocks further to Mill to see the charming early-Italian style *Church of St. Michael and the Archangel* at 424 SW Mill.

Portland Mall

Tour #4

Follow the seasonal banners that fly over the Portland Mall to find a wealth of art, fountain wizardry, green trees, hot pretzel and dog vendors, and many other pleasurable sights.

The red brick pavement will lead you from W. Burnside south on 5th to SW Madison and back again via 6th. Art, fountains, and flowers are placed at regular intervals on both mall streets. For descriptions of the art, see Art in Public Places; for more information on Tri-Met, the metropolitan area's mass transit system, see Transportation. Ask at the Tri-Met Customer Assistance office, 522 SW Yamhill (heart of the Mall), for a Mall walk map.

Old Town

Tour #5

The remains of early Portland lie in the area along the west bank of the Willamette River now known as Old Town. Although the metropolis of the small port town once lay along the harbor and on First Avenue, that enemy called progress has removed most of the original city.

Several preservation-minded groups are working to upgrade what remains from SW 2nd and Oak and north to Everett.

For the longest walk start at SW 2nd and Oak (across from the Police Station), and while you are there, step around the corner to 3rd to search out the **Portland Outdoor Store,** a one-of-a-kind enterprise which stocks western and eastern riding clothing, gear, hunting and fishing equipment, and even some Indian jewelry.

Just south from the parking lot is **Victoria's Nephew,** an excellent stop for lunch or high tea, either at the end or the beginning of your trip.

As you walk along 2nd, you will pass the **Hazeltine Building,** on the west side between Pine and Ash, where local historians have recorded high-water marks from flooding during the 1800's. Flood control is one of the kinder changes brought to this city of iron fronts, Victorian lace, and Gothic arches.

The brightest star in the area is the **Skidmore Fountain,** ★ located just at the end of Ankeny. This narrow lane transports you back to the days of horse and buggy or the earliest Model As. (Nearby is the **Waterfront Park** ★ plaza.)

The fountain splashes next to the newer fire station on 1st and is well worth a stop, but first duck down the alley toward **Dan and Louis' Oyster Bar**. The oyster shells tucked neatly around the bases of young trees as well as the scent of salty seafood will lead you there.

Just across 2nd, on the river side, is the **New Market Theatre**. Now a parking garage, this historic building, a registered landmark, is still waiting in the wings for its day of restoration.

Heading west on Ankeny (Dan and Louis' is a good lunch stop), just across the street is the **Green Dolphin Book Store** as well as **The Source**, a mixture of new and old oddities. This cluster provides an especially good side trip for a rainy day since many of the doorways are canopied, and the narrow street will cut the cold wind.

With energy to spare, however, retrace your steps back down Ankeny, put your fingers to the wind to find the river, and head east toward 1st. This is a walk to the main shopping area of Old Town which avoids crossing Burnside, the main intersection of the city which flows heavily with traffic during all waking hours.

At the Skidmore Fountain if you look up and to the right, you will see the top of the mast of the Battleship *Oregon* and next to it the American flag, giving you a good idea of the

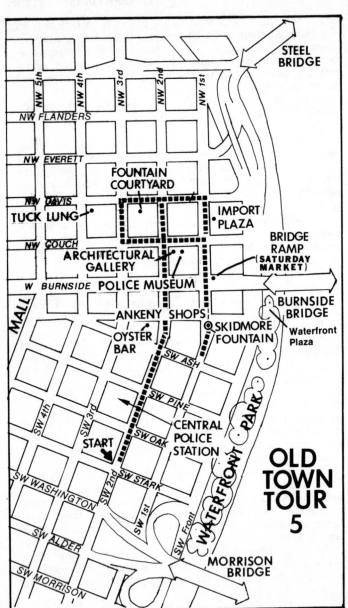

strength of the wind as well as the patriotism of city fathers. The mast is a landmark of Portland's new Waterfront Park.

Turn left, walk under the bridge, and be sure to stop for a tour of the Saturday Market (providing that it is Saturday or Sunday), a mecca for young artists. If you covet a piece of pottery, a bit of wood carving, or anything else for sale, give in to your whim and buy it. Many of these artists travel considerable distances for the market and do not return every week. Certainly their wares vary with their moods, which makes the market a new experience every week. The market is open Saturdays 10 a.m.-5 p.m. and Sundays from 11 a.m. to 5 p.m. May to mid-Dec.

Coming up under the bridge, you will face the bright light and Couch Street. Just beyond the traffic light on the right is *Import Plaza*, the largest of the direct shipment stores in the city. Import Plaza has a large parking lot to the north of the building as well as one across the street. These will be the first to fill up, so if you start your tour at this end and cannot find a parking spot here, drive on south to Oak Street. Also in the Import Plaza building is the Oregon Mountain Community (see Shopping).

But before you load yourself down with baskets, piñatas, and other bulky items which may make you a sidewalk hazard, turn left on Couch to visit two museums in one of the newest of the Old Town restorations—*Capt. John H. Couch Square*, ★ at the southeast corner of 2nd and Couch. The *Architectural Preservation Gallery* ★ and the *Portland Police Museum* ★ are neighbors on the second floor of the Couch Square building. If you want elevator service, enter *Norton House*, another renovation at the southwest corner of 1st and Couch, elevate to the second floor and use the passageway to Couch Square.

Import Plaza maintains a parking lot across 1st where stand the two smokestacks from the Battleship *Oregon,* the "Bull Dog of the Navy" whose 14,000-mile dash from San Francisco around South America to join the fleet off Cuba was a celebrated event of the Spanish-American War. Decommissioned, the *Oregon* was a floating museum in Portland from 1925 until it was cut up for scrap in World War II.

Just across the parking lot with the stacks, to the west, lies the heart of the shopping center known as Old Town. It says so in bright red letters, so don't worry, you can't miss it.

What you may miss, however, are some of the shops you found the last time you visited. Like the breeze from the river, some of these owners drift back and forth and sometimes away all together, so it is pointless to locate many specific shops.

Do cross the street at NW 2nd and Davis. On 4th near Davis lie most of the Chinese restaurants of the downtown area. At the southeast corner of 4th and Davis is the elegant new home of the *Tuck Lung Grocery and Restaurant*, a spacious building in an Oriental motif with an open walkway around the second level. Squint a little to the north and spot the *Fong Chong Chinese Grocery* at 4th and Everett, also worth a visit.

The *Fountain Courtyard* proves that many beautiful moments lie behind the old brick facades in the area. Enter this center of calm which is the core area for four buildings, either on Davis between 2nd and 3rd or on 2nd between Davis and Couch. Either way you will pass a variety of stores on the way to the fountain. It still seems that there should be some laundry flapping in the breeze about four stories up, but the courtyard has become park-like.

Another innovation around the corner to the south is *Couch Street Galleries*, a combination of you-name-it decor with a nonsexist restroom labeled "Ye Old Outhouse," which might come in handy. Like most of the old buildings, the restroom has a skylight, keeping it bright, and is reasonably clean.

There are two ways to return to your car, if you left it across Burnside. You can make this same trip in reverse, reworking the many shops and picking up those items you admired the first time around. Or you can head directly south on 2nd, crossing Burnside. The route along 2nd will take you past a couple of "antique shops." A good spot to catch a bus going south to the Portland Mall is at 5th and Couch.

Walking Tour Postscript

For more walking tours, try *The Portland Walkbook* (Victoria House) by Peggy Robinson.

ENTERTAINMENT
A Full House

PORTLAND is alive and well after 5 p.m. From black tie symphony opening nights to a barefoot hassle with an electronic tennis game in the corner tavern, the city provides a wide variety of entertainment for all ages.

Specifics concerning road shows, arias, or drum beats are difficult to compile, but the following listings contain the most dependable sources to initiate a good evening. The local newspapers are the best source for up-to-the-minute information.

Theater

In addition to road stars who play the Portland Civic Auditorium, Portland supports many small theater groups offering a constantly changing script. For information on live theater productions call:

Portland Civic Auditorium—Box Office at 222 SW Clay (248-4496).

Portland Civic Theatre—1530 SW Yamhill (226-3048) has a long and excellent reputation for good locally produced shows. Mainstage productions run concurrently with Blue Room theater in the round. Curtain time for each is 8:30 p.m. Civic's SRO (Summer Repertory Onstage) is a popular summer series. Children's plays frequently are scheduled for Saturday matinees at this largest of the community theaters which also offers year-round classes in acting and theatrical technique.

Other Theaters and Stages

Firehouse Theater—1436 SW Montgomery (248-4737). Theater and dance on stage, classes in both for ages five through adult.

Lake Oswego Community Theatre—156 SW Greenwood Rd., Lake Oswego (635-3901), regular performances, year around including musicals and drama.

The Long Goodbye—tavern at 300 NE 10th (228-1008) has downstairs location for cabaret-style theater by New Theater Company among other groups.

Mark Allen Players—Benson Hotel Dinner Theatre, 309 SW Broadway (228-9611), weekends. Anyone who has ever seen Mark Allen's productions appreciates this director's talents.

New Rose Theater—904 SW Main (222-2487). Season subscriptions are available for a wide scope of theatrical productions.

Paramount Theater—1037 SW Broadway (226-0034). Touring rock shows, also Trail Blazers games on closed circuit television.

Portland Black Repertory Theatre—call 281-5658 for a taped listing of performances and stages. Offers a variety of musical and drama productions on several Portland stages.

Present Tense—Dinner Theater at the Cosmopolitan Airtel, 6221 NE 82nd (255-6530).

Production Company—215 SE 9th (231-5715). Serious theater; classic and contemporary.

Pub Theater—1900 NW 27th (221-0666). Presents playlets on weekends. Food, beer, wine, and soft drinks available.

Storefront Actors' Theatre—6 SW 3rd (248-0199) has moved to new quarters in Skidmore Old Town but the blend is still the same. Unusual contemporary theater, some original drama; also sponsors a children's touring group.

Sumus Theatre Ensemble—Wilson Center for the Performing Arts, YWCA, 111 SW 10th (227-5558 for advance tickets). High-minded productions on weekends; group of serious actors also give a variety of classes in all aspects of the theater.

Willamette Repertory Theatre—Willamette Center, SW Front at Taylor (226-1605), Fri.-Sat., comedy and drama in the new luxurious theatre on the waterfront. Mark Allen is the managing and artistic director.

Theater footnote: The ***Oregon Shakespearean Festival Assn.***, Ashland, 97520, provides the state's outstanding theatrical venture with three theaters and two seasons including some non-Shakespeare. Portland ticket outlet is The Ticket Place (Frederick & Nelson), 521 SW 5th (227-5558).

Ticket purchasers must come in person to reserve Shakespeare tickets.

Mime

Portland Mime Theatre (285-6928) silently drifts throughout the state in regular performances during the fall and summer months. Regular performances in Portland's parks are scheduled during the summer months through the Park Bureau. Call the theater for performance dates and times.

Oregon Mime Theater—P.O. Box 486, Lake Oswego, 97034 (636-2068) appears regularly in the Portland area; also tours the country.

Dance

Portland, says the Oregon Journal's Martin Clark, has become a "traffic jam of ballet companies" often performing all over themselves. Dance is definitely on the move in the city which less than two years ago offered no more than a half dozen choreographed groups. Keeping the beat, en pointe or otherwise, are so many companies of dance that the curtain rarely falls. Some of the best (alphabetically) are:

Ballet Fiesta, 1710 SW Taylor (222-2302). Maria Moreno, director, leads this professional Hispanic dance company which performs and teaches dances of Spain.

Ballet Workshop—6433 NE Tillamook (282-5061). A student-oriented dance workshop sponsored by the Portland Bureau of Parks and Recreation. The workshop is seen in concert during the summer at the Washington Park amphitheater.

Cirque—716 SW 16th Ave., a full-time school of dance which appears in informal concerts in hall and outdoors during the summer months. They have been known to perform on tennis courts—the dance (not the stage) is the thing.

Country Dance Community—2735 SE Main (232-7939) hosts old-time community dances for the general public and teaches country dances including those of South Appalachia and the British Isles. Members are seen in performances.

Moving Space Inc.—215 SE 9th (231-3138) is a performing group which also offers classes in visual experience.

Northwest-Repertory Dance Co.—3636 SE 21st (232-1932). Keith Martin, director, teaches and leads this group in performances of modern dance.

Oregon Festival Ballet—9609 N. Van Houton (289-7388), John W. Gardiner, director.

Portland Ballet Co.—Pythian Bldg. (227-6867) is the prima donna of ballet in the city. This dance company, under the direction of Jacqueline Shoemaker performs year-round in Portland and throughout the state. The season at Lincoln Hall, Portland State University, includes a children's program and lecture demonstrations, according to manager Pamela Hulse.

Portland State University Dance Program—P.O. Box 751 (229-4401). Nancy Matschek is the director of this university program which sponsors dance concerts at the college with a local company.

College Theaters

University of Portland, Lewis and Clark College, Portland State University, and Reed College have theater schedules during the school year. *Portland State Players* perform in the mainstage theater and Studio Theater of newly renovated Lincoln Hall. PSU also sponsors *Coaster Theater* at Cannon Beach in the summer.

For reservations and ticket information about Portland State theater, dance, and music performances, call PSU Box Office (229-4440).

Special Screenings

Several movie houses in the Portland area screen for a selected audience. The Portland Art Museum as well as the main branch of the Multnomah County Library offer out-of-the-ordinary motion pictures from time to time, so check local newspapers for the latest billings.

Especially noteworthy is the Northwest Film Study Center, 1219 SW Park (221-1156). The center presents films Thurs., Sat., and Sun., including classics, comedy, retrospective series, and a wide variety of screen drama. In addition, courses on film making, especially geared to adults, teachers, and children are offered year-round. Call the center for current films and show times or ask to be added to the mailing list to rent your own 16 mm classics. Members of the Northwest Film Study Center enjoy reduced admissions to center showings and to certain movie houses in Portland and vicinity.

The *PSU Film Committee* sponsors series showings Fri. and Sat. evenings during each term in Room 75 at Lincoln Hall. Call PSU Box Office (229-4440) for dates and times.

For additional information about film series and festivals check the newspaper entertainment sections: *Oregon Journal,* Thursday; *The Oregonian,* Friday; and *Willamette Week.*

These theaters can be counted upon for films with a difference, whether they be vintage or Renaissance:

Bagdad III—3702 SE Hawthorne Blvd. (236-6116)

Cinema 21—616 NW 21st (223-4722)

Clinton St. Theatre—2522 SE Clinton (238-8899)

5th Avenue Cinema—510 SW Hall (224-6038), near PSU

Fine Arts—SE Hawthorne & 20th (235-5005)

The Guild—829 SW 9th (226-0044), downtown

Joy—11959 SW Pacific Hwy., Tigard (639-1482)

The Movie House—1220 SW Taylor (222-4595), downtown

Sherwood Oriental—Sherwood (625-6887)

Music

Portland is filled with music the year around, and the score ranges from Beethoven to bluegrass, from the preschool set to the Old Time Fiddlers. Four colleges and universities and countless auxiliaries see to it that at one time or another every score has its day.

For traveling musical offerings, you can ask to be put on the mailing list of the Portland Civic Auditorium to receive a monthly calendar of events. You must ask in writing: Civic Auditorium, 222 SW Clay, Portland, 97201. For day-to-day listings consult the local newspapers.

Major Groups

Oregon Symphony Orchestra—1119 SW Park (228-1353) was founded in 1896 and is one of the oldest symphonies west of St. Louis. The 85-member orchestra, under the direction of director and conductor James DePreist, presents more than 100 performances for residents of Oregon and Washington each year, including: 36 classical performances at Portland Civic Auditorium, 15 pops concerts conducted by Norman Leyden, low-priced Sunday afternoon family concerts featuring light classical selections presented in an informal manner, three performances of Handel's *Messiah* with the Portland Symphonic Choir, special youth concerts for elementary and high school students, and special concerts featuring world renown soloists from both the classical and popular fields of music.

Portland Opera Association Inc.—922 SW Main (248-4741, 248-5322), traces its roots to the first operatic performance given in the Northwest by a company which arrived in Portland in 1867 sailing by steamer from San Francisco. Portland's association with opera is by no means a newly-hatched thought. The Portland Opera Association was incorporated in 1964, the heir of many former interest groups which brought music to the city. Current programs include four productions a year with three performances of each in Sept., Nov., March, and May. Visiting artists of world stature join an excellent local orchestra and chorus at the Civic Auditorium.

Portland Junior Symphony—922 SW Main (223-5939) was founded in 1924 to provide opportunities for gifted young musicians to study great orchestral compositions. The Junior Symphony, which has had just two conductors in its 52 years, consists of two orchestras: the symphony, known as the Portland Youth Philharmonic, and the Preparatory Orchestra. Young musicians are heard in four regular concerts at the Portland Civic Auditorium as well as in-school concerts. The orchestras, each with 100 or more players, have no lower age limit. Players are judged solely upon ability and may remain with the group until the age of 21. The organization also offers scholarship opportunities through lessons and summer camps for its members.

Chamber Music Northwest—P.O. Box 751, Portland, 97207 (229-4079). Founded in 1971, this group offers an annual five-week summer season of concerts at Reed College from June through August. Top-ranking national performers are in residence for the intensive and widely-varied concert season. Picnic suppers on Reed's spacious lawns precede the concerts.

New Oregon Singers—Cascade Building (227-5800) is an amazing group of energetic young people who spread the "gospel according to Oregon." This group, which performs contemporary as well as red-white-and-blue tunes, raises its own money through local appearances to tour military installations across the United States and abroad. Their ability to take themselves (not their music) lightly and fill the front row with beautiful faces and figures has made them a part of nearly every hoopla event in the city.

Concerts in the Parks—The park bureau, 1107 SW 4th (248-4287) sponsors more summer music, free of charge, than any other organization. Under its careful planning the public can meet at Washington Park from late July through Aug. for a three-week program of the best in Oregon music. Included on the bill is apt to be a recent musical comedy, the Oregon Symphonic Band, folk dancers, sounds of the big bands, ballet, barbershop quartets. At Laurelhurst Park, band concerts are performed Sun. at 5 p.m. in July and August. Jazz, country, and soft rock groups play lunch concerts in two downtown parks during July and August. Listen for these sounds at O'Bryant Square, Chapman Square, and Waterfront Park. Across the river at Holladay Park, near the Lloyd Center, Wed. is lunch concert day. Other park entertainment includes music in the Volcano at Mt. Tabor Park, Shakespeare in the Parks throughout the city, and symphonic band concerts at Laurelhurst Park.

Colleges and Universities

Music is always in the air on college campuses. Following is a list of regular groups, although many offer impromptu groupings. For further information, call the music departments of the college.

Lewis and Clark College—0615 SW Palatine Hill Rd. (244-6161). Lewis and Clark College Community Band, Wind Ensemble, Stage Band. The Lewis and Clark College Choir, Chamber choir, College community Chorus and the Collegium Musicum, Renaissance and baroque music for voice and instruments.

Portland State University—724 SW Harrison (229-3011). University Chorus, Chamber Choir, Madrigal Singers, Wind Ensemble, Sinfonietta, Concert Band, Stage Band. During the fall, winter, and spring terms at PSU, free Brown Bag Concerts are performed in Room 75 of Lincoln Hall, Tues. and Thurs. at noon.

Reed College—3203 SE Woodstock Blvd. (771-1112). Collegium Musicum, String Quartet, Chamber Ensemble, Choir, and impromptu groups. Collegium Musicum offers free spring and Christmas concerts of early music performed by singers and players of authentic reproductions of old instruments.

University of Portland—5000 N. Willamette Blvd. (283-7228). University of Portland Community Symphony Orchestra, Concert Choir, Chamber Singers, Wind Ensemble, Chamber Ensemble, Jazz Ensemble. Solo recitals and mixed groups also are featured. The university will mail out a bi-monthly calendar of activities for those interested.

Other Music Groups

Chamber Music Society of Oregon (282-2826) offers free concerts regularly.

Early Keyboard Society, P.O. Box 40402, Portland, 97240 (233-0401) is one of the oldest and most prominent groups of its kind.

Friends of Chamber Music, P.O. Box 751, Portland, 97207 (229-4029).

Oregon Repertory Singers, P.O. Box 894, Portland, 97207 (227-3929). Gilbert Seeley directs 3 concerts a season, beginning with Christmas.

Portland Chamber Orchestra, P.O. Box 544, Portland, 97207.

Portland Community Concert Assn., 620 SE Manchester (236-4865) brings 6 concerts a year to the city from ballet to orchestra, instrumental to choral groups.

Portland Symphonic Choir, P.O. Box 1517, Portland, 97207 (226-1631).

After Dark

Portland offers hot and cool running music all over the town as it continues to prove why musicians are one of the city's major exports.

Now that the young men and women of the Willamette Valley are not concerned with preparing for the spring planting, many of them spend the long rainy months experimenting with chords, beats, and novel patterns. Unique taverns and lounges display these new talents.

No one knows Portland music like John Wendeborn, critic for *The Oregonian*. A musician himself, this gentle man speaks the language and listens for beats with a difference.

His orchestrations for nightlife vary from a string quartet through Dixieland, a fast-dying art form from in the music field.

Just barely upstaging Wendeborn during the summer months is the act next to the elephant house at Washington Park Zoo, when musicians gather every Wednesday from late June through August to perform during a summer program called *Your Zoo and All That Jazz*. Admission to the zoo is all it takes for the performances, which promise a rain check for a Thursday show, if necessary. Pack a picnic dinner, or purchase wine, cheese, and fruit at the site for music with a special aroma during the summer. A call to the zoo will give you the weekly performance.

Another special entertainment spot for music lovers under legal age is Portland Skate and Disco, 418 SE Main (236-9171). Billed as "rock'n rollerskate" this moving spot features table tennis Mon., Wed., and Sat. during the morning hours, with live music on Fri. and Sat. nights. Dancers can follow the bands on skates or flat footed, according to preference. Those who know, say the emphasis is on rock, rather than disco beats.

Portland's newest music spot for those under 21 is Urban Noize, 525 SE Stark (231-0233). Club owners schedule live rock and plan to showcase out-of-town bands. Other activities include a discotheque and movies.

Drawing crowds on the adult circuit for its Las Vegas-style entertainment is the Showplace Lounge at the Sheraton-Airport, 8235 NE Airport Way (288-7171), where rock show bands perform 6 nights a week. Dance sets between shows make the evening complete. Shows start at 9 except for Sun. when the lounge is closed.

For dancing only, a current favorite is the Tiffany Lounge at the Red Lion Motor Inn, 310 SW Lincoln in Portland Center (221-0450).

Lounges

Beachcomber, 40 N. Lake, Lake Oswego (636-6677). Jazz and popular music; jam sessions Sun.

Jazz De Opus, 33 NW 2nd (222-6077). Jazz always, sometimes live and always according to the preference of the purists.

Key Largo, 31 NW 1st (223-9919). Soft jazz Thurs.-Sat., live.

Monte Carlo, 1016 SE Belmont (238-7627). Jazz, contemporary, popular music with dancing and entertainment.

Tuck Lung, 140 NW 4th (223-1090). In addition to a fortune cookie, this venerable restaurant serves up jazz. No cover.

Taverns

Accuardi's Caffe-Bar, 135 NW 5th (227-3661). Funk and jazz, live nightly.

Buffalo Head Tavern, 6900 SW Nyberg Rd., Tualatin, on east side of I-5 freeway (638-8232). Rock.

Chuck's, 823 SW Front (226-0256). Live music, mostly jazz. Also outstanding restaurant.

Darcelle XV, 208 NW 3rd (222-5338). A gay tavern which caters to straights during a female impersonator show 5 nights a week.

Depot, 5021 SE Powell (775-8278). Rock, Wed.-Sat.

Earth, 632 NW 21st (227-4573). Variety of good rock, folk, jazz, Tues.-Sat.

Euphoria, 320 SE 2nd (235-4300). Traveling names, touring bands; some jazz, mostly rock. Tues.-Sun.

Faucet, 6821 SW Beaverton-Hillsdale Hwy. (297-2702). Dancing with rock; game room. Music, Wed.-Sat.

Foghorn's Harbor, 1134 SW Jefferson (227-4209). Acoustic guitar Fri.

Gazebo Gallery, 11 SW Mt. Jefferson Terr., Lake Oswego (635-2606). Open 6 days a week. Wine and music, lunch and dinners in a gallery surrounding. Closed Mon.

Helm, 1301 NE Broadway (288-1814). Jazz 5 nights a week at this long-established Portland spot.

Horse Brass Pub, 4522 SE Belmont (232-2202). English pub atmosphere. Singalongs, folk, ragtime, and Irish melodies, Fri.-Sun.

Long Goodbye (see Theater), 300 NW 10th (228-1008). Jazz, sometimes live, RB, and rock, Tues.-Sun.

Ninth Street Exit, 215 SE 9th (232-8216). Live rock.

Nut Loft Deli, 17210 SW Shaw, Aloha (649-3354). Jazz, bluegrass, Fri. and Sat.

Hobo's Inn, 120 NW 3rd (224-3285). Formerly Old Town Strutters' Hall, now moving out with jazz, Fri.-Sun.

Old Orleans Alley, 519 SW 11th (242-1124). Dixieland, 2 shows nightly, Wed.-Sun.

Orange Peel, 6327 SW Capitol Hwy. (246-1530). Live rock, Tues.-Sat.

PC and S Tavern, 1036 SW Morrison (no phone). Folk and jazz.

Pub Theatre, 1900 NW 27th (224-1431). The Irish are alive here.

Rockcreek, Rt. 1, Box 188, Hillsboro (645-3822). Country, bluegrass, folk, jazz, 7 days a week.

Silver Moon, 432 NW 21st (221-1919). Mostly rock.

Tippers, 11342 SE Powell Blvd. (761-5252). Live rock.

Vat & Tonsure, 822 SW Park (227-1845). Occasional classical ensembles, good food.

White Eagle, 836 N. Russell (282-6810). Oldest tavern in rock. Live music Mon.-Sat. "If you have a good group, you can play on the weekend; otherwise your turn will come early in the week" according to owner.

Wreck of the Hesperus, 1200 NE 102nd (252-0965). All live rock, Tues.-Sat.

Discotheque

Earthquake Ethel's Roadhouse, 2970 SW Cedar Hills Blvd., Beaverton (643-1647). Teenage disco dance parties Sat. afternoons.

Fast Eddie's for Ribs, 1800 SW 1st Ave. (228-2117). Eat those on the plate and then move yours to the beat.

Great Gatsby's, 10235 NE Halsey (253-2874). Dining and disco dancing.

Maxie's, Red Lion—Jantzen Beach, 909 N. Hayden Island Dr. (283-4466). Dinner with a difference plus disco.

Steamers, Chumaree-Rodeway Inn, 8303 NE Sandy Blvd. (256-5211). They're talking about the engines, not the clams, but buttered clams are featured on the menu. Disco is on the lounge floor.

Electronics

Television Stations

KATU-TV Channel 2, the ABC affiliate
KGW-TV Channel 8, the NBC affiliate
KOIN-TV Channel 6, the CBS affiliate
KPTV Channel 12, nation's leading independent station
KOAP-TV, Channel 10, the educational station

Radio Stations

Easy Listening
KUPL—1330 AM 98.5 FM
KJIB—99.5 FM
Listener Supported
KBOO—90.7 FM
Middle of the Road
KARO—1480 AM
KEX—1190 AM
KYTE—970 AM 101.1 FM
KUIK—1360 AM
Country & Western
KWJJ—1080 AM
KRDR—1230 AM
KGAR—1550 AM
Educational/Public
KOAP—91.5 FM
KBPS—1450 AM

Talk
KKEY—1150 AM
KXL—750 AM—95.5 FM
KYXI—1520 AM
Rock
KGON—92.3 FM
KGW—620 AM
KKSN—910 AM
KPAM—1410 AM—97.1 FM
KINK—102 FM
KMJK—107 FM
KQFM—100 FM
KLLB—101 FM
Religious
KPDQ—800 AM—93.7 FM
Sounds of '40s
KLIQ—1290 AM

Photo: David Falconer

Portland Mall with its exclusive bus lanes is a major downtown attraction. Bus travel is free on mall and within 340-block area designated as Fareless Square except from 3 to 7 p.m. weekdays.

TRANSPORTATION
Getting Around is Half the Fun

E VER since the covered wagons rolled across the Oregon Trail from Missouri, Portland has been luring travelers over the mountains. The 20th century version of the Old Oregon Trail is I-84, which, interestingly enough, carries transcontinental motor and bus traffic along an approximate version of the covered wagon route.

Remnants of the Oregon Trail and the Barlow Road, which provided wagon passage over Mt. Hood to Portland, are marked for motorists as they whisk in or out of Portland via I-84 or U.S. 26.

More recently Portland has become a major West Coast terminal for air travel to and from the Orient and other parts of the world.

A railroad passenger center, Portland is not. Those once-glamorous east-west trains, the *City of Portland* and the *Portland Rose,* have disappeared like the covered wagons before them. Although AMTRAK once completely eliminated all passenger routes east from Portland, it has restored limited service via *The Pioneer,* which travels to Salt Lake City and makes connections with transcontinental trains headed farther east. AMTRAK also provides service north to Seattle and south to San Francisco.

Airlines

Portland International Airport has emerged from major terminal expansion with many new features, including underground escalator service to and from the parking areas;

decor which is distinctly Northwest in mood; and a children's area with semi-private facilities for parents with infants, including child-size furniture.

Red cedar paneling, warm red and blue carpeting, suspended fabric panels illustrating Oregon wildflowers, and natural plantings all work together to capture the mood of the Pacific Northwest environment. An excellent restaurant, Port West (249-4850), serves the airport.

Major airlines serving Portland are: Air California (241-8005), Alaska (224-2547), Braniff (224-5030), Continental (224-4560), Delta (228-2128), Eastern (224-7550), Republic (224-5252), Northwest Orient (226-3211, domestic; 226-6091, international and Hawaii), United (226-7211), and Western (225-0830).

Commuter airlines flying out of Portland International are: Cascade (249-4920), to eastern Oregon, Washington, Boise, and Lewiston, Idaho, and Air Oregon (249-4480), to points all over the state.

Airport Transportation

DART (Downtown Airport Rapid Transportation—223-2139) offers the most convenient way to get to the airport, short of a free ride with spouse or friend. DART sends buses back and forth frequently for $2.75 a passenger.

Also providing ground transportation to Portland International from their areas are: Beaverton Airporter (649-2213); Lake Oswego Airporter (636-3639); Hut Limousine Service, from the Salem-Woodburn area (1-363-8059); and Vancouver Airporter, Longview-Woodland Airporter, and Hood River Airporter, which also serves Mt. Hood and Timberline Lodge (same Portland number for all three: 285-4040).

If you're staying near the airport, the new Sheraton Inn and most other hotels and motels provide transportation to and from the terminal.

If you choose to drive yourself to the airport and "board" your car there while you're away, you can park in the long-term parking facility operated by the airport. A free shuttle bus will take you to the terminal. Short-term parking is also available. None of the airport parking is under cover. Private shuttle parking is offered near the airport.

In the short-term parking area are a number of reserved spaces near the terminal building for automobiles carrying passengers with wheelchairs. Elevator service from the tunnel to the terminal area augments the escalators.

AMTRAK

Portland's revered red brick Union Station, 800 NW 6th (248-1146) is interesting for itself and as a landmark AMTRAK passenger station. Built in 1890, the station has a 150-foot clock tower and a red tile roof visible from many downtown sites. A good restaurant, Wilf's (223-0070), occupies part of the building. Three trains leave Portland daily for Seattle; the Coast Starlight leaves daily for Los Angeles at 4:05 p.m.; and The Pioneer leaves daily for Salt Lake City at noon.

In addition, under the experimental Willamette Valley commuter service, two trains (in addition to the Coast Starlight) travel the valley to and from Eugene. The trip between Eugene and Portland takes 3 hours.

Call this toll-free number for AMTRAK Intercity Rail Passenger Service Information and Reservations: 1-800-421-8320. Baggage room number is 223-2663.

Buses

Tri-Met

Tri-Met, the Portland metropolitan area's excellent tri-county public bus system, is trying harder and harder to lure commuters out of their automobiles—and seems to be succeeding.

Of the many new services and features Tri-Met has initiated, the Portland Mall, completed in early 1978, is making the greatest impact on the downtown scene.

Wide brick sidewalks, planters, park benches, trip-planning kiosks, flower stalls, kiosks for public notices, and passenger shelters with televised schedule information are making the mall a place where people want to gather, shop, work—and board the bus.

Tri-Met's buses travel exclusively on two or three lanes on 5th and 6th from Burnside to Madison, whisking passengers through downtown more quickly. Streets crossing the mall continue to carry cars and other vehicles. Private vehicles are allowed limited access to the mall.

Fareless Square—Complementing the mall scheme is Tri-Met's already established, popular Fareless Square policy. Fareless Square is a 340-block area downtown where you can ride free except from 3 to 7 p.m. weekdays. It extends from the river west to the Stadium Freeway (SW 13th or 14th) and from the Stadium Freeway on the south as far north as Hoyt.

Let's suppose you're staying at the Hilton Hotel on 6th and want to have lunch in the Old Town area. Just hop any bus in front of your hotel and travel north to Oak. Walk through the U.S. Bank Plaza east toward the river and you're near the heart of Old Town—free. Or ask your driver if the bus you're riding continues across Burnside to NW Couch or Everett, which is even closer to the heart of Old Town. You'll still be within Fareless Square. (See Walking Tours.)

Generally, all southbound buses travel through downtown on 5th and all northbound buses on 6th; all go the entire length of the mall.

Get a Fareless Square map for details on free travel outside the mall. You must exit from the front of the bus (to pay your fare) if you have boarded free in Fareless Square and have traveled beyond the boundary.

Customer Assistance Office—Located in the center of downtown at 522 SW Yamhill, this handy drop-in center is staffed with clerks who sell tickets, monthly passes, and are generally helpful. The center is stocked as full as a magazine stand with all of Tri-Met's schedules and other information.

Trip-Planning Kiosks—Eight trip-planning kiosks are located on the mall to help Tri-Met passengers reach their destinations. Each is equipped with a television screen and keyboard that will automatically answer route and scheduling queries. Using a map installed in the kiosk, a passenger determines desired line number, then pushes a button on the keyboard for line number, day of the week, and direction intended. The screen replies with a listing of bus arrival times and locations for the specified route.

Fares—You pay 65¢ to ride Tri-Met within a 5-mile radius of downtown. Beyond the 5-mile radius (Zone 3) to downtown, the fare is 90¢. Exact change or ticket must be dropped in the fare box. Students and Honored Citizens ride for less.

The rate for high school students with ID cards is 45¢. The rate for younger students is 45¢. Children in grades one through six need not carry ID cards, but seventh and eighth graders must. ID cards are available at schools. Children under six riding with an adult ride free.

Honored citizens may use an ***Honored Citizen*** card or Medicare card to qualify for 10¢ fares during weekday nonrush hours (9 a.m.-3 p.m.) and free rides on weekends and evenings after 7 p.m. The rest of the time they pay the regular fare. Honored Citizen cards, which are issued to disabled or legally blind persons, as well as to persons over 65, are available at the Customer Assistance Office.

Books of tickets may be purchased at the Tri-Met Customer Assistance Office or at trip-planning kiosks or at over 100 ticket outlets around town. VISA cards are accepted at the Tri-Met office but not, generally, at other outlets. Nor can you charge your Tri-Met ticket book on a downtown store account.

Monthly passes, costing $14 (students), $21 or $29 (Zone 3), are also available at the Customer Assistance Office as well as other ticket outlets. They are transferable so anyone in the family can use them.

Transfers are issued to passengers who must take more than one bus to reach their destination. All transfers are good for as long as two hours to provide for shopping time in between buses.

Pets—No animals are allowed on Tri-Met buses unless they are in a container or cage—with the exception of seeing-eye dogs.

Tri-Met Routes—Covering three counties, Tri-Met obviously operates plenty of routes. You can ride the air-conditioned buses as far as Canby, Molalla, and Estacada to the south; Hillsboro and Forest Grove to the west; Vancouver, Wash., to the north; and Boring, Sandy, and Troutdale to the east. Tri-Met offers a **System Map** which shows all bus routes, gives a description of points of interest along each route, and contains service area, Fareless Square, and Portland Mall maps. Get your copy at the Customer Assistance Office. A scaled-down version is in the Portland phone book. Separate route schedules are available at more than 300 outlets in Tri-Met's service area. By pursuing them, you'll be amazed at all the places Tri-Met goes and the schedules it keeps at odd hours. Seven colorful symbols identify geographic areas within the Tri-Met System. Call for fares outside the 5-mile zone.

Bus Shelters—Among Tri-Met's more than 600 passenger shelters system-wide are 31 "super" shelters on the Portland Mall. You board your bus at the shelter marked with the symbol for your destination. (Cross mall routes are served on Morrison or Yamhill.) In each shelter is a television screen showing the next three departure times (from the first mall stop) of all buses serving that shelter; maps; pay phone; seating for four; and protection from the weather for up to 100.

Park-and-Ride Stations—Many areas are designated around the metropolitan area. You may park your car free all day and ride Tri-Met wherever you want to go. For the Park-and-Ride nearest you, call 233-3511. A west Portland transit station has been erected at SW Barbur & Capitol Hwy. for Tri-Met passengers.

Freeway Travel—Whether you're busing or driving, if you've been on I-84, locally known as the "Banfield," you've noticed the signs that say "Buses and 2-Person Carpools Only." These signs designate a special lane which Tri-Met uses for express "flyers" weekdays on the busy Banfield. The special lanes run from NE 39th to 82nd eastbound and from NE 82nd to Holladay westbound. Restrictions are imposed only during rush hours.

Sports and Special Events Shuttles—Tri-Met operates shuttle buses for sports and special events. Call 233-3511 before the event for details.

24-Hour Route and Schedule Information—Direct dial your bus route for schedule information. Each route has its own phone number. See telephone directory for listings by route number.

Handy Phone Numbers—Route and Schedule Information, weekdays, 8:30 a.m.-4:30 p.m. (233-3511), Lost and Found (238-4855), Charters (238-4853), Complaints and Suggestions (238-4909).

Inter-City Buses

Two transcontinental bus lines serve Portland: Greyhound Bus Lines, 509 SW Taylor (243-2323, for nationwide information; 243-2313, Seattle only) and Trailways Bus System, 500 NW Broadway (228-8571).

Important to Portland-Vancouver commuters is Tri-Met's Vancouver-Portland line #5. Fare is $1; a monthly pass costs $35.

Taxis, Special Cars

Biggest cab companies in town are Broadway Cab (227-1234) and Radio Cab (227-1212). Don't try to hail a cab in Portland; phone ahead. Special phones are provided in many busy locations for ordering cabs.

Medi-Car Wheel Chair Transport Service, 2535 NW Upshur (227-2555), provides expert, cheerful help for the handicapped.

PLACES TO STAY
"Room service, please..."
to "Tenting Tonight"

With the exception of the Benson Hotel, built by retired logger Simon Benson in 1913, Portland offers little in the way of historic lodgings. But the hotel-motel growth during the 1970s promises that history may yet have a chance to speak in Portland as innkeepers challenge one another in a battle for better rooms and more exotic residents

George Washington did not sleep in any of Portland's hotels, but the late President Taft spent some time stuck in a bathtub at the old Portland Hotel, according to a late and very colorful newspaper photographer. Neither the president, the hotel, or the photographer are here today to substantiate the story, but had the picture been taken (the photographer just a second too late), Portland might have made the hotel industry map.

Jimmy Carter quietly broke his stay-at-home tradition by spending a night at Portland's new Marriott Motor Hotel just after its completion. And when former President Gerald Ford first visited the city, he greeted locals at the Benson. Being a good politician, he crossed the river the following year to shake hands at the Lloyd Center Sheraton (now the Red Lion) and finally endeared himself to management and Republicans alike by visiting the Hilton Hotel on his final visit west.

The National Trust for Historic Preservation ironically chose the contemporary Hilton for its meeting a few years ago. Zsa Zsa Gabor called for hairdressing services to her suite at the Benson, while George Hamilton held court at the Jantzen Beach Thunderbird. James Beard makes his reservations at the Mallory Motor Hotel, and Katharine Hepburn, in her classic style, chose none of the above, sublet a private apartment and took a taxi to Jimmy Corno's to pick out her own fresh vegetables.

Innkeeping is on a definite upswing in the Portland area with many new accommodations. And for those traditionalists, the older establishments continue to keep rooms well appointed and clean with hallways safe at night.

Following is a selection of tested, expensive to moderate rooms, all of which are friendly and comfortable. Rates are subject to constant change along with the U.S. dollar, but quality is not. For your convenience we have arranged them by area.

Hotels and Motels

West Side (downtown)

The Benson on Broadway—309 SW Broadway (228-9611). 330 rooms. A "classic" among hotels. The Benson was recently renovated from lobby to penthouse, although the rare materials selected by Simon Benson in 1913 remain intact, including Circassian walnut paneling imported from Russia, Italian marble stairways, and sparkling chandeliers. Even if you are a local, stop by the lobby cocktail lounge in the afternoon for a sip of Perrier just to slip into the turn-of-the-century mood now given gently, but grandly given, to this beauty. A Western International Hotel, home of Trader Vic's and the Holiday-award London Grill. Pay garage. Moderate to expensive. All credit cards, including United Air Lines.

Hilton Hotel—SW 6th & Salmon (226-1611). 500 rooms. Panorama restaurant on the 23rd floor, not open Sun. Outdoor swimming pool on the terrace also caters to guests and to the delight of the employees of the Public Service Building across the street. On the main floor find The Trees (see Restaurants). Although this hotel is part of an international chain, the waitresses have learned to "speak Portland." Waitress Kay Scroggins crocheted all the bright potholders for the individual coffee pots at the tables. Pay garage. Credit cards. Moderate to expensive.

Imperial Hotel—400 SW Broadway (228-7221). 170 rooms which still serve as a stopping place for eastern Oregon cattlemen. Comfortable, with room enough to swing your lariat. Restaurant and bar. Credit cards. Moderate.

Mallory Motor Hotel—729 SW 15th (223-6311). 160 rooms. Quiet, out-of-the-way home-away-from-home (NYC) for gourmet James Beard; also where Medford, Oregonians stay when they visit the Portland Clinic. Dining room, cocktail lounge. Credit cards. Moderate.

Marriott Hotel—1401 SW Front (226-7600). 506 rooms, almost half of them facing the Willamette River with windows opening to catch the river's breeze. Two restaurants and a lobby bar in a setting which can only be described as traditional Marriott. However, it will no doubt weather in and become more Portland than Pittsburgh as the months go by. Full range of services, pets allowed. Complete health club including exercise room, indoor swimming, hydrotherapy massage pools, men's and ladies' saunas, and game room. Outstanding gift shop, certainly the best of its kind in the city. Airport limo service. Parking under the hotel. Meeting facilities for 2,200 theater-style and 1,500 for a banquet. Credit cards. Moderate to expensive.

Riverside West Motor Hotel—50 SW Morrison (221-0711). 138 rooms, some overlooking the Willamette River. Close to shopping areas. Dining room and lounge. Credit cards. Moderate.

East Side (Coliseum-Lloyd Center)

Cosmopolitan Hotel—1030 NE Union (235-8433). 175 rooms. Rooftop pool and dining, live entertainment. Best Western Motel. Credit cards. Moderate to expensive.

Hyatt Lodge—431 NE Multnomah (233-5121). 80 rooms. Close to Memorial Coliseum and Lloyd Center. Credit cards. Moderate.

Kings Way Inn—420 NE Holladay (233-6331). 97 rooms and suites. A Best Western motel. Covered parking. Moderate. Credit cards.

Thunderbird/Red Lion Motor Inn—Lloyd Center (288-6111). This Northwest chain has puchased the former Sheraton-Portland with the promise of a $5 million remodeling and renovation program. A 15-story tower addition will add 250 guest rooms to the complex, giving it a total capacity of 526 guest rooms and making it the largest hotel in the state. Meeting rooms and the 10,000-sq.-ft. ballroom will be remodeled, and 12 smaller meeting rooms will be added. The motor inn is directly adjacent to Lloyd Center, one of the Northwest's largest shopping centers. ★ Restaurants, outdoor pool, lounge. Credit cards. Moderate to expensive. Free Parking.

Thunderbird Motor Inn Downtown—1225 N. Thunderbird Way (235-8311). 220 rooms. Opposite the Memorial Coliseum. Dining room and cocktail lounge overlooking the Willamette River (see Restaurants). Meeting facilities and banquet halls. Credit cards. Moderate.

TraveLodge at the Coliseum—1441 NE 2nd (233-2401). 243 rooms. A fine motel. Restaurant and lounge with live entertainment; within walking distance of the Coliseum and the Lloyd Center. Credit cards. Moderate.

Airport

Cosmopolitan Airtel—6221 NE 82nd (255-6511). 100 rooms, three minutes from the airport. Indoor-outdoor pool and tennis courts, live entertainment and dancing. Credit cards. Expensive.

Fortnighter Best Western Motel—4911 NE 82nd (255-9771). 52 suites with some kitchenettes. Close to airport. Credit cards. Moderate.

Ramada Inn—7101 NE 82nd (255-6722). 140 rooms adjacent to airport; 24-hour courtesy limousine. Restaurant and lounge with live entertainment. Credit cards. Moderate.

Sheraton Inn Airport—8235 NE Airport Way (288-7171). 152 rooms. Although this is located at the end of the runway, the rooms are soundproofed and beautiful. Lobby, cocktail lounge, and restaurant feature all Oregon woods. Entertainment nightly is of Las Vegas quality. Meeting facilities. Credit cards. Moderate to expensive.

Outlying Innkeepers

Greenwood Inn—10700 SW Allen Blvd., Beaverton (643-7444). 200 rooms located well out of downtown area but close to Washington Square.★ Live entertainment with "name" celebrities. Convention facilities 15 minutes from city center. Credit cards. Moderate to expensive.

Holiday Inn—I-5 at Stafford Rd. (682-2211). 175 rooms in this masterpiece in the Holiday chain. Restaurant and cocktail lounge, indoor swimming, banquet rooms to 600. Immediate freeway access to city center. Credit cards. Moderate.

Nendel's Inn—9900 SW Canyon Rd. (297-2551). 108 rooms, outstanding restaurant (see Restaurants). Heated pool and convention facilities 10 minutes from downtown. Credit cards. Moderate.

Ramada Inn—7125 Nyberg Rd., Tualatin (638-4141). 104 units in sylvan setting just south of Portland on I-5. Coffee shop, restaurant, live entertainment, pool. Credit cards. Moderate.

Red Lion Motor Inn—Jantzen Beach—909 N. Hayden

Island Dr. (283-4466). 320 rooms on the Columbia River. Part of Portland's largest motel complex all facing the Columbia River. Close to airport and Jantzen Beach Shopping Center. Credit cards. Moderate to expensive.

Thunderbird Motor Inn at Jantzen Beach—1401 N. Hayden Island Dr. (283-2111). 351 rooms here and across the river on the Washington side, plus 159 more at the **Thunderbird Inn at the Quay**, (285-0636). And this is only a start for this luxurious motor inn, which will add a 16-story tower with 300 additional rooms. Fine restaurants and cocktail lounges with windows overlooking the Columbia. Large convention center. Located on I-5 just 10 minutes from the airport. Next door to Jantzen Beach Shopping Center.★ Credit cards. Moderate to expensive.

State Parks

Ainsworth State Park, Columbia River Scenic Route, 37 miles east of Portland, 45 trailer sites.

Champoeg State Park, off US 99W, 7 miles east of Newberg. Tents and trailers; trailer dumping station but no hookups.

Fort Stevens State Park, off U.S. 101, 10 miles west of Astoria, tents and trailer sites with hookups. Trailer dumping station. Reservations. Open year-round.

Beverly Beach State Park, U.S. 101, 7 miles north of Newport. Tents, trailer sites with hookups. Reservations. Open year-round.

Listed immediately above are two of the largest state camping facilities on the Oregon Coast. There are many others and not all require reservations.

Fees at state parks range from $3 ($5 nonresident) per night for primitive tent campsites to $5 ($8 nonresident) for a trailer campsite with hookups and sewage disposal.

Reservations are accepted by mail or in person—not by phone—at 15 state parks which take them. Reservation requests must include a $4 deposit, which will be applied toward the first-night campsite fee. If reservations are cancelled by 6 p.m. on date you planned to arrive, a $4 raincheck will be issued for future use at any state park (until Dec. 31 of the following year). Campsite Information Center (1-800-452-5687; Portland, 238-7488) provides current information on availability of campsites and will accept cancellations but not reservations; operates Mon.-Fri. 8 a.m.-5 p.m. from spring to early Sept. For additional information, visit or call the Portland Travel Information Center, 12345 N. Union at Jantzen Beach (285-1631). It is open May-Oct.

An *Oregon Parks* map and directory is available from most travel information outlets.

Destination Resorts

Coast

Inn at Otter Crest offers 300 rooms and suites. Park your car at the office and be shuttled down wooded paths to the rooms which climb the cliffs. Facilities include year-round swimming, tennis, saunas, a putting green, and trails. Restaurant and cocktail lounge. Reservations: Otter Rock, 765-2111; toll-free (in Oregon) 1-800-452-2101.

Salishan Lodge rooms are on the 18-hole golf course★ and tucked up in the kinnikinnick. Restaurant, coffee shop, lounge, year-round covered swimming pool, sauna and hydro-therapy pool, men's and ladies' gym, playground, and covered tennis courts. (764-2371).

High and Dry

Black Butte Ranch, about 10 miles west of Sisters on Hwy. 20, keeps a low profile in central Oregon but with two 18-hole golf courses, four swimming pools, stocked fish ponds, a recreation barn, and much more, this resort is a popular insiders' retreat. With the Three Sisters mountains in clear view, the place, once a working ranch, is one of Oregon's finest resorts, offering fine dining, as well. Phone 595-6211 for reservations, information about rooms, condominiums, and home rentals. Black Butte is an enterprise of Brooks Resources Corp.

Kah-Nee-Ta Vacation Resort affords an opportunity to spend some time with the Indians. Stay in a tepee (complete with firepit and cement floor) or take one of the 140 rooms with air conditioning. Heated pools, hot mineral baths, golf, and a restaurant with Indian cuisine. For reservations, call 553-1112.

Sunriver, 15 miles south of Bend, 211 guest rooms and suites. Swimming, golf, tennis, fishing, horseback riding, boating, nature tours, skiing (at Mt. Bachelor just 40 minutes away), bicycling (rentals), restaurant, coffee shop, and cocktail lounge. Private landing strip for small aircraft. (593-1221).

Timberline Lodge ★ (see also Getting Away From It All) offers overnight accommodations on the slopes of Mt. Hood. Activities include heated pool, day and night skiing all week, a ski shop with ski rental and school, a restaurant, and convention and banquet facilities. For reservations, 226-7979.

Valley

The Village Green blossomed into a multimillion-dollar resort simply because Oregonians were intrigued with luxurious accommodations in the middle of nowhere. Located just off I-5 (south of Eugene), this development includes 96 luxurious rooms and suites, swimming pool, a 9 hole pitch-and-putt golf course, tennis, bowling, and a visit to Railroad Town, USA. (942-2491).

Photo: Greater Portland Convention and Visitors' Assn.

Photo: Lisa Stone, Portland Parks

It's "batter up!" all summer as the Portland Park Bureau offers a full range of fastpitch and slowpitch programs for adults and children in parks throughout the city.

SPORTS AND RECREATION

Fun and Games for Every Season

SNOW in the mountains, fat salmon and trout in the clear rivers, lots of water for boating, and thousands of miles of scenic hiking trails are persuasive reasons to choose Portland as a place to live.

Many do and then want to seal the state off from more newcomers. You won't hear them boasting that in Oregon you can golf year-round and ski all summer—on real snow. But, you can.

With all of this plus a fair-sized shopping list of spectator sports, Portland is the kind of place where even the non-athlete has to read the sports pages to survive in social conversations.

Spectator Sports

Professional Franchises

Portland supports two major league professional sports franchises, the 1977 World Champion Portland *Trail Blazers* of the National Basketball Assn., with home games played in the Memorial Coliseum, 1401 N. Wheeler (235-8771, general offices; 239-4422, ticket information; 238-4636, coming events recording) and the Portland *Timbers* of the North American Soccer League, home games played in Portland Civic Stadium. Portland is also the home of the Class AAA baseball *Beavers*. The *Portland Winter Hawks* of the Western Hockey League play a lively season at the Memorial Coliseum in the fall and winter months.

Portland **Trail Blazers**—Season runs October through March; tickets, by mail only, from the Trail Blazer Ticket Offices, 700 NE Multnomah (234-9291). Home games can also be

137

seen on closed-circuit television at the Paramount Theatre, 1037 SW Broadway.

Portland **Timbers**—Season runs May-Sept., games played at Portland Civic Stadium, 1844 SW Morrison (248-4345). Tickets are sold at the stadium and Timbers ticket office, across from the stadium on SW 18th (226-4625).

Portland **Beavers**—Season runs early April to early September at Portland Civic Stadium, 1844 SW Morrison. For additional information call 223-2837. Beaver office is at 1205 SW 18th, near the stadium.

Portland **Winter Hawks**—Season runs October through March; games played at Memorial Coliseum. Hawks office is at 1401 N. Wheeler (238-6366).

Parimutuel Betting

Portland Meadows Horse Race Track, 1001 N. Schmeer Rd. (285-9144). Season runs early Nov.-late April.

Multnomah Kennel Club Dog Race Track, NE 223rd, between Halsey & Gilsan, Fairview, about 15 miles from the city (665-2191). Season runs May-Sept.

Other Athletic Events

Basketball—The Memorial Coliseum reverberates each Christmas season with the Far West Classic, recognized nation-wide as the finest college basketball tournament going. Pacific Athletic Conference (PAC-10) University of Oregon and Oregon State University host the annual affair. During the regular college season, the many fine smaller schools in the area play regularly. The best of these are Portland State University, University of Portland, and Lewis and Clark College. The University of Portland, a member of the West Coast Athletic Conference, plays all of its home games at the Memorial Coliseum.

Track and Field—The last Saturday in January, each year, the Memorial Coliseum hosts the Portland Invitational Indoor Track and Field Meet. Athletes from all over the world compete in one of the slickest track meets in the nation.

Auto Racing—Rose City Speedway, 9727 N. Union (285-2269). Super stock, jalopy, and speed-stock racing begin the last of March, and programs, sometimes including dragsters and formula road racing (particularly through the summer months), continue into late fall. The facilities are good and the track is easily accessible.

Wrestling—This sport can be seen weekly at the Portland Sports Arena, 8725 N. Chautauqua (289-4222).

Archery and Bowhunting

Public archery ranges are available at Washington Park in southwest Portland and East Delta Park in north Portland. Bring your own targets. Visitors or new residents from the more populous eastern parts of the country might be interested in knowing that archery is more than just a fun and games sport in Oregon. Our hunting season includes a special month-long period for bowhunting. Call or write the Oregon Fish and Wildlife Department, 506 SW Mill, P.O. Box 3503, Portland, 97208, (229-5403), for details.

Badminton

Co-ed badminton play is scheduled Tuesday evenings during the school year at Cleveland High School, 3400 SE 26th, under sponsorship of the Park Bureau (248-4315). Free play and informal instruction are offered.

Baseball, Softball

Portland Park Bureau offers a full range of fastpitch and slowpitch softball programs for adults and children throughout the city.

In addition, Portland has one of the bigger and better Little League Baseball programs in the country. As well as pee wee, minor, and major league teams, the Portland Little League sponsors a Little League softball program for girls. (Girls also play on regular Little League teams.) Other baseball programs include Babe Ruth, Pony League, and American Legion, for youth, and Casey Stengel League for adults.

Additional information about Little League and other baseball programs is available from the Park Bureau sports office (248-4325).

Softball becomes a popular spectator sport Fridays, Saturdays, and Sundays in the summer when scores of fans pay the nominal ticket price for a chance to watch exciting adult play at

Farragut Park, N. Farragut and Kerby, or Erv Lind Stadium at Normandale Park, NE 57th & Halsey.

Basketball

Organized basketball is so popular in Portland, home of the NBA champion *Trail Blazers*, that school and community center gymnasiums are precision-scheduled for every day of the hoop season. The Park Bureau offers competition in Goldenball Basketball for grade and high school teams. In recent seasons, 260 boys' teams and 60 girls' teams have scheduled play through the Park Bureau.

In addition, some 200 Portland Basketball Assn. teams compete in the commercial, industrial, church, major, 6-foot and under, and 35-and-older divisions at Portland high schools. Sponsored by the Park Bureau, this city league was described in a local newspaper, *Willamette Week*, as "the Park Bureau's answer for frustrated, aging athletes with a lust for competition."

For information about basketball for grade school girls and adult women, call the Park Bureau (248-4325).

In summer, Pepsi-Cola/NBA Hotshot Basketball competitions are conducted in neighborhood parks, with the winners going on to district and city competitions which in turn lead to a state playoff and competition at Portland *Trail Blazer* games. Boys and girls age 9-18 are eligible and if interested should speak with the directors at their local parks. For more information about Park Bureau basketball programs, call 248-4325 or 248-4315.

Bicycling

Bicycle tours in the Portland area are scheduled just about every weekend of the year, so there's no need to worry about finding your way around the city or countryside if you're a newcomer or a new cyclist.

Portland Wheelmen Touring Club conducts rides on weekends. For information about upcoming rides and membership write to 2605 SE Yamhill, 97214.

More organized bicycle touring is one demonstration of an increased emphasis on safe bicycling practices by local and state authorities and cycling enthusiasts.

Bicycle touring in the Portland area escalated when state funding became available to construct bicycle paths. Now, cyclists are encouraging use of many lightly traveled roadways which are perfect for the sport if proper safety rules are followed.

The **Bicycle Commuter Service**, 1914 SE Ankeny (233-BIKE) will provide you with a personalized commuting route and information on parking. Call between 10 a.m. and 4 p.m. The service also sponsors clinics in bike maintenance and safe riding.

The city's **Bicycle and Pedestrian Program**, 621 SW Alder, Portland 97205 (248-4407), is an important source of cycling information. Working with the **Citizens' Bicycle and Pedestrian Advisory Committee**, it coordinates all city programs for bicyclists, including Park Bureau bike clinics for children and adults.

The children's clinics are held in the parks as part of the summer playground program. In the summer and fall, adults can attend a series of clinics to learn how to maintain their bikes, the best biking places around Portland, and tips on bike touring. Call the bike program number above for schedules.

The city program publishes a *Portland Bicycle Map* which is available at City Hall, bicycle stores, the Portland Convention and Visitors' Association, and other locations for $2. Portland streets are rated by color from easy to very difficult. Accompanying information includes bridge maps, safety tips, bike laws, and a repair shop list.

Bicycle Trips

Some popular bicycle trips and bicycle areas are listed here—a compilation of the favorites of a number of cycling friends. If you're serious about touring, buy *55 Oregon Bicycle Trips* by Nick and Elske Jankowski (Touchstone). It is full of pictures, maps, and helpful suggestions.

Eastmoreland Ride—Route along SE 28th circles Eastmoreland Golf Course and provides access to Reed College and Crystal Springs Rhododendron Garden.

SW Fairmount Boulevard—Fairmount Blvd. in southwest Portland is a winding road which draws a 4-mile circle around Portland Heights and borders the base of Council Crest Park. You can start at any point on the circle. Fairmount is a lovely, wooded road edged with hillside residences. It's narrow, so stay alert on the curves. The grades are gentle.

Scenic Figure-8 Trip—Travel the Fairmount circle and then take SW Talbot Rd. to SW Patton where Patton joins Humphrey Blvd. at St. Thomas More Church. Travel Humphrey northwest to Hewett Blvd. Follow Hewett back to Patton.

Multnomah Falls Ride—For the rider who is in good condition, a beautiful ride is to Multnomah Falls, 35 miles east of Portland in the Columbia Gorge. Cyclists recommend going to the Columbia River Scenic Highway via SE Stark and returning to Portland via NE Halsey.

Terwilliger Boulevard—You can park near the Carnival Restaurant, 2805 SW Sam Jackson Park Rd., where Terwilliger begins its incline toward the University of Oregon Health Sciences Center, to begin this lovely park-lined ride of about 3 miles (one-way). This is an established bike route and is well signed. To avoid the rather steep incline at the beginning, you can leave your car at a scenic parking area about 1½ miles up the road from the Carnival. Travel through Terwilliger Blvd. Park and past the Health Sciences complex. Notice the Totem Pole at the Hillvilla Restaurant on your left★ (see Art in Public Places). Your path will pass under busy SW Capitol Hwy. and put you on the boundary of peaceful George H. Himes Park, a good picnic spot. You'll find tables at Terwilliger and SW Nebraska. The bicycle path ends at Barbur Blvd.

Terwilliger-Tryon Creek State Park—An extension to the Terwilliger ride takes you on to Tryon Creek State Park★ to the south. To achieve this, cross a major intersection at Barbur (where the Terwilliger bike path ends) and continue south across a bridge over I-5. You're still on Terwilliger. Continue on it through the Burlingame shopping area, past Collins View School to a fork at Boones Ferry Rd. At this point, a bike route (well marked) begins which takes you into Tryon Creek State Park. The distance from the end of the Terwilliger bike path to the beginning of the Tryon path is about 1½ miles.

Sauvie Island—Country roads and pleasant beaches are your reward for pedaling on Sauvie Island,★ a rural agricultural retreat formed by the confluence of the Willamette and Columbia Rivers. To get there, take U.S. 30 (one of the roads to Astoria) going northwest to the Sauvie Island Bridge about 10 miles from Portland. Immediately after crossing the bridge, you'll see a park, where you can leave your car if you're not cycling all the way. Follow Reeder Rd. to the sand beaches on the northeast side of the island. One of these is dubbed

"Social Security Beach" because it is a pensioners' favorite fishing ground and the "headquarters" for "plunking," a peculiar technique of angling using a rod, rod holder, and cow bell, which is rigged to ring when a fish strikes the line. Unfortunately, salmon fishing has been curtailed on the Sauvie Island beaches and varies from year to year depending on run forecasts.

Mary Young State Park—Three miles south of Lake Oswego between State Hwy. 43 and the Willamette River is Mary S. Young State Park, which contains a designated bike path.

Bike Postscripts

• The Burnside Bridge sidewalk is recommended for a safe crossing of the Willamette. See *Portland Bicycle Map* for other suggested bridge crossings.

• For bicycle spectators, the Portland Rose Festival offers an exciting event: the Bicycle Road Races at Mt. Tabor Park. Also scheduled during the Rose Festival, held each June, is the Bicycle Track Race at Alpenrose Dairy. Rose Festival events are widely publicized in the metropolitan press. In addition, you can generally watch bicycle races Thursday nights in August and September at Alpenrose and Tuesday nights for 16 weeks starting in May at Portland International Raceway at West Delta Park.

• Moto-cross racing programs for kids aged 7 to 18 are sponsored by the YMCA at the Y's East Clackamas Community Center (see YMCA entry in this section). The Y has developed a Y-BMX race course in Gladstone.

• For help with do-it-yourself bike repairs go to the *Bicycle Repair Collective*, 1912 SE Ankeny (233-0564), open Mon.-Sat. from 10 a.m.-6 p.m. For a $12 membership fee, you can use the shop, the tools, and the consultants—and get a newsletter, as well. An adjustable rate schedule accommodates one-time customers. Classes in bike maintenance are sometimes offered at the shop. Classes in bike repairs are also sponsored seasonally by the Park Bureau and the YMCA.

Some recommended bicycle shops are:

Action Sports, Inc., 3480 SW Cedar Hills Blvd., Beaverton (644-3636).

Beckwith Schwinn Cyclery, 4235 SE Woodstock (774-3531); 1045 E. Powell, Gresham (665-5538).

Bike Gallery, The, 5201 NE Sandy (281-9800), open Sun. Ask
    about Moto-cross racing here.
Cycle Craft, SW 12th & Morrison (222-3821). The place for in-
    formation about bicycle racing. Also rents bikes.
Cycle World, 13807 SE McLoughlin, Milwaukie (654-6888).
Hook's Cyclery, 7850 SE Stark (253-1191).
Northwest Bicycles, 2108 NW Glisan (248-9142). Equal treat-
    ment for a child's broken one-speed.
Phil's Schwinn Cyclery, 701 NE Broadway (281-4036).

Bird Watching

Wintering area for ducks and geese and stopover for
migrant birds, including sandhill cranes, is the Sauvie Island
Wildlife Management Area, operated by the Oregon Fish and
Wildlife Dept. During the hunting season (Oct.-Feb.), the area
is off limits to all visitors except for hunters. Best bird watching is in late winter and spring. In addition to waterfowl, you
can see pheasant, eagles, and hawks. Call 621-3488 to find out
which birds have checked in. The area keeps a checklist.

Other close-in watching areas are:

The Crystal Springs area surrounding the lake at the Rhodo-
    dendron Test Gardens ★ (Feb.-April).
Pittock Wildlife Sanctuary, a good place to see the pileated
    woodpecker and ruffed grouse year-round and, in
    spring, black-throated gray warblers, Townsend warblers,
    and Wilson's warblers.
An area known as the Oaks Bottom, which is being developed
    in southeast Portland as a wetland bird sanctuary. Call
    the Audubon Society (292-6855) for more information.

Boating

Portland's riverways are wide enough and deep enough that
small recreational craft, from sleek rowing shells to power
speedboats, have plenty of room to maneuver around the
barges and ships that comprise the every-day river traffic.

Many of the big yacht clubs and moorages are located on the
Columbia River along NE Marine Drive between NE Union
and points east of the Portland International Airport. Other
moorages are located on Sauvie Island, Hayden Island, and on
the Willamette south of downtown Portland.

"Boating is a way of life for those who take it seriously,"

says retired *Oregon Journal* columnist Ed Goetzl, who once observed that Portland is one of the few places where you can catch a 30-pound salmon during your lunch hour—if you have a boat. (*The Portland GuideBook* makes no guarantees.)

In a motorboat, sailboat, or canoe, you can explore 200 miles of shoreline in the metropolitan area alone. Favorite haunts of boaters include Ross and Hard Tack Islands between the Ross Island and Sellwood Bridges, south of the downtown area; Coon Island and Collins Memorial Marine Park (Columbia County) in the Multnomah Channel opposite Scappoose, north of Portland; and Government Island and Lady Island on the Columbia. The locks at Willamette Falls at Oregon City and at Bonneville Dam east of Portland on the Columbia are free and easily negotiated.

Boaters who know the river shoreline say a good place to moor your boat temporarily for downtown access is at the old harbor patrol dock on the west side of the river at the foot of Clay. There is no boat-launching ramp there.

Houseboat communities in the Portland area are not unusual and offer an attractive alternative lifestyle. The houseboat colony that calls itself the Portland Rowing Club (it still owns some shells) is moored on the east side of the river above the Sellwood Bridge. Others moor at Oaks Park and at Hayden Island in the Columbia.

Free courses in basic safe boating—motor and sail—are conducted by U.S. Power Squadron Units in the area and by various flotillas of the U.S. Coast Guard Auxiliary. For additional information call the U.S. Coast Guard in Portland (221-6344 or 6345) or write the Portland Power Squadron, P.O. Box 1441, Portland, 97207.

A safe boating correspondence course is offered by the Oregon Marine Board, 3000 Market, NE, No. 505, Salem, 97310—a handy substitute for the classroom instruction if you arrive in the state at a time when classes are not being offered. The Marine Board also issues an *Oregon Boaters Handbook*.

Every motorboat and every sailboat 12-feet long or longer—any sailboat with auxiliary power—must be registered with the State of Oregon Marine Board.

Every powerboat must carry at least one fire extinguisher and one Coast Guard-approved personal flotation device for each passenger.

For water skiing, the Willamette, south of Sellwood Bridge, and the Columbia are popular as are the lakes and reservoirs of

Photo: David Falconer

Just by leaning into the wind, summer sailors get a closeup view of metropolitan Portland. Handy moorages make sailing a lunchtime treat when the wind is on the rise.

the Portland area. Central Oregon and the Coast have many lakes where powerboat owners in the Portland area go for skiing and pleasure boating.

Sailing

"The Willamette River is a good place to learn to sail because you have to be alert every minute," said one sailor somewhat cynically. Most sailing in the metropolitan area is confined to the Willamette and Columbia Rivers, and most boaters agree that river sailing is tricky. On the Columbia, when the northeast breezes combine with the current to take you downstream in a hurry, it's a hard tack back.

Nonetheless, sails dot the river in summer, many of them flying from small boats. Favorite small boat classes are *Thistle, Lightning, 470, 505, Coronado, C-Lark, Karalle, Laser,* and *Sunfish.* A popular small craft sailing club is the Willamette Sailing Club at 6336 SW Beaver, north of Willamette Park on the Willamette River's west side. Take time on warm, breezy summer evenings to watch a race there.

Sailing classes for all ages are offered by Lewis and Clark College (sailing dock number is 636-8504); Portland State University (229-3407 or 3412); Portland Community College (777-8020); and Reed College (771-1112).

While sailing and powerboating seem to dominate the local water scene, the Willamette, Sandy, and Clackamas Rivers and nearby lakes and reservoirs provide good water for canoeing and rowing.

Canoeing

Launch your canoe upstream and paddle downstream to any of a number of destinations on the Willamette River.

If urban sightseeing by river is your desire, try putting in at Mary S. Young State Park near West Linn and paddling downstream under bridges, past river-bank homesites to the highrises of downtown Portland. The working cranes at Zidell Explorations Inc. (a sophisticated junkyard) are an interesting sideshow. You'll get a different perspective of the Portland skyline than you do by car. The Cathedral Park★ Ramp is probably the best spot to take out. Watch for debris in the river there. The whole trip will take a full day, and of course you'll need a pick-up at the end. For a shorter trip, take out at one of the many boat ramps south of the city.

For a rural **Willamette River** drift, try a trip from the Newberg boat ramp at Newberg (near the Herbert Hoover house) downstream to Willamette Park in West Linn, at the mouth of the Tualatin River. Bass fishing is good here. River enthusiasts warn: watch out for poison ivy on the tempting islands that dot the river course.

A good drift on the **Sandy River** is from Oxbow County Park to Dabney State Park.★ Both parks provide good facilities for putting in and taking out. The drift is about six miles.

Ramps, Rentals, Charters

Following is a list of boat ramps in the Portland stretch of the Willamette:

Cathedral Park Ramp (east side, under St. Johns bridge)
Willamette Park (west side, south of downtown)
Staff Jennings Ramp (west end of Sellwood Bridge)
Marine Drive (on the Columbia near the airport)

Many more ramps are available in the Milwaukie, Oswego, and Oregon City areas to the south and in the Sauvie Island area to the north.

Canoe rentals are common in the Portland area. For the Sauvie Island area, try Brown's Landing (1-543-6526) and for the Oregon City area, Sportcraft Landing (656-6484). For canoe drift parties, Sportcraft will truck canoes up the Willamette. For Sandy River shuttle service, try River Trails Canoe and Raft Rentals in Troutdale (667-1964). In addition, you can let Yachts-O-Fun do all the work for you and charter the Cruis-Ader Princess (285-6665).

Oregon River Tours, by John Garren (Touchstone), provides detailed information about river running.

Call Lute Jerstad Adventures, P.O. Box 19527, Portland, 97219 (244-4364), about guided float trips.

Northwest Outward Bound School (243-1993), OMSI (248-5938), and the YWCA (223-6281) conduct occasional float trips.

Rowing

A rowing renaissance is under way in Portland. An enthusiastic group of adults and students have organized the Station L Rowing Club, which takes its name from an auxiliary power plant at its moorage beneath the east end of the Marquam Bridge. The club was formed to promote the return of intercollegiate rowing to the Willamette. Reed and Lewis and Clark College students pay $25 a year as student members; adults pay $50. Family memberships are $75 annually. The club's membership is open. For further information call 774-4995 or 286-2840 (eves.).

Body Building and Weight Lifting

Matt Dishman, Mt. Scott, and University Park Community Centers, all operated by the Portland Park Bureau (248-4315), have weight rooms and offer classes or open time in body building and weight lifting year-round.

Bowling

More than 25 bowling alleys are operated in the Portland area, many of them offering food service and child care. Billiard facilities are available at some bowling alleys. For more information about bowling, call: Portland Bowling Assn. (239-7163); Greater Portland Women's Bowling Assn. (239-7160); or Greater Portland Junior Bowling Assn. (254-0931).

Boxing and Wrestling

Boxing and wrestling programs are offered through the Park Bureau at a number of community centers and high schools. Call the Park Bureau (248-4325) for more information.

A Wrestling Fitness and Development Program for grade school youth is sponsored by the Park Bureau in cooperation with the Portland high school wrestling coaches during the winter.

Bridge

In addition to Park Bureau bridge programs at some community centers, there are at least three bridge clubs in Portland. Ace of Clubs Bridge Center, 9364 SW Beaverton-Hillsdale Hwy., Beaverton (292-1437); Gateway Bridge, 10751

NE Fargo (252-5630); and Portland Bridge Center, 2717 NE Broadway (287-4445).

Chess

Each spring some 5,000 chess players compete for a chance to play in *The Oregonian*-OMSI ★ annual chess tournament, a big event in the Northwest. OMSI also offers chess instruction from time to time.

Fencing

Beginning, intermediate, and advanced fencing are offered by the Park Bureau for ages 10 through adult at a variety of locations and at some Community Schools operated jointly by the Portland Public Schools (249-2000) and the Park Bureau. Clinics or demonstrations may be arranged at your school or for your club. Call 248-4325 for more information. Call Salle Auriol Fencing Club, 13939 NW Cornell Rd. (645-8485), about private lessons.

Fishing

Salmon, steelhead, and rainbow and cutthroat trout are the glamour fish from the lakes and streams.

Willamette River—Famed for its run of spring chinook salmon in March, April, and early May and for sturgeon from Feb.-May. The fishery is the length of the lower river and Willamette Slough.

Clackamas River—Steelhead in the lower river, from River Mill Dam to Clackamas, in Nov.-March, and for rainbow trout in the upper river, May-Sept.

Eagle Creek—This Clackamas tributary near Estacada is good for winter steelhead Dec.-Feb., and for jack salmon and coho, late Oct.-Dec.

Sandy River—Fish the lower river from Marmot Dam to Troutdale for steelhead, Dec.-March, and for coho and fall chinook, Oct.-Nov.

Molalla River—Above Wagon Wheel County Park, steelhead, March-Apr., and rainbow trout, May-Aug.

Salmon River—This tributary of the Sandy is good for rainbow trout from June-Sept.

Sauvie Island Wildlife Management Area Lakes and Sloughs—Panfish, bass, catfish, March-Sept.

Sauvie Island Beaches, (Columbia River side)—Steelhead, salmon, jack salmon, and searun cutthroat (harvest trout). Seasons have recently been curtailed on spring and summer runs of salmon.

Licensed fishing guides in the area include:

Dud Nelson (654-5311)

Dennis Mobley (761-1310)

For more information about guides, write for the *Oregon Guides and Packers Directory*, P.O. Box 132, Sublimity, OR 97385. Listings include whitewater guides.

For up-to-date information on what fish are striking where, call the recorded outdoor information number of Oregon Fish and Wildlife (229-5222).

Fishing Postscript

Fishing docks within the city include one at Cathedral Park,★ which offers access for the handicapped, and locations along the waterfront promenade in downtown Portland, including the floating dock at Waterfront Park.★ Sloughs at West Delta Park are stocked with warm-water fish. Try your luck.

Charters

The cost of salmon at your neighborhood market is out of sight, you say? So you decide you want to charter a boat to hook fresh fish and have some fun at the same time.

Nearly every town on the coast berths charter boats, but there are charters and then there are charters. Charters by the hour are a poor investment, for the captains rush to return to shore and pick up the next load whether or not you've limited out. We offer you the very best in two areas. If they're full, they'll recommend someone else. Wise fishermen who take the recommendations usually take home a limit of chinook or silvers.

Prices for salmon excursions run out of the economy class, but you'll get your money's worth with the better skippers. Pick up licenses and salmon tags at a modest fee from sport shops and most charter-boat operators on the coast. The season usually runs from May 1 to Oct. 15, give or take a couple of weeks.

Photo: David Falconer

Fresh salmon for supper is no novelty to Portlanders who have learned to join lines just below Willamette Falls during the spring and fall Chinook runs.

Boats usually leave dockside between 5-6 a.m., so a word of warning: easy on the drinks the night before. Get at least six hours of solid sleep. If you've never been on the ocean, take a motion sickness pill (*Dramamine* or *Marazine*) at least an hour before leaving the dock as insurance. Your stomach will thank you for it.

Bring your own lunch and beverages, other than coffee, aboard. Most cafes open at 4 a.m. on the coast and will prepare a lunch for you while you eat breakfast.

Warrenton—For larger groups who want to be together in one boat and don't want steerage treatment, Bud Charlton's Warrenton Deep Sea Charters is the answer. Capt. Charlton operates three boats for 12 passengers and a couple with small capacities. Charlton is in the business for your enjoyment, not his profit and loss statement. He is a pro's pro and will get you fish if there are any in the ocean. He furnishes tackle and bait. Reserve well ahead (861-1233).

Depoe Bay—This is a unique area for deep-sea fishing. From Depoe Bay the fishing waters are only a 10-minute boat ride, compared to approximately one hour from the Astoria area. For this reason, Depoe Bay charter-boat skippers offer four-hour trips, and these can be worthwhile. Charter costs are somewhat less expensive here, and most boats get in two trips a day.

Stan Allyn's Depoe Bay Charters (765-2345) is one of the best known among the large operators in the area, although there are many other worthwhile skippers. Allyn is usually booked well ahead of time, so call in advance to be sure of your trip time.

Newport—Call Don Christenson of Sea Gull Charters (265-7441) if you're after salmon or tuna in the Yaquina Bay area. Don's charter operation is located at 343 SW Bay Blvd. in Newport.

All the coastal fishing areas have a good supply of charter skippers; lists are often available from Chambers of Commerce.

Fly Fishing

When the Cascade rivers have expended their rush of cold, spring snowmelt, fly fishing picks up and is best during summer evenings. Closest to Portland for the fly angler in July and August is the Clackamas above North Fork Reservoir along with its tributaries, Oak Grove Fork and Collowash Rivers. A run of summer steelhead is now being established in the Clackamas. Summer steelhead are available in the Big Nestucca and Wilson Rivers on the northern Oregon Coast.

There is also nearby fly fishing for these wild warrior steelhead in southwest Washington on the Kalama, Washougal, and Wind Rivers during spring and summer months.

East Fork Hood River, Badger Creek, and White River on the east side of Mt. Hood National Forest are pleasant streams, but the most noted is the lower Deschutes River, which has a special fly-only area.

After a brief sojourn in the saltchuck, the searun cutthroat return to the coastal rivers. Fly fishing with bright attractor patterns is pursued in the lower reaches, near tidewater, for cutthroat starting in August and continuing into September. Nearest Portland or west of the Coast Range are the Kilchis, Big Nestucca, Little Nestucca, Trask, Wilson, and Necanicum Rivers for these searun trout.

The *Oregon Journal* and *Oregonian* both carry weekly fishing reports. Detailed information can be obtained from the Oregon Fish and Wildlife Dept., 506 SW Mill, P.O. Box 3503, Portland, 97208 (229-5403).

A large casting pool in Westmoreland Park is available for bait, spin, or fly casting practice. Fly fishing classes are offered from time to time at Portland Community Centers (248-4315).

Shellfish

Going after Pacific shellfish is something to tell the folks back East about. Try digging for razor clams on a minus tide along the Pacific surfline, or venture onto the bay flats in search of cockle, butter, littleneck, softshell, or gaper clams. Some are best steamed or eaten on the halfshell, others are great for chowder, and the razor clam is the prize when quick-fried in butter and a fresh bread crumb jacket.

Dungeness crab is considered superior to all others by epicures, and moorages on Nehalem, Tillamook, Netarts, Siletz, Yaquina, and Alsea bays offer crab rings and bait plus friendly advice on how to use them.

Or, consider a "crabbing package" such as that offered by the Embarcadero Resort Hotel in Newport. The package includes complete crabbing gear and an excursion on Yaquina Bay. The hotel thoughtfully provides an outdoor kitchen for cooking crab.

Football

Pop Warner football (tackle) for 6th, 7th, and 8th grade boys is conducted through the Park Bureau program. Sponsors pay team fees. The Park Bureau also coordinates seven-man touch football competition for adults and sponsors nine-man flag football programs for grade school boys. Call 248-4325 for more information.

Golf

The Portland metropolitan area supports more fine golf courses per capita than nearly any other city in the United States. Many public courses are available for play, and a number of the fine private clubs are accessible if you're a member of a club in your home town or know a member of one of the local clubs.

Nearly every course is playable year-round. A broad spectrum of challenges faces the hacker or the scratch player. Greens fees are generally quite reasonable at the public courses and only slightly more expensive at the private clubs.

Listed below are public courses in order of toughness.

Meriwether National Golf Club, Hillsboro (648-4143)— About 15 minutes from downtown, 18 holes, 7042 yards, par 72. Long, lots of water, bunkers, limited clubhouse facilities; plan to shower at your motel.

Forest Hills Country Club, Cornelius (648-8559)—20 minutes from downtown, 18/6244/72; best manicured of all public courses with rolling hills, many bunkers, and quite a bit of water and tall fir trees. Local favorite. If you have time, it's worth the drive. Good clubhouse facilities. Call ahead for tee time.

Eastmoreland Municipal Golf Course, 2425 SE Bybee Blvd. (775-2900)—18/6522/72. A contrast in nines; one fairly mundane, the other beautiful with water on every hole. Gets heavy play, so call ahead. Modest clubhouse facilities. Plan to shower at motel.

West Delta Park Golf Course, 3500 N. Victory Blvd. (289-1818)—18/6397/72. Robert Trent Jones designed course; many bunkers, not too long or too many trees or water; lots of doglegs. Needs to mature and get more attention from city. Modest clubhouse.

Gresham Golf Course, 2155 NE Division, Gresham (665-3352)—18/6500/72. About 18 miles from downtown. Challenging course with a little bit of everything for the golfer. Fun to play, and at times can be an ego builder. Good clubhouse facilities.

Rose City Municipal Golf Course, 2200 NE 71st (253-4744)—18/6493/72. Rather pedestrian layout with about five interesting holes. Lots of trees, little sand or water. Gets heavy play. Modest clubhouse facilities. Shower at motel. Close to town.

Colwood National Golf Course, 7313 NE Columbia Blvd. (254-5515)—18/6432/72. Fun course for average golfer; a little sand, a little water, a lot of trees. Jets at nearby Portland Airport sometimes make the hearing difficult. Very friendly people; shower facilities adequate.

Broadmoor Golf Course, 3509 NE Columbia Blvd. (281-1337)—18/6155/72. Sporty, tight course with a little sand and quite a few trees; slick greens. Close to town; also close to airport. Shower facilities adequate.

Mt. View Golf Course, 27195 SE Kelso Rd., Boring (663-4869)—18/6214/72. Tight course with some beautiful holes. About 22 miles from town. Some sand, some water.

Progress Downs Golf Course, 8200 SW Scholls Ferry Rd. (646-5166)—18/6496/72. No sand, no water, little trouble except for a few small trees. Does have one of the city's finest restaurants, The Stock Pot. If you like to golf, then eat, with the emphasis on the latter, this is your course.

Glendoveer Golf Course, 14015 NE Glisan St. (253-7507)—Oldest 36-hole course in Oregon. 6368/74; 6066/72. Gets heavy play and little maintenance from county. Beautiful fir trees and narrow fairways provide most of challenge. Not very long and has very little sand; lots of rough, some intended, some unintended. Shower in your room.

Top O'Scott Golf Course, 12000 SE Stevens Rd. (654-5050)—18/5544/70. If you like to see a view of the city along with a pleasant outing while swinging a golf club, this is the place. Not a great challenge, but a fun course—good for the ego.

Executive Courses (Public)

Charbonneau Golf Club, Wilsonville (682-1717)—27/4260/64. New, beautiful executive course running through a fine housing development. Lots of sand; good challenge despite short length. Off I-5 about 15 minutes south of downtown. The course will fool the good golfer and bedevil the average one.

Portland Meadows Golf Course, 901 N. Schmeer Rd. (289-3405)—9/2180. Nine holes inside a horse race track. If you have some time before the races, during the season, this is where the action is.

Par-three Courses

Rivergreens Golf Course, 480 River Rd., Gladstone (656-1033)—18/2380/54. Along the Willamette River about 12 miles SE of town. Easy to reach and fun to play.

Lake Oswego Park and Recreation Golf Course, 17525 Stafford Rd. (636-8228)—18/2725/54. Very similar to Rivergreens except it is on a hill, overlooking Portland. Well-manicured greens; some traps; easy to play in 2 hours.

Private Golf Clubs

Portland has some of the finest private clubs in the Northwest, and all are accessible to the traveler, providing he belongs to a reciprocal private club in his home town or knows a member in Portland. Recommended, in order of toughness, are:

Portland Golf Club, 5900 SW Scholls Ferry Rd. (292-2778)—18/6714/72. Robert Trent Jones redesigned course; lots of trees, water, and sand. Location of several PGA tournaments; beautifully manicured, tortuous greens; superb facilities; some caddies; carts. Call ahead for starting time.

Oswego Lake Country Club, 20 SW Iron Mountain Blvd., Lake Oswego (635-3659)—18/6584/71. Beautiful, exquisitely manicured hillside course with very tight fairways, abundant sand, water, and small, slick greens. Outstanding facilities, some caddies; gasoline carts.

Waverley Country Club, 1100 SE Waverly Dr. (654-6521)—18/6324/72. Oldest course in Oregon (1913). Site of National Amateur in 1970. Comparatively short; very tough with lots of bunkers and trees. No water, but vicious greens. Magnificent colonial clubhouse with all other facilities to match. Caddies, carts.

Columbia-Edgewater Country Club, 2138 NE Marine Dr. (285-8354)—18/6598/72. A fine all-around challenging golf course with abundant sand and water as well as trees. Site of many PGA tournaments. Very friendly membership. Carts, some caddies.

Tualatin Country Club, Tualatin (638-5432)—About 15 minutes from downtown. 18/6324/72. Demanding tight course, well bunkered. Well manicured. Nice clubhouse. Carts, some caddies.

Coastal Golf (Astoria to Newport)

Astoria Golf and Country Club (private), Warrenton—18/6486/72. Outstanding course laid out on rolling sand dunes with water, sand, and sometimes wind that provides the ultimate challenge to all golfers. Well manicured in a beautiful setting. Probably the best coastal golf north of the Pebble Beach area. Fine, new clubhouse with excellent facilities. Carts. Call ahead.

Gearhart Golf Club (public), Gearhart—18/6147/72. Challenging, windswept seaside links. Not much sand or water, very dry fairways. Nice greens. Gets heavy play during the summer months. Carts available, showers not. Pleasant cocktail lounge and coffee shop.

Seaside Golf Course (public), Seaside—9/2610/36. Pleasant, fairly easy family-style golf course. Some challenging holes to help wile away a pleasant afternoon. Good restaurant, no showers.

Neah-kah-nie Golf Club (public)—Along the Coast Highway at Manzanita—9/1804/29. Sidehill course best suited for family play. Good view of the ocean. Can be an interesting challenge for medium to long iron players.

Alderbrook Country Club (public), Tillamook—18/5810/72. A truly fun golf course. Don't let the shortness of the course fool you. There are some holes that can bite you. This course requires good, strong legs or cart. Good clubhouse facilities.

Neskowin Golf Course (9/3021/34) and *Hawk Creek Hills Golf Club* (9/2910/34) (public), Neskowin. Both in a small, isolated resort area. Both courses are sporty with no overwhelming challenges. Shower in your motel.

Salishan Golf Club (public), Gleneden Beach—18/6437/72. Bring lots of golf balls. If you hit into the rough, you probably won't find your ball. Long, well-trapped course with a little water. Beautiful view of ocean. Some holes on course, particularly the 7th, border on the unfair. Course is absolutely unforgiving. Fine pro shop and coffee shop. Carts are available and almost a necessity, considering the steepness of the front nine.

Agate Beach Golf Club (public), Agate Beach—9/3002/36. Pleasant course to play. Host pro and owner, Bill Martin, is very accommodating with well-stocked pro shop and pleasant coffee shop. Last four holes quite sporty. Ideal for the golfing family. On a windy day, it's a tiger. Change and shower in your room.

Mountains, Desert

Black Butte Ranch, near Sisters—Two courses, Ranch (18/6308/72) and Glaze Meadows (18/6290/72). Both spectacular with marvelous doses of scenery, sand, woods and water. Back nine of Ranch Course and front nine of Glaze Meadows give delightful view of surrounding mountains and are very tricky with much sand and water and very few flat lies. Tough courses with views that make one not readily care about a high score.

Bowman's at Welches, operated by Red Lion (18/6008/68)— Resort course with some challenging holes. Gets heavy play. Third nine (9/3100/36) at Rippling River across road, more picturesque, harder.

Kah-nee-ta, Warm Springs (18/6587)—Golf course at Kah-nee-ta, luxury resort on the Warm Springs Indian Reservation, in the sage desert of central Oregon.

Sunriver, south of Bend (18/6605/72)—Long, flat, well-trapped, some water, and hard. Wind comes into play frequently. Good view of Mt. Bachelor. Second 18 under construction which should be in play in 1981.

Gymnastics

Gymnastics is an increasingly popular athletic activity among young people and adults in Portland. Most Park Bureau programs offer classes as do the YMCA (223-9622) and YWCA (223-6281).

In addition, the Park Bureau (248-4315) conducts a gymnastic program for boys and girls in grades 1-12 during the summer at Jackson High School. The three-week sessions are open to all youth, experienced or beginner for a reasonable fee.

For private instruction call Portland Gymnastic Center (639-5388).

Hiking

Oregon hiking trails are so popular in summer that many appear to be pedestrian freeways. The true wilderness seeker soon learns to hike midweek or in places that have not been publicized in books like this. The crowd thins in proportion to the number of miles you're willing to hike, but not necessarily when you're mountain climbing. Even though proportionately fewer persons claim peaks, climbing routes become congested, as there are only so many ways to the top. Literally hundreds of people will reach the summit of Mt. Hood on any number of good climbing days during May and June.

Because there is so much to learn about hiking, backpacking, and climbing, we recommend good books, maps and equipment, and membership in one of the climbing and hiking clubs in the Portland area. Hikes are sponsored by various Park Bureau community centers. Hiking information and guidance are also available from the YMCA and YWCA.

An ongoing hiking program is part of the Park Bureau's burgeoning outdoor recreation program (248-4018). Hikes depart from Overlook House, 3839 N. Melrose, each Wednesday at 8 a.m. most months of the year. Trails in the Gifford Pinchot, Mt. Hood, and Willamette National Forests are among the destinations as are special neighborhoods in and near the city. Car pools are used for transportation. The hikes occur rain or shine—winter, too.

The Park Bureau also sponsors such programs as wilderness backpacking, mountaineering and basic backpacking workshops, and many other outdoor recreation activities. Call for more information.

August is the most popular hiking month in the mountains because by then, in a typical year, the snow has melted from the trails and the mosquito hatch has passed. September is an ideal month to hike—no mosquitoes and fewer people. Trails in the Columbia Gorge and at the coast can usually be used year-round.

Clubs

Most widely known mountaineering club in the area is the 2600-member **Mazama Club,** 909 NW 19th (227-2345). To become a member, you must climb a peak with a living glacier. This sounds rather restrictive but Mazama programs are geared to helping potential members reach the top and return.

When you see a new crop of Mazamas headed for the top of Mt. Hood in late spring or early summer, it's "like the Himalayan Army," someone once said.

Also worth noting are the **Trails Club** of Oregon, P.O. Box 1243, Portland, 97207, and the **Sierra Club,** which has an Oregon office at 2637 SW Water (222-1963). Both the Mazama and Trails Clubs have lodges on Mt. Hood.

Gear, Guides, Books

Where to go for climbing and hiking gear? Mountain shops (see Shopping) offer equipment to buy or rent and freeze-dried food. (Check your grocery store for the food, first, if you're economy minded.)

If you need a professional leader call:

Johann Mountain Guides, P.O. Box 2334, Lincoln City, 97367

Lute Jerstad Adventures, P.O. Box 19527, Portland, 97219 (244-4364)

Many useful guidebooks which are as practical as they are attractive have been written about Oregon hikes, including:

62 Hiking Trails—Northern Oregon Cascades, by Don and Roberta Lowe (Touchstone), an excellent hiking guide; *60 Hiking Trails—Central Oregon Cascades,* also by the Lowes (Touchstone); *Hiking the Oregon Skyline,* by Charles M. Feris (Touchstone); *Short Trips and Trails, The Columbia Gorge,* by Oral Bullard and Don Lowe (Touchstone); and *A Hiker's Guide to the Oregon Coast Trail,* by David E.M. Bucy and Mary C. McCauley (Oregon State Parks and Recreation).

For mountain climbers, *Freedom of the Hills,* published by the Mountaineers in Seattle, is considered a classic hiking-climbing text for the area.

Some of the best hikes in Oregon are in national forests in the Cascade range. To acquaint visitors and residents with the features of these areas, the U.S. Forest Service (USFS) and the National Park Service (NPS) jointly maintain an information office on the ground floor of the Multnomah Building, 319 SW Pine (221-2877). Many maps of wilderness areas are available there, some free, some for 50¢. (Especially good is *Forest Trails of the Columbia Gorge.*) Maps that provide the most detailed hiking information are U.S. Geological Survey topographic maps. Some are available from the USFS-NPS information office. They are also sold at J.K. Gill Co., 408 SW 5th, and Captain's Nautical Supplies, 817 SW 2nd (227-1648).

Short Hikes

The Portland-area is blessed with a seemingly endless list of day hike destinations, most of them suitable for spring, summer, and fall months. Here are a few day hikes, ideal for family outings.

Urban Hikes

Wildwood Trail—Within the city limits, huge Forest and Macleay Parks offer miles of hiking trails, including the 25-mile wooded Wildwood Trail, which begins at the Western Forestry Center and winds through the Arboretum and Pittock Acres★ and ends deep in Forest Park on Springville Road between Skyline and Leif Erikson. The Wildwood Trail has been designated a scenic trail by the National Trail Act.

Upper Macleay-Wildwood Loop—A lovely wooded loop hike, particularly in spring when the trillium and elderberry are in bloom, is on the Upper Macleay Trail to a junction with the Wildwood Trail which brings you into the Macleay Trail and back to your starting point. To reach the start, take Burnside west. Turn right on Macleay Blvd. (about half a mile west of 23rd) and wind uphill past Warrenton to a cul de sac where Macleay terminates. Find good parking and trail markers. Follow the Upper Macleay Trail about ¼ mile to a three-pronged junction. Take the center trail winding downhill and looping back to a junction with Wildwood and Macleay (not to be confused with Upper Macleay) Trails. Follow Macleay back to your car. Allow one hour at the most for this 1½-mile hike.

Arboretum Trails—Start at the Western Forestry Center★ on the Wildwood Trail, which leads you to various trails that lace the Hoyt Arboretum.★

Marquam Nature Trail—This newly acquired nature trail, when complete, will take the hiker on a 7½-mile trek (one-way) from Council Crest Park,★ where Marquam Ravine begins, to Willamette Park on the Willamette River—from the highest to the lowest points in the city. Some sections of the trail are already complete. Call the Park Bureau (248-4315) for an up-to-date report.

Oaks Bottom—A network of trails in a wetland bird sanctuary on the east side of the Willamette, accessible from the Sellwood Park parking lot at the northeast corner of the park, SE 7th and Miller.

Group tours on the Forest Park trails and arboretum trails

can be arranged by calling 228-8732. A brochure about Forest Park and a map of all hiking trails within the park may be requested by writing the Park Bureau at 409 SW 9th, Portland, 97205, or by calling 248-4315.

Columbia Gorge Hikes

Wahkeena-Perdition Loop—For this 3-mile hike which takes in views of Wahkeena and Multnomah Falls, park your car at the Wahkeena Picnic Ground on the Columbia River Gorge Scenic Highway. Follow Trail #420 for nearly half a mile to a junction with Perdition Trail #421. Take Perdition for nearly a mile to a view of Multnomah Falls. Continue on to the junction with Larch Mountain Trail #441, 1.1 miles from Multnomah Falls Lodge. Follow #441 north to the lodge. Head west on Scenic Hwy. 300 feet until you find return trail (#442) near rock outcropping. Follow trail #442, which parallels the highway, west to Wahkeena picnic ground.

Horsetail Falls-Oneonta Gorge Loop—Your departure point for this spectacular 2.5-mile waterfall hike can be reached only via the Columbia Gorge Scenic Route. Park at Horsetail Falls, two miles east of Multnomah Falls. Trail #438 climbs via switchbacks for about ½ mile to a passage behind Upper Horsetail Falls. Children love this. After passing "through" the falls, proceed less than ½ mile to a viewpoint overlooking deep, dark Oneonta Gorge, a narrow cleft in a basalt bluff, and the Columbia Gorge. Continue another ½ mile to Oneonta Trail, #424, which descends in an easterly direction to the Columbia River Scenic Highway, ½ mile west of the Horsetail Falls parking area. A very abbreviated version of this is to Upper Horsetail and back.

Eagle Creek and Punch Bowl Falls—Eagle Creek Trail in the Columbia Gorge (not to be confused with Eagle Creek, a tributary of the Clackamas River) will take the serious hiker as far as Wahtum Lake, 13 miles away. For the family day hike, however, we recommend a 2-mile trip up the Eagle Creek Trail to Punch Bowl Falls, a wonderful geological "waterworks." To get to your departure point, travel east on I-84 to the Eagle Creek Fish Hatchery, a mile east of Bonneville Dam. Travel south to the end of the dirt road and park. (Use picnic area parking lot on weekends to avoid congestion at the trailhead.) Trail #440 rises through forest and past mossy rock walls. After 1½ miles, you'll reach a short side trail to Metlako Falls.

A half mile further you'll see the side trail to Punch Bowl Falls. This trail descends to the river for a close look at the punch bowl as it receives a massive spill of water from a spout in the basalt. At this point, you can either return or proceed 1.7 miles further to Tenas Campsite.

Watch small children on all hikes in the Columbia Gorge. Trails often wind up and down steep canyons, and the very features that provide interesting and spectacular viewpoints can make the terrain dangerous for unpredictable youngsters.

Mt. Hood Forest Hikes

Ramona Falls—A beautiful walk from late July through October is to Ramona Falls on the Upper Sandy River on the western side of Mt. Hood. Take U.S. 26 heading east to the town of Zigzag and travel north on the Lolo Pass Road, which you'll find opposite the Zigzag Ranger Station. Travel Lolo Pass Road north more than 4 miles to Road #S25. Turn east and drive for another 3 miles. Walk from the parking area to the Sandy River Trail, #797. Cross the bridge over the Sandy River. Continue on the Sandy River Trail to the Upper Sandy Guard Station and to Ramona Falls, where you'll find a pleasant forest camp and the 100-foot falls.

Salmon River—To reach your departure point, travel east on U.S. 26 and, just before reaching Zigzag, turn south on the Salmon River Road, #S38. Travel for 5 miles past the Green Canyon Campground to the north end of the Salmon River Bridge (about one more mile), where you'll find minimal parking. The trail, #742, is marked. The first 1¾ miles make an easy family hike along and above the Salmon River. Wildflowers are abundant in June.

Other Hikes

Clackamas River Trail—This hike is on a beautiful reach of the Upper Clackamas River near the Ripplebrook Ranger Station. Take Oregon 224 east through Estacada. About 25 miles southeast of Estacada is the ranger station. Drive east and then south less than a mile to Rainbow Campground. The Riverside Trail, #723, heads south for 2½ miles along the Clackamas River to Riverside Campgrounds.

Silver Creek Falls State Park—You can pick your own hike in this inspiring spot 26 miles east of Salem on Oregon 214. The park contains 14 waterfalls and many trails. It is a sightseeing favorite and usually crowded on fair weather weekends.

Saddle Mountain—One of Oregon's most attainable and beautiful mountain tops—especially rewarding for the novice hiker—is Saddle Mountain, 3,283 feet above the Oregon coast near Seaside. Departure point is Saddle Mountain State Park 2 miles off U. S. 26, 14 miles east of Seaside. The trail is well marked at the parking lot and is usually climbable from March to December. The hike is 6 miles round trip; elevation gain, 1,663 feet. Coast moisture keeps Saddle Mountain ever green. Wildflowers there are spectacular in the spring.

Hiking Postscript—For most hikes, allow 25 minutes per mile.

Horseback Riding

If you've just moved to town and want to enroll your daughter or son in a riding class, the best places to call are:
Horsemanship West, 19713 S. Molalla, Oregon City (656-9113).
Lake Oswego Hunt, 2725 SW Iron Mountain Blvd., Lake Oswego (636-9993), for eastern instruction.
Sunset Farms and Stables, 5000 NW 242nd, Hillsboro (648-6782), also for eastern instruction.
Sunwood Farms, Rt. 1, Box 439, Scholls Ferry Rd., Beaverton (649-3930), for show jumping and riding instruction.

For pleasure riding, Tryon Creek State Park has beautiful bridle paths, but you have to bring your own horse.

For trail riding by the hour in a ranch environment with all the amenities, call the ***Flying M Ranch,*** Rte. 1, Box 95C, Yamhill, 97148 (662-3222). Trail rides, tennis, fishing, swimming, and good dining (Fri.-Sun.) are offered in a riverside setting 45 miles southwest of Portland. Flying M also promotes its airstrip and banquet facilities. Overnight camping facilities available. Overnight trail rides, too.

Though it's farther from Portland, the ***Rock Springs Guest Ranch,*** a few miles west of Bend, deserves special mention in any section on horsemanship. Donna Gill has combined her widely respected expertise in riding with her talents as an innkeeper at this beautiful family ranch, where riding is the primary activity, but tennis, swimming, and fishing follow closely behind. Annual horsemanship clinics attract riders from all over the state. Address is 64201 Tyler Rd., Bend, 97701 (1-503-382-1957).

Hunting

Information about hunting seasons and regulations is available from the Oregon Dept. of Fish and Wildlife (229-5403). Tom McAllister's annual *Oregon Journal Hunting Calendar,* a handy billfold-size folder, is available in September at the *Oregon Journal,* 1320 SW Broadway, or at sporting goods stores and other outlets throughout the state.

In the Portland area, the only public hunting grounds are at the well-managed Sauvie Island Wildlife Management Area. You can hunt there during the three-month waterfowl season. Reservations are required to hunt the east side of the area. On the west side, it's first-come, first-served. Make reservations by mail or phone. Mailing address is 506 SW Mill, P. O. Box 3503, Portland, 97208.

Hunter safety training programs sponsored by the National Rifle Assn. are conducted annually. Watch the newpapers for announcements or call the state agency number.

Trap and skeet shooters are welcome at the Portland Gun Club, 4711 SE 174th (665-9977).

Ice Skating

Ice skating rinks in the Portland area where competitive figure skating is supported are:

Funworld Ice and Roller Skating Center, 1210 NE 102nd (255-4644).

Valley Ice Arena, 9300 SW Beaverton-Hillsdale Hwy. (297-2521), headquarters for the Carousel Figure Skating Club.

The same rinks host teams of the Portland Amateur Hockey Assn. Businesses support the various teams in the same fashion as Little League baseball. Play starts in the fall and continues into February and March. Call the rinks for additional information.

If competition isn't for you, you can still skate for fun at any of the above rinks or try what is probably the best known rink in town at the **Lloyd Center** (288-6073), where hundreds of shoppers pause to watch pleasure skating there night and day.

Ice skaters transplanted in Portland from the East and Midwest will find little here in the way of outdoor pond skating, but on those few occasions when the weather is cold enough to freeze a pond, or when the ice age returns, try the Westmoreland casting pond, the lake at Laurelhurst Park, or Smith Park, northwest of West Delta Park Golf Course.

Kite Flying

Kite-flying is airborne in Portland, and the sociable place to do it is West Delta Park, where kite flyers gather Sunday afternoons. Portland also has a store that sells only kites. It's **Windplay** at 212 NW Couch (223-1760).

Lacrosse

For information about the Portland Lacrosse Club, call Chris Hatcher at Oregon Episcopal Schools (246-7771).

Lawn Bowling

Westmoreland Park has lawn bowling facilities.

Model Airplanes and Boats

Model plane flying is allowed at East Delta Park; model boat sailing, at Westmoreland Park.

Motorsports

Portland International Raceway, 1940 N. Victory Blvd., at West Delta Park (285-6635) offers a full schedule of motorsports events throughout the year. In addition, the raceway is available for recreational riding at certain times. A sample of the activities sponsored at the raceway, which is a focal point of activity for cycling and driving in the northwest, includes Porsche Club Autocross, motorcycle road races, motocrosses, grudge drags, and bicycle races.

Auto and motorcycle repair and maintenance courses are offered by Portland Community College's Community College's Community Education Division (244-6111).

Oriental Martial Arts

Judo, karate, kung-fu, and other forms of self-defense training are offered both publicly, through Park Bureau and Community School programs, and commercially. Instruction for both men and women is also available at the YMCA and YWCA.

Racquetball, Handball

Since the first edition of *The Portland GuideBook*, racquetball has blossomed into nearly a full page of listings and ads in the *Yellow Pages*.

The indoor sport is particularly popular during the rainy season; is space efficient; and its courts double as handball courts.

When racquetball became so popular a few years ago, the City of Portland altered its plans for a new tennis facility in the *St. Johns Racquet Center.* The center, with 4 racquetball-handball courts and 3 indoor tennis courts, is at 7519 N. Burlington (286-6411). There are hourly and seasonal court fees.

Among the private racquetball clubs, *Lloyd Center Courts,* 815 NE Halsey (287-4594), offers a full array of facilities—courts for racquetball and handball, an indoor jogging track, weight room, saunas, steamroom, and pro shop. For membership information, call the club.

The *YMCA Metro Fitness Center* (see YMCA listing in this chapter) has six racquetball/handball courts. The *Neighborhood Athletic Assn.* (282-2254) leases handball courts at Neighborhood House, 029 SW Hamilton. The *Jewish Community Center,* 6651 SW Capitol Hwy. (244-0111) has handball and racquetball facilities for its members. Call the membership secretary for further information.

Racquetball classes are available at the St. Johns Center.

Road Running and Track

Portland offers road runners unparalled scenery, a variety of terrain and weekly T-shirts if they go for the organized events.

In addition, Portland and Oregon runners support a first-class club—*Oregon Road Runners*—and boast one of the top-rated running events in the country—the *Cascade Run Off,* a 9.32-mile race which starts and finishes in downtown Portland.

If you're a visitor, you can start some of your best runs right outside your hotel door.

From the *Marriott Hotel,* exit at the riverfront entrance (front door), cross Front Avenue and head for the waterfront promenade. You can travel north as far as the Steel Bridge, about 1 mile, with the city skyline on one side of you and the river traffic on the other.

From the *Red Lion Inn* in *Portland Center,* ★ start your run at the south end of the center and head north through its secluded corridors to Market. For a longer run, travel on to Clay, Columbia, or Jefferson, turn east and run until you encounter the waterfront promenade described above. Return by way of Ira's Fountain, ★ on 3rd between Clay and Market, the biggest public shower in town.

If you're staying at the *Hilton,* head west to the nearby South Park Blocks★ and run south to the Portland State University Campus. ★ Continue south through the campus until you reach SW Hall, turn east, travel to SW 4th, and enter Portland Center where shortly you'll come to another of the city's favorite watering places, the Lovejoy Fountain. Both PSU and Portland Center have plenty of fountains and sculpture to look at en route.

If you're a guest at the *Benson,* you're favored with a jogger's map. Ask at the desk for one or all three: to Duniway Park-Terwilliger Blvd. (see below); to Washington Park; and to the waterfront for the run along the promenade.

The maps in the Walking Tours section of this book can be adapted for your downtown runs.

Crowning Portland's jogging terrain is its 2-mile exercise and jogging trail, maintained by the Park Bureau. The jogging and bike trail takes you from Duniway Park, near downtown, up Terwilliger to within ¼ mile of the Hillvilla Restaurant at 5700 SW Terwilliger. Twenty exercise stops provide diversion and a workout. There's a perfect point on the course where each runner is silhouetted against a Mt. Hood-city skyline backdrop. (Take a friend with a camera.)

Many joggers visit hilly, woodsy Washington Park, where they choose 4-, 6-, and 10-mile treks. The dirt trails of Forest Park are also popular.

On the east side of the river, runners visit the Eastmoreland area, which encompasses the Eastmoreland Golf Course, Reed

College, and the Crystal Springs Rhododendron Garden;★ Oaks Bottom and Sellwood Park; Laurelhurst Park;★ and Mt. Tabor Park,★ where they run past a crater in an extinct volcano and on to the top for a view of the city.

Also worth noting:

• Running clinics are conducted throughout the year by various organizations and clubs, including the YMCA, Oregon, Road Runners, Multnomah Athletic Club, and the Park Bureau. The Park Bureau (248-4315) offers regular jogging schedules at some centers. The Park Bureau will also tell you which all-weather track is closest to you.

Portland State University sponsors a jogging and adult fitness program conducted Mon., Wed., and Fri. from 5 to 6 p.m. Call the PSU health and physical education department (229-4401) for more information.

• Oregon Road Runners Club, P. O. Box D, Beaverton, 97075, sponsors many runs, capped by the annual *Portland Marathon,* run in late October. Write about joining the club.

• A calendar of runs and upcoming events for the coming week appears every Friday in the sports section of the *Oregon Journal.*

• For more runs and running information, buy *Running Around Portland* by John Perry and Buzz Willits. This guide to the best running in the Portland and Vancouver areas is published by RAP Press, 2655 NW Overton, Portland, 97210.

• Portland Track Club, an Amateur Athletic Union Club, sponsors cross country and track programs for boys and girls aged 7-15. For additional information, call 245-7930 or 644-5737.

• The All-Comers Track and Field Meets for children all ages. Call the Park Bureau (248-4325) for more information.

Roller Skating

Roller skating, once confined to a few rinks and sidewalks, is seen all around the town now. The cushioned ride that the new roller skates provide on hard concrete has something to do with the revival of the sport, which seems to have surpassed skateboarding in popularity. If you can't afford to buy those expensive skates, rental vans roll to the best skating spots.

One rental operator, *Achilles Wheels* (248-9910), visits Laurelhurst Park on weekends.

Another, *Cal Skate & Sport* (223-0245), promotes rental

rollers for skating at Willamette Center, where it is permitted in a covered arena at the northeast corner of SW 1st and Salmon. If the rental outlet isn't open at the arena, the Cal Skate shop is close by—at SW 2nd and Salmon.

Like skateboarding, roller skating is prohibited on downtown streets except in those areas mentioned above and on the waterfront promenade.

While commercial rinks become more and more glamorous, the best buy in Portland is still the Park Bureau's public rink at the Mt. Scott Community Center, 5530 SE 72nd (774-2215). Phone for hours. Skating is free and skates rent for 25¢ an hour. This is possibly the only large rink in the world operated by a city park bureau.

Private rinks include:

Beaverton Roller Skate Center, 3495 SW Cedar Hills Blvd. (643-6655)

Oak Park Roller Skating Rink, at the foot of SE Spokane near the east end of the Sellwood Bridge (236-5722)

Funworld Ice and Roller Skating Center, 1210 NE 102nd (255)4644).

Skate World, 1220 NE Kelly, Gresham (667-6543)

Oregon City Roller Skate Center, 1622 Molalla (656-0644)

Imperial Skate and Paddle Place, 418 SE Main, east end, Hawthorne Bridge, (236-9171)

Scuba Diving

Classes in scuba diving are offered by Portland Community College (244-6111).

Skateboarding and Surfing

The hills of Portland provide irresistible skateboarding terrain. With the flexible boards and urethane wheels, the sport is still popular here. Hospital emergency rooms, where the injuries are being treated, will testify to this. THE place for skateboard problems is *The Surfer,* 2840 SE Powell (235-7983). Don't be fooled by the greying proprietess. She knows all there is to know about skateboards, roller skates, and surfboards, can apply a mean socket wrench, and runs Mrs. A's Typing Service on the side. All this goes on in a tiny area behind the counter where Mrs. A's typewriter shares space with everything from ball bearings to "Pure Juice" wheels.

Skateboarding is permitted on the old soapbox derby road in Mt. Tabor Park.

Skiing

Snow depths measured in the hundreds of inches on nearby Mt. Hood make Portland a skiing center in the Pacific Northwest.

At Government Camp, 58 miles from Portland, are two ski areas, Multorpor-Ski Bowl and Summit Ski Area (for beginners), both at about the 4,000-foot elevation. At the 6,000-foot level are Timberline, ★ at the end of a spur road 6 miles from Government Camp, and Mt. Hood Meadows, a few miles north of Government Camp on Oregon 35.

With construction of the Palmer Chairlift, which runs from the 7,000-foot to the 8,500-foot level on Mt. Hood, Timberline boasts the first year-round ski resort served by ski lifts on the North American continent.

The lift spans the Palmer Snow Field, a permanent snow area about 1½ miles long and 2 miles wide, which has always been known to be covered by deep snow, even in the drought of 1976-77.

At Timberline, snow is so plentiful that during the past 20 years, the ski season has opened three times before Halloween and practically every year by Thanksgiving. In 1973-74, Timberline recorded 310 inches of snow by March and had 200 inches left by June.

Some skiers refer to Mt. Hood's heavy, moisture-laden snows as "Mt. Hood cement," but they still flock to the mountain. Those seeking lighter, drier snow and sunnier weather will drive the extra 125 miles to Mt. Bachelor, considered to be Oregon's best ski area, in the central part of the state near Bend. With its varied open terrain for the packed slope skiers and its forested slopes holding virgin powder for the deep snow skiers, Bachelor is a favorite weekend and vacation area for Portlanders as well as Californians and Washingtonians.

The larger Oregon ski areas with their day lodges and ski shops are open weekdays as well as weekends during the ski season, are well patrolled for accidents, provide ski instruction, and illuminate slopes for night skiing.

Following is a list of ski areas according to location. Lift rates change from season to season. Some areas offer season passes. Call the numbers listed for more information.

Multorpor-Ski Bowl—(1-272-3522). Mt. Hood's oldest ski area and the closest to Portland at Government Camp. Here are some of the steepest ski slopes of any area on Mt. Hood. Slopes suitable for intermediates and beginners as well. Night skiing. Equipped with 4 chairs, 8 rope tows, one ski jump. Two day lodges, ski shop, rentals, instruction. Overnight accommodations in Government Camp or in nearby Rhododendron.

Summit Ski Area—Located at Government Camp (1-272-3351), this area is for beginning skiers. Day lodge and ski shop.

Timberline—(226-7979). Home of one of the first chairlifts in the U. S., Timberline boasts a lodge that is a Northwest showplace. Facilities in addition to the big lodge are a ski shop, ski school, and lights for night skiing. Runs are generally intermediate. On a clear day, the famed Magic Mile run and the new Palmer Snow Field run are spectacular; in a white-out, you can't tell up from down. Late-season skiing at Timberline is one of its best features, especially since the Palmer lift was constructed. Facilities include 4 chair lifts and 2 rope tows. Accomodations at the lodge.

Mt. Hood Meadows—(1-337-2222). Newest ski area on Mt. Hood, located on the southeast slopes of the mountain with terrain for all levels of skiing. Season normally continues through June. Spacious day lodge. Seven chair lifts, 3 rope tows. Rentals, ski shop, ski repair, ski school, including cross country instruction.

Cooper Spur—(1-386-2777). Take either I-84 east or U. S. 26 to get to this small but pleasant intermediate ski area, which is about halfway between Hood River and Government Camp on Oregon 35. At the 4,000-foot elevation, this area has one T-bar, 1 rope tow, a day lodge, ski shop, school, and night skiing.

Mt. Bachelor—(1-800-452-6872). About 180 miles from Portland, 20 miles west of Bend on the Cascade Lakes Hwy. At a base elevation of 6,500 feet, Mt. Bachelor offers Oregon's most varied skiing terrain. Eight chair lifts, 1 rope tow, 3 day lodges, 2 ski shops, rentals, and a ski school. No lights. Overnight accommodations at nearby Bend, at resorts on the highway, or at Sunriver Resort, south of Bend.

Hoodoo Ski Bowl—(Ask operator for Hoodoo 2). About 75 miles east of Salem at Santiam Pass off U. S. 20 at 4,700 feet. Three chairlifts, 3 rope tows, 2 lodges, ski shop, lights, ski school.

Ski Schools and Instruction

Portland skiers, novice and advanced, can choose from an abundance of good ski school programs offered each winter. Transportation is generally provided from various pick-up points in the area to the mountain.

Mt. Hood Meadows offers a Ladies' Day program midweek, with transportation provided if desired. The Meadows also has weekend bus service with pre-sold seating.

To help would-be skiers prepare themselves both physically and psychologically for the sport, the Park Bureau recommends its *Dry Ski School,* geared for persons 14 years and older. The series of classes also includes first aid, coping with winter weather, search and rescue, and even a showing of ski fashions.

Other ski schools and programs worth noting:

Jaycee Ski School, 824 SW 5th, Portland, 97204 (227-5656)
Instruction at Timberline for all ages in downhill and Nordic. Also a special program for 5-7-year-olds.

Nordic Ski School, P. O. Box 10529, Portland, 97210 (297-6102). This special program in cross-country skiing is the oldest continuously operating cross-country ski school in Oregon. Sessions consist of a lecture in Portland and snow lessons on Mt. Hood.

Western Ski Pros, 2039 SE 103rd Dr., Portland, 97216 (253-8524). Lessons for all ages weekends at Timberline. Also sponsor Mogul Mice, a program for ages 6-16 at Timberline, and Lollipop, a program for ages 4-7, also at Timberline.

Snow Reports

For local and regional ski conditions dial:
Mt. Hood Meadows (227-Snow)
Mountain Shop (281-8886)
Multorpor-Ski Bowl (224-9221)
Timberline Lodge, summer or winter (222-2211)
Mt. Bachelor (1-800-452-6872)

For the state police road and weather report, call 238-8400.
U. S. Weather Bureau Forecast—255-6661.

Sno-Park

A Sno-Park permit is required to park your car on roads or lots plowed by the Oregon State Highway Dept. Skiers, snowmobilers, or other winter sports enthusiasts can buy these permits at ski areas and other places authorized to sell them by the Department of Motor Vehicles. Cost is $5 for the season or $1 per time.

Ski Organizations

Oregon Nordic Club, P. O. Box 3906, Portland, 97208.
Cascade Ski Club, P. O. Box 721, Portland, 97207, sponsors a full junior racing program and has a lodge on Mt. Hood.

Ski Touring

Ski touring (Nordic skiing) is attracting more and more downhill skiers away from long lift lines and turning former nonskiers into new ski enthusiasts. Mt. Hood's late spring snow pack makes the sport particularly attractive.

The Oregon Nordic Club as well as the Mazamas, Trails Club, and Sierra Club (see Hiking), conduct cross-country tours on weekends in the winter. The Nordic Ski School offers a comprehensive program of instruction, including a lecture and field trips, with rentals provided.

Cross-country rentals are available at Government Camp, Mt. Hood Meadows, and in Portland.

For up-to-date information on the best ski touring in the Mt. Hood area, call the Zigzag Ranger Station (224-5243). The forest rangers will direct you to the several signed trails in the area. For advice about ski touring in the Bend area, call the Mt. Bachelor Ski Area.

For an easy ski tour on open terrain, try the Summit Meadows tour southeast of Government Camp in the Mt. Hood National Forest. Park adjacent to the State Highway Dept. station at Timberline Junction and walk to Still Creek Road. Ski on snowbound road to meadows and return.

Skiing Postscript

• Some skiers consider the ultimate in spring recreation to be skiing the corn snow on Mt. Hood in the morning and winding up at the Red Lion Inn at Bowman's for a round of golf in the afternoon. Bowman's, offering excellent food and accommodations, is 14 miles west of Government Camp at Welches.

• For detailed information about ski touring, read *Oregon Ski Tours* by Doug Newman and Sally Sharrard (Touchstone).

Sky Diving

Sky divers do their thing at Western Sport Parachute Center (654-0718) at Shady Oaks Air Park, 2 miles west of Estacada on Heiple Road, and at Donald, Pacific Parachute Center (1-843-3616), Sheridan Airport.

Sled Dog Racing

While not in the league with soccer or basketball, sled dog racing is a growing organized sport in Oregon, with meets usually occurring in central and southern Oregon and in adjoining Western states. Where there is no snow for workouts, the dogs pull sleds on wheels. For additional information, contact the Cascade Sled Dog Club through the Yukon Kennel, 10895 Sunnyside Rd. SE, Jefferson, 97352 (1-362-3368).

Snowmobiling

If you've moved to town with your snowmobile and want to try it out, check with the U. S. Forest Service in the area where you're headed to learn on which roads snowmobiling is permitted. Two good areas to start with are Frog Lake, southeast of Government Camp on U. S. 26, and the Larch Mountain Road, accessible from the Columbia River Gorge Scenic Highway. Other popular areas on Mt. Hood are north of the White River Bridge, on Oregon 35, and ½ mile east of Government Camp in the Still Creek Campground area.

Mt. Hood Snowmobile Club, 17994 S. Merry Meadow Ct., Oregon City, 97405, welcomes members and provides good access to information on places to go.

Soccer

As in other areas, soccer is the "in" sport in Portland, especially since the Portland *Timbers* adopted the city. At many parks, you can see kids bouncing the ball off each others' heads and knees either in informal play or scheduled matches. A full-scale grade school and high school soccer program for boys and girls is sponsored in the fall by the Park Bureau

(248-4325). Teams are accepted from schools, community centers, boys clubs, or any other youth service organization and number well over 100, with some 3,000 individuals participating. Entry deadline for the fall season is mid-August.

Hundreds of adults play in leagues for every skill level organized by the Oregon Soccer Football Assn. (774-0263). The Oregon Youth Soccer Assn. (222-4069) administers play for ages 7-18 in Portland and in most of the outlying areas, including Beaverton, Lake Oswego, and Gresham. Both associations are affiliated with the U. S. Soccer Federation. For information about clinics for coaches and referees call the Park Bureau or the OSFA.

Lewis and Clark College (244-6161) conducts a summer soccer clinic.

Squash

Nerve center of squash in Portland is the private Multnomah Athletic Club, though the YMCA★ has opened a new building at Duniway Park with excellent squash and handball facilities.

Swimming

Pools

Three indoor pools and 11 outdoor pools are operated by the Park Bureau, all free of charge. Pool hours vary. Outdoor schedules, with the exception of port-a-pools, are generally Mon.-Fri., 9 a.m.-8 p.m., and Sat. and Sun., noon-8 p.m., but check with each pool or the Park Bureau for public swim times. Other activities are often scheduled in the pools.

Indoor pools, open year-round, are:
Buckman, 320 SE 16th (235-0704)
Columbia, 7701 N. Chautauqua (283-9302)
Couch, 2033 NW Glisan (227-6075)

Outdoor pools, open summer months only, are:
Creston, SE 44th & Powell (774-9113)
Dishman, 77 NE Knott (249-9077)
Grant, 2300 NE 33rd (249-9992)
Montavilla, 8219 NE Glisan (254-4101)
Mt. Scott, 5530 SE 72nd (774-9215)
Peninsula, 6400 N. Albina (285-4222)

Pier, foot of N. Seneca, St. Johns (240-9016)
Sellwood, SE 7th & Miller (238-9216)
Wilson, 1151 SW Vermont (246-9179)

A port-a-pool at Woodlawn Park, NE 11th and Dekum, is open Mon.-Fri. from noon-6 p.m. as is Abernethy Port-a-Pool, 2421 SE Orange.

Schedules for the indoor pools vary to accommodate many different groups and activities. Lessons are given at most pools. Call the pools or the Park Bureau (248-4010) for an indoor pool schedule; ask about family swims, public swims.

Swim Instruction

Many excellent swim instruction programs are available for adults and children in the Portland area.

The Park Bureau sponsors a "Learn to Swim" campaign at local public pools in June and a city-wide swimathon in August.

Swimming instruction of various kinds is offered at two YMCA centers—the John R. Leach, 6036 SE Foster (775-4396) and the Northeast, 1630 NE 38th (281-1169); and at the YWCA, 1111 SW 10th (223-6281).

Reed College (771-1112) and Lewis and Clark College (244-6161) offer swim lessons for children. Call for more information.

Recreational Swimming

Portland Community College (244-6111) opens its pool at the Sylvania Campus, 12000 SW 49th, for public swimming at certain times. Call for schedule and fees.

Mt. Hood Community College Aquatic Center offers public programs at its indoor and outdoor pools and hydrotherapy pool (adults only). Call 667-7243 for schedules for adults and children, including preschoolers, winter and summer. Center is at south end of the campus at 26000 SE Stark in Gresham.

Several close-in parks mentioned elsewhere in this book offer good lake and river swimming.

Tennis

Portland is fortunate to have a municipally owned and operated indoor tennis center which tennis players agree is first rate.

In addition to the 4 indoor courts, the Park Bureau maintains nearly 100 outdoor tennis courts throughout the city of which 60 are lighted for night play. Lighted courts may be used until the midnight curfew hour.

Unlike the indoor center, which operates under a reservations system, most of the outdoor courts are available on a first-come, first-served basis, although some at Washington Park may be reserved by calling 248-4325.

At the *Portland Tennis Center*, 324 NE 12th (233-5959) at Buckman Park, hours of operation are 9 a.m.–10 p.m. from July 1 to Sept. 30 and 6:30 a.m.–11:15 p.m., Oct. 1 to June 30. Court times are generally one hour in length. Reservations must be made and there is a fee. Fees from Oct. 1–June 30 are: Adult singles, $3.25 each, from 6:30 a.m.–5 p.m. weekdays (nonprime time), and $4, weekday evenings after 5 and all day Sat. & Sun. (prime time); adult doubles, $2 each, nonprime time, and $2.50 each, prime time; junior singles (20 and under), $2.25, and doubles, $1.50 each (nonprime time only). During prime time, juniors are charged adult fee.

Court fees from July 1 to Sept. 30 are: adult singles, $2, and doubles, $1 each; junior singles, $1, doubles, 50¢.

Reservations may be made one day in advance by calling 233-5959 or 233-5950. Anyone wishing to reserve a court more than a day ahead (and up to 7 days) is charged $1 extra. You may purchase one court time per week for the same day of the week and the same time on a quarterly basis. Costs during the rainy seasons are $104 for nonprime time and $130 for prime time. From July 1 to Sept. 30, cost is $52.

The center rents ball machines and offers private and group lessons. The facility also includes a players' lounge with full view of the tennis courts; a pro shop; dressing rooms and showers for men and women, with lockers and towels available; and a balcony with seating capacity for 300.

Another city-operated indoor tennis center is in *St. Johns* at 7519 N. Burlington (286-6411). The 3 indoor courts are operated much as the Portland Tennis Center is (see Racquetball).

Lewis and Clark College (244-6161) offers summer tennis lessons.

The Oregon State Tennis Tournament is held in July every year at the *Irvington Club*, 2131 NE Thompson (287-8749), which is a magnet for indoor and outdoor tennis competition throughout the year. The 78-year-old private club has 4 indoor courts.

A privately operated public indoor tennis facility is the **Western Racquet Club**, 8785 SW Beaverton-Hillsdale Hwy. (297-3723), with 4 indoor tennis courts and 8 racquetball-handball courts.

Across the Columbia River in Vancouver, Wash., is the **Vancouver Tennis Center**, a municipal facility like Portland's.

Following is a list of the outdoor public courts in Portland, with the total number indicated first; lights (L), if any, second; and practice backboard (PB), if any, last:

West

Burlingame Park, SW 12th & Falcon—1
Gabriel Park, SW 45th & Vermont—8 (L), PB
Hamilton Park, SW 45th & Hamilton—2
Jackson High School, 10625 SW 35th—4 (L)
Lair Hill Park, SW 2nd & Woods—1 (L), PB
Portland Heights, SW Patton & Old Orchard—2 (L), PB
Washington Park, SW Kingston—6 (L)
Willamette Park, SW Macadam & Nevada—4 (L)
Wilson High School, 1151 SW Vermont—2

Southeast

Berkeley Park, SE 39th & Cooper—2 (L)
Brooklyn Park, 3830 SE 14th—2 (L)
Clinton Park, SE 55th & Division—4 (2-L)
Col. Summers Park, SE 20th & Taylor—2 (L), PB
Creston Park, SE 44th & Powell—2, PB
Essex Park, SE 79th & Center—2
Glenwood Park, SE 87th & Claybourne—2 (L)
Kenilworth Park, SE 34th & Holgate—2
Laurelhurst Park, SE 37th & Stark—2 (L), PB
Lents Park, SE 92nd & Steele—2 (L), PB
Marshall High School, 3905 SE 91st—2
Mt. Scott Park, SE 72nd & Harold—2, PB
Mt. Tabor Park, SE Salmon, between 60th & 69th—2, E. side; 3 (L), W. side
Sellwood Park, SE 7th & Miller—4 (2-L)
Westmoreland Park, SE 22nd & Bybee—2 (L)
Woodstock Park, SE 47th & Steele—2, PB

Northeast

Alberta Park, NE 19th & Killingsworth—2
Buckman Field, NE 12th & Everett—8 (6-L), PB

Fernhill Park, NE 38th & Simpson—2
Glenhaven Park, NE 79th & Siskiyou—4
Irving Park, NE 7th & Fremont—4 (L), PB
King School, 4906 NE 6th 2, PB
Montavilla Park, NE 82nd & Glisan—2, PB
Rose City Park, NE 62nd & Tillamook—2 (L)
U.S. Grant Park, NE 33rd & Thompson—6 (L), PB

North

Columbia Park, N. Lombard & Woolsey—2 (L), PB
Jefferson High School, 5210 N. Kerby—3
Northgate Park, N. Geneva & Fessenden—2 (L)
Peninsula Park, N. Portland Blvd. & Albina—2 (L), PB
Pier Park, N. Seneca & St. Johns—2

Volleyball

Portland Volleyball Assn. organizes some 150 men's, women's, coed, and grade school girls' teams for fall practice and competition Sept.-Nov. Program is coordinated by the Park Bureau. Call 248-4325 for more information.

YMCA

The epitome of keep-in-shape programs and facilities in Portland is the new *Metro Fitness Center of the YMCA* of the Columbia-Willamette at 2831 SW Barbur (223-9622).

At the edge of Duniway Park in southwest Portland, the big green facility is accessible to Duniway's running track, playing fields, jogging trails, and bike paths. It includes a large gymnasium, exercise rooms, an indoor track, a 6-lane 25-meter pool with a bubble top, 6 regulation handball/racquetball courts, and 2 squash courts.

With all of this and Portland a fitness-conscious town, it's not surprising that the new Metro Center is already full, with 5,000 adult members and many more waiting to join. You can get on the waiting list by making a $50 deposit with the membership office which is refundable if you change your mind.

What makes the Metro Center special is its cardiovascular health program which evaluates an individual's capacity for exercise, then prescribes the proper exercise program. The center also provides a YMCArdiac program of exercise therapy for post-heart attack victims.

Children cannot join the Fitness Center but may work out with their parents on weekends.

The Y also operates the **John R. Leach Center**, 6036 SE Foster (775-4396); the **Northeast Family Fitness Center**, 1630 NE 38th (281-1169); and three community centers: East Clackamas, 10879 SE Main, Milwaukie. (653-2464); West Clackamas, 420 N. State, Lake Oswego (636-1212); and North, 4815 NE 7th (287-2523), which will be moving to a new location. The Leach and Northeast centers both have swimming pools.

The YMCA Outer East Youth Service Center is at 2005 SE 82nd (777-3921).

In addition, the Y operates the **Commonwealth Fitness Center**, 421 SW 6th (223-7643), a fully equipped downtown exercise facility with sauna and locker rooms. Initiation fee is $100; monthly rate, $18.

YWCA

Fitness and personal growth programs geared to the entire family operate year-round in the convenient facilities of the **Downtown YWCA**, 1111 SW 10th (223-6281) and at two YW satellites.

The downtown building includes a large gymnasium for basketball, volleyball, aerobic dancing, gymnastics, and exercise. In the "body shop," personalized exercise is prescribed, including use of the Universal Gym and other equipment. There is a 75-foot-long 6-lane swimming pool.

Among the programs that make the YWCA special are swim instruction for disabled children and adults and post-mastectomy water/land exercise therapy.

The YWCA also operates the **St. Johns YWCA**, 8010 N. Charleston (286-5748), with a community fitness center, and the **Northeast YWCA**, 126 NE Alberta (288-5173).

A free newsletter listing activities at all YWCAs and a membership application and registration form are available by phoning the Downtown YW.

PARKS
Community Play

FROM 3,700-acre Forest Park to tiny mini-parks in the central city, Portland's system of 160 public parks (not including some small or undeveloped areas) has much to offer citizens and visitors.

For example, you can reserve a park or a baseball field for your wedding, play tennis, picnic in the rain under shelter, swim free, hike, bike, watch your child in a Little League game, swing, slide, or read a best seller under a Douglas fir tree. You can sniff roses, ogle huge rhododendrons, or feed ducks.

For complete information or to arrange for permits for park use by groups of 50 or more, call the Park Bureau (248-4315). Tennis and swimming facilities are listed separately under sports.

Community Recreation Programs

Summer, fall, winter or spring, public use of Portland's 11 community centers and 14 swimming pools (11 outdoor) is free, so get your tax dollar's worth by visiting the center nearest you.

Each center offers its own program with recreation specialists. Some have gyms, others craft facilities such as looms and kilns. One even has a roller rink. All offer a full schedule of classes, some of which carry fees.

A guide to the city's recreation programs is published quarterly by the Park Bureau. Phone 248-4315 to get on the mailing list. An illustrated *Portland Parks* map, also published by the Park Bureau, will help you find your way to your child's basketball, soccer or softball games.

In addition to the community centers and pools (listed under Sports), the Park Bureau operates an indoor tennis center, a motor raceway, and several cultural centers.

Regular programs of the Park Bureau are expanded in summer to more than 50 locations around the city, including many city parks and playgrounds not used in the spring, fall, and winter months.

Sports Fitness Camps provide a full morning or afternoon of rapid-fire athletics for boys and girls ages 9-13 at both east-and west-side locations. Three 3-week sessions are scheduled each summer. A small fee is charged.

The 11 community centers are:

Fulton, 68 SW Miles (244-8449); Hillside, 653 NW Culpepper (223-8992); Matt Dishman, 77 NE Knott (282-1460); Montavilla, 8219 NE Glisan (254-4101); Mt. Scott Center and Roller Rink, 5530 SE 72nd (774-8156 and 774-2215, rink); Overlook House, 3839 N. Melrose)282-2053); Peninsula, 6400 N. Albina (285-4222); Sellwood, 1436 SE Spokane (236-4022); St. Johns, 8427 N. Central (286-1551); University, 9009 N. Foss (289-2414); Woodstock, 5905 SE 43rd (771-0784).

Community Schools

The Portland School District cooperates with the Park Bureau in sponsoring Community Schools which offer adult education, usually in the evening, and programs for children in the afternoon. The programs are designed for and by the neighborhoods and feature hundreds of low-cost classes, workshops, and recreational activities. Most popular classes in recent years are aerobic dance, jazz dance, gymnastics, self-defense for women, family movies, ceramics, and weatherization. For more information, call the Community School nearest you from the following list:

Abernethy—2421 SE Orange (235-6610)
Alameda—2732 NE Fremont (284-1686)
Atkinson—5800 SE Division (777-3256)
Binnsmead—2225 SE 87th (771-0121)
Bridlemile—4300 SW 47th (222-3919)
Brooklyn—3830 SE 14th (235-7588)
Gregory Heights—7334 NE Siskiyou (255-6641)
Irvington—1320 NE Brazee (288-1537)

Markham—10531 SW Capitol Hwy. (246-2972)
Metropolitan Learning Center—2033 NW Glisan (241-0299)
   Northwest Community Theater developing there.
Mt. Tabor— 5800 SE Ash (234-6974)
Ockley Green—1315 N. Ainsworth (285-8269)
Portsmouth—5103 N. Willis (285-5609)
Scott—6700 NE Prescott (281-3451)
Sunnyside—3421 SE Salmon (235-5674)
Woodmere— 6540 SE 78th (777-2527)

Cultural Facilities

Elaborate schedules are planned for both children and adults at these city-wide cultural recreation facilities:

Ballet Workshop, 6433 NE Tillamook (282-5061); Children's Museum, 3037 SW 2nd (248-4587); Community Music Center, 3350 SE Francis (235-8222); Firehouse Theater, 1436 SW Montgomery (248-4737); Little Loom House, 8427 N. Central (246-7000); Multnomah Art Center, 7780 SW Capitol Hwy. (246-2706); Theatre Workshop, 511 SE 60th (235-4551).

In addition, a specialized recreation program for mentally and physically handicapped individuals is offered at many locations (248-4328). Day and resident camp programs are offered handicapped persons in summer at Camp Ky-O-Wa, near Dodge Park on the Sandy River. Call 248-4328 to request a camp brochure.

Structured classes carry a minimum registration fee, but in summer more free activities are offered than at other times of year.

At Council Crest Park, atop Portland's southwest hills residential area, Labaree Memorial Fountain, "Mother and Child," by Frederic Littman, satisfies spiritual as well as physical thirst.

ART

Galleries and Art in Public Places

Owning sculpture or a painting by a well-known local artist carries plenty of status in Portland where regional names enjoy the patronage of art collectors. Mention your Louis Bunce, Tom Hardy, Amanda Snyder, Carl Morris, and, above all, your C.S. Price,★ and you're launched—without the help of any New York galleries.

Fortunately for the buyers and artists, Portland has experienced a proliferation of small, intimate art galleries during the past 15 years. Some are commercial, some nonprofit. Several are located in the Old Town section of the city, a convenience for tourists who want to "do" a group of galleries all in one day. Virtually all the galleries show regional or local work, some of it inspired by Oregon's coast and mountain scenery; much of it abstract; less of it objective.

The Portland Art Museum's long-established Rental Sales Gallery★ has helped to stimulate interest in local art by making it possible to rent a painting and apply the rental fee toward purchase if you decide to buy.

Four excellent college and university galleries are included in the list below, which contains, we believe, the most tenacious outlets on the gallery scene. Schedules change so it's best to call before you go.

Galleries

Oregon School of Arts and Crafts—8245 SW Barnes (297-5544). In the Julia E. Hoffman gallery, rotating exhibits show work by contemporary artists and craftsmen as well as arts and crafts of folk and primitive cultures. Gallery talks arranged on request. In the gift gallery, books, prints, sculpture, ceramics for sale. Nonprofit society has been operating since 1906. Hours: Mon.-Fri., 8 a.m.-10 p.m.; Sat., 9 a.m.-4 p.m. (Summer schedule varies.)

Attic Gallery—1313 NW Kearney (228-7830). Paintings, sculpture, drawings, ceramics, and prints take their turn in rotating shows at this gallery which outgrew small quarters in a home on Portland Heights. Among the featured artists are Amanda Snyder, Sidonie Caron, Liza Jones, Peter Giltner, Elizabeth Rocchia, and many others. Hours: Tues.-Sat. noon-5 p.m.

Blackfish—325 NW 6th (224-2634). This is an artist-owned cooperative gallery. Mixture of new talent and well-established reputations represented in exhibits of paintings, sculpture, drawings, some photographs. Hours: Tues.-Sat., 11 a.m.-5 p.m.

Camerawork—Lobby, Good Samaritan Medical Center Nursing Education Building, 2255 NW Northrup (228-6509). Rotating exhibits, primarily by local and regional photographers. Physician-photographer reviews portfolios of would-be exhibitors. Hours: Mon.-Fri., 9 a.m.-5 p.m.; Sun., noon-5 p.m.

Contemporary Crafts Gallery—3934 SW Corbett (223-2654). Three exhibition spaces feature the work of outstanding regional and national artists in clay, glass, wood, jewelry, textiles, paper, and mixed media on a monthly schedule. Established in 1938, Contemporary Crafts Assn. is a nonprofit organization. Hours: Tues.-Fri., 11 a.m.-5 p.m.; Sat. 11 a.m.-4 p.m.; Sun. 1-4 p.m.

Courtyard Gallery—2190 W. Burnside (227-2775). Hours: Tues.-Sat., 11 a.m.-4 p.m.; Sun. by appointment.

Fountain Gallery—117 NW 21st (228-8476). Leading artists of the Pacific Northwest, such as Carl Morris, Louis Bunce, Mike Russo, and Horiuchi, are represented in this major private gallery. Gallery owner Arlene Schnitzer presents a large collection of contemporary sculpture, paintings, prints, and drawings. Hours: Mon.-Sat., 11 a.m.-5 p.m.

Gallery West—4836 SW Scholls Ferry Rd. (292-6262). Sculpture, watercolors, original prints, oil paintings, weavings, batiks, ceramics, representing 60 professional Northwest artists. Wide range of styles. Hours: Tues.-Sat., 11 a.m.-5 p.m.; Sun., 1-4 p.m. Call for directions because gallery is difficult to find for first-time visitors.

Image Gallery—1017 SW Morrison, Room 307 (224-9629). In addition to presenting work by excellent local and regional artists year-round, the Image is known on the West Coast for its presentations of Canadian Eskimo sculpture. The gallery's proprietors, Jack and Barbara McLarty, have traveled to Ottawa and Montreal to select pieces. Hours: Tues.-Sat., noon-5 p.m.

Northwest Artists Workshop—117 NW 5th (223-3210). Second floor gallery in same building with Center for Visual Arts. If you follow trends in art, this is the place to go. Call for hours.

Oregon Society of Artists—2185 SW Park Pl. (228-0706). Regular exhibitions of generally traditional work are presented by society, made up of retired professionals, art hobbyists, and others. Hours: Daily, except Mon., 1-4 p.m.

Portland Art Museum Rental Sales Gallery—SW Park & Madison (226-2811). Hours: Tues.-Sat., noon-5 p.m.; Sun., 2-4 p.m.

Portland Center for Visual Arts—177 NW 5th (222-7107). Nothing like it on the West Coast, it's said. PCVA shows contemporary art in all media; also a center for theater, dance, music. Noncommercial. Hours: Tues.-Sun., noon-6 p.m.

Portland Community College's North View Gallery—In the Communications-Technology building, Sylvania Campus, 12000 SW 49th (244-6111). Call for exhibit schedule and hours.

Portland State University's Galleries—Smith Memorial Center (229-3020). Hours: Mon.-Fri., 7 a.m.-10 p.m.; Sat., 9 a.m.-10 p.m. except in summer. Call for summer hours. Also on the PSU campus is the Art and Architecture Gallery, 299 Neuberger Hall. Hours: Mon.-Fri., 9 a.m.-5 p.m. when there is an exhibit. Call ahead (229-3515).

The Poster Gallery—205 SW 1st (223-1712). If you can't find just the poster to suit your need or your mood here, you probably won't find it anywhere. Posters are contemporary, funky, old-fashioned. Hours: Mon.-Sat., 10 a.m.-5 p.m.

Reed College's College Center Gallery—3203 SE Woodstock (771-1112). Usually five exhibits a year by regionally or nationally important artists. Hours: Sat. & Sun., noon-5 p.m. or by appointment. Summer alumni art shows—hours: 9 a.m.-5 p.m., weekdays.

Sunbow Gallery—206 SW Stark (221-0258). Significant pieces such as wall hangings, furniture, and pottery share space in this imaginative gallery with some moderately priced gift items such as fanciful papier mâché puppets, marbled papers, and much more. Hours: Mon.-Sat., 11 a.m.-5 p.m.

University of Portland's Clark Memorial Library Gallery—5000 N. Willamette Blvd. (283-7111). Library hours.

Art in Public Places

Once art is in place in Portland, it's likely to remain there.

The Elk Fountain, honoring a former mayor, still occupies the middle of downtown Main Street despite attempts to remove it as a traffic hazard.

And while the Portland International Airport underwent a major overhaul, its Louis Bunce mural, "Communication," and the wall it's glued to remained untouched.

The Skidmore Fountain ★ maidens have stayed put since 1888, inspiring renovation of the neighborhood surrounding them in the historic Old Town area.

Four C.S. Price canvases commissioned in 1936 by the PTA for the Beach School auditorium were almost relocated by the school district administration some 30 years later but saved for Beach when the irate PTA secured a lawyer and produced proof of ownership.

A tour of the city's public art collection turns up several treasures which were completed for the Lewis and Clark Exposition in 1905. "They seemed to be quite busy at that time trying to make it look like something was here," one observer of the art scene commented. In the last 15 years, new buildings have brought much new art to Portland, i.e., the Lawrence Halprin fountains and considerable sculpture.

At the Evan H. Roberts Memorial Sculpture Mall, adjoining the Portland Art Museum, and at the museum's new interior sculpture court, a range of styles may be viewed, from Renoir to Hepworth.

Controversial or ridiculed works survive in Portland, too.

Georgia Pacific Co.'s marble nudes on SW 5th downtown have been dubbed "Three Groins in the Fountain" or "Men's Night at the 'YW'," but admirers point to the 190-ton piece of white marble from which they're carved with pride. The five figures are supposed to symbolize growth and awakening.

Decide for yourself about two controversial paintings hanging in the Civic Auditorium's first balcony foyer. They were commissioned for the building when it was completely re-modeled in 1968, but some of the town fathers were so outraged when they saw the works that city hall relegated them to a back room. Time passed and the art community seethed. Finally, the artists and one of the town mothers, former Mayor Connie McCready, combined to get the work out of hiding and up. Jack McLarty's "Man's Past and the Garden of Possibilities," a sectional allegorical painting which "performs" both in opened and closed positions, is considered the most controversial, although now few remember there was a controversy.

Art on the Mall

Equal in magnitude to the art commissioned for the Lewis and Clark Exposition and as controversial as the auditorium art is that which was purchased for the **Portland Mall** in 1977.

The collection of fountains, sculpture, and graphics—20 in all—is as abstract as the Lewis and Clark statuary is historic. No match here for Washington Park's "Sacajawea" unless it's "Kvinneakt" (Norwegian for "nude woman") who skims along the 5th Ave. Mall with her cape flying behind her.

Despite the debate, Portland has already assimilated its newest public art collection, valued at nearly $700,000, and the odds are that the new pieces will stay firmly planted on the mall even if the vehicles of future generations are forced to slalom around them.

Two large fountains lead the mall art procession, one at **5th & Ankeny** and the other at **6th and Pine**. On 5th, water spews from an arc-shaped collection of stainless steel pipes into a pool fronting on a small three-level park or amphitheater.

On 6th, a monumental sculpture by Lee Kelly rises more than 20 feet from the center of a pool. Water falls in continuous sheets over the smooth stainless-steel surface of the intersecting rectangular planes. Kelly received the top commission in a mall art competition.

Both fountains are lighted at night and like the others on the mall were designed by Lawrence Halprin and Associates of California.

On 6th between **Washington & Stark**, west side, is a fountain constructed of a series of carnelian granite cubes in "step" formation rising from the sidewalk to a maximum height of 5 feet. The water activity is flowing, spilling, and splashing against surfaces in the fountain.

Another mall fountain, at **5th & Yamhill**, east side, is an attempt to capture the idea of the well as a social gathering place and is an arrangement of granite blocks featuring six bubbling pools in which the water is strictly contained.

Other mall art:

5th, East Side—between Stark & Oak, stainless steel rectangle, Bruce West; at Washington, "Kvinneakt," hooded nude woman in bronze, Norman Taylor; between Alder & Morrison, "A Cat in Repose," poised feline in polished limestone, Kathleen Conchuratt; between Madison & Main, abstract interlocking forms of Indiana limestone weighing 10 tons, Don Wilson.

5th, West Side—between Alder & Washington, copper-sheathed redwood abstraction, Melvin Schuler.

6th, West Side—between Madison & Main, steel and porcelain enamel, John Killmaster; between Taylór & Yamhill, triangular planes of aluminum painted black, placed in oval rust-colored granite reflecting pool/fountain, Robert Maki; between Morrison & Alder, "Talos No. 2," a bronze figure looking like an abstract Don Quixote but actually named for the warrior whom Zeus chose to defend the Island of Crete, James Lee Hansen; between Alder & Washington, painted steel planes, Ivan Morrison.

6th, East Side—between Stark & Oak, "Matrix III," steel and ferro concrete in circular form set on a pedestal, Charles Kelly.

In addition to the statuary and fountains, the mall art includes six graphic designs for the cylindrical poster kiosks placed at major bus stop areas on the mall. Artists are Susanna Kuo (two designs), Candace Coleman, Byron Gardner, Candace English, Jerry Scheideman.

Downtown

Bank of California—407 SW Broadway. Mushroom-shaped bronze fountain, 10 feet in diameter, in enclosed courtyard visible from main lobby, Robert Woodward; untitled bronze fountain, reminiscent of rocks and leaves, Aristides Demetrios.

Central Library—SW 10th & Taylor. Two paintings by C.S. Price, "Indians" and "Pioneers;" also a study sculpture of horses by Tom Hardy—all on third floor; on third-floor landing, "Library Piece," sculpture/mural, Brent Jenkins, 1976 (see Walking Tours); in Children's Library, a 4-panel painting, "The Four Seasons," by Jack McLarty.

Chapman and Lownsdale Squares—between SW 3rd & 4th, Salmon & Madison. Bronze Elk Fountain dividing the two squares, and incidentally, the street between them, Roland H. Perry, animal sculptor, and H.G. Wright, architect, 1900; in Lownsdale Square, the northern of the two parks, the Second Oregon Volunteers Memorial (Spanish-American War), featuring a bayonet-charging soldier, Douglas Tilden, 1904.

Civic Auditorium—SW 3rd between Clay & Market. The Ira C. Keller Fountain (across the street facing the building), Lawrence Halprin, 1970. Inside, orchestra level: "Sculpture No. 1," Bruce West; "Memory From the Shore," painting, James McClintock; first balcony level: "Man's Past and the Garden of Possibilities," painting, Jack McLarty; "The Magician's Screens," painting, George Johanson; "Mistral –3," sculpture, Frederick Littman; "In Reflection," painting, Sally Haley; bronze bust of William VanHoogstraten, first conductor of local symphony, Marie Louise Feldenheimer; second balcony level: "Monument," 83-inch-high welded steel modern sculpture, Manuel Izquierdo; "Love Rug," painting, Frank Elliott.

Equitable Center—1300 SW 6th. Paintings, main floor, Shirley Gittelsohn and LaVerne Krause.

Far West Federal Savings—444 SW 5th. "Forms Found in Nature and in the Tools of Man," pleasant fountain amidst downtown din, Bridge Beardslee, 1972.

Federal Building—1220 SW 3rd. Columbia River Gorge inspired untitled sculpture by Dimitri Hadzi, 1976. The 10-foot-high basalt piece weighs more than 7 tons and is placed on the east terrace of the building above SW 2nd.

First National Tower—between SW 4th & 5th, Jefferson & Columbia. "Birds and Water," welded bronze sculpture, Tom Hardy. (Extensive art collection inside may be toured. See Industrial Tours.)

Georgia-Pacific Building—SW 5th & Taylor. "The Quest," sculptured marble fountain featuring five nude figures, Count Alexander von Svoboda, 1970; "Perpetuity," redwood surrounding bronze seedling sculpture, symbolizing growth, von Svoboda, 1970; in underground tunnel to parking garage, sculpture, 16 modules of welded steel covered with chrome, Bruce West.

Hilton Hotel—SW 6th between Salmon & Taylor. Bronze lilypond, Tom Hardy.

Lownsdale Square—See Chapman Square.

Mohawk Galleries—SW 3rd between Morrison & Yamhill. Interior courtyards display fountains and statuary in this gallery which is really an office building.

O'Bryant Square—between SW 9th & Park, Washington & Stark. Contemporary fountain, honoring first mayor of Portland, Donald W. Edmundson and Evan Kennedy, 1973.

Orbanco Building—1001 SW 5th. "Folded Circle, Blue Line," a 4,000-pound stainless steel circle split along the line of a large blue "L," Fletcher Benton, 1980. Piece is inside the lobby entrance at 5th & Salmon.

Oregon Historical Center—1230 SW Park. In the Bishop Courtyard, a charming urban sanctuary which forms the Broadway access to the center, a bronze "Beaver," by Tom Hardy, commissioned in 1970 by the C.M. Bishop family to commemorate Oregon's state animal; on landing between main and second floors, "Forest Belle," a wooden ship's figurehead dating back to 1877, on loan from City of Portland.

Pacific Northwest Bell/Capitol II Building—735 SW Stark. In lobby, stainless steel hanging wall sculpture with burnished surface and red lacquer highlight, Lee Kelly, 1971.

Pittock Block—921 SW Washington. On semicircular wall above bank of elevators in lobby, eight rectangular stainless steel panels, each divided into curvilinear spaces of polished steel, Bruce West, 1977.

Portland Art Museum—north of Jefferson between SW 10th & Park. Evan H. Roberts Memorial Sculpture Mall, 1970, features "Dual Form," Barbara Hepworth, 1965, and "Split Ring," Clement Meadmore, 1969.

Portland Center—south of SW Market between 1st & 4th. Lovejoy Fountain, Lawrence Halprin, 1966; in American Plaza area, large "Druidic" sculpture of rusted monuments faced with segmented orange panels, Lee Kelly; Pettygrove Park, between SW 1st & 4th, Market & Harrison, large bronze figure, Manuel Izquierdo, 1977; west wall of 200 Market building, on 3rd Ave. Mall between Market and Pettygrove Park, yellow folded aluminum plane sections, Douglas Senft, 1976. (We have been waiting for the Izquierdo to appear at Pettygrove ever since we wrote the first edition of *The Portland GuideBook* in 1976. As this edition—our third—went to press we were still waiting. Izquierdo promises it will be in place soon, so perhaps when you read this it will be.)

Portland State University—on face of Neuberger Hall, between Hall and Harrison, bronze panels at eye level depicting various kinds of sea life and flora of Oregon, Tom Hardy, 1962; opposite Neuberger on the west side of the Park Blocks, "Holon," sculpture by Don Wilson, 1980, which honors the late Gordon Hearn, founding dean of PSU's School of Social Work. In South Park Blocks portion of campus, near Montgomery, "Farewell to Orpheus," Frederic Littman, 1973.

South Park Blocks—from SW Salmon & Park to PSU. Small plaza containing one of Benson drinking fountains; Shemanski Fountain, with its classical bronze figure of "Rebecca at the Well," Oliver Barrett, 1926; statue of Abraham Lincoln, George Fite Waters, 1928; equestrian statue of Theodore Roosevelt, A. Phimister Proctor, 1922.

Standard Plaza—1100 SW 6th. "Ring of Time," sculpture based on the mathematical phenomenon of the Moebius Strip, Hilda Morris, 1966.

Terry D. Schrunk Plaza—between SW 3rd & 4th, Madison & Jefferson. One of a number of identical ornamental drinking fountains located throughout downtown. Designed by A.E. Doyle, original 20 were given to city by logger-philanthropist Simon Benson. Additional ones have been cast for new locations.

U.S. National Bank—321 SW 6th. Bronze doors depicting allegorical scenes of Oregon history, A.E. Doyle, 1917. (View when bank is closed.)

Water Services Building (City of Portland)—SW 6th & Montgomery. In lobby of basement auditorium, where it has been relegated from a more prominent spot in the main lobby, a controversial three-sectioned oil-on-acrylic painting, "Columbia," featuring a water-related environmental image, Jon Masterson, 1975. (Here is one instance where the proponents of keeping a piece where it belongs lost.)

Old Town

Area at river end of SW Washington & Front—Not exactly art but still statuary, the foremast of the Battleship USS Oregon, commissioned in 1896, was obtained by the city in 1943 and subsequently planted here. The ship's smokestacks and anchor are across Burnside to the north in the parking lot of Import Plaza, a shopping bazaar.

Old Town Parking Lot—SW 1st & Davis. Butterfly, painted to look like a huge screen, covering entire wall of building at south end of lot, Joe Erceg.

Import Plaza Building—NW Front & Davis. Wall mural of historic Old Town building, Bill McCabe, Julie Nielsen, William Hawkins, 1980.

Skidmore Fountain Plaza—SW 1st & Ankeny, Skidmore Fountain, with its two maidens and inscription "Good Citizens are the riches of a city," Olin Warner, 1888. Fountain honors Stephen Skidmore, who left a bequest for a fountain for the "horses, men, and dogs of the city." As usual, the women were left to carry the load, in this case, the font.

Waterfront Park—SW Front & Ankeny. Large metal rectangular screen at staging area, Bruce West.

Southwest

Council Crest Park—Laberee Memorial Fountain, "Mother and Child," romantic bronze drinking fountain supports figures silhouetted against scenic natural backdrop, Frederic Littman, 1956, who says fountain depicts "joy."

Hillvilla Restaurant—5700 SW Terwilliger. Totem pole carved by Chief Lelooska of Ariel, Washington, 1961.

Triangle Plaza—SW 19th & Burnside. David Campbell Memorial Fountain, a sculptural fountain and bronze plaque erected in memory of a Portland fire chief killed on duty, Avard Fairbanks, sculptor, E.F. Tucker, architect, 1928. Other Portland firemen killed on duty are named here, too.

Washington Park—"Sacajawea," bronze statue of woman Indian guide, Alice Cooper, 1905; "Coming of the White Man," bronze statuary of two natives, H.A. MacNeil, 1904; in Rose Gardens, Beach Memorial Fountain, large contemporary sculpture of burnished metal posts set in pool, a memorial to the man who gave the phrase "City of Roses" to Portland, Lee Kelly.

Washington Park Zoo—Once dreary restroom entrances inside main gate have been transformed into jungle scenes in bold, whimsical murals by Peter Giltner, 1978. Snake, crocodile, hippo are there with many friends. Also at the zoo: a memorial sculpture court of animals, including a bear with nursing cubs, by different artists; "Sleeping Badger," by Tom Hardy; and at the entrance, outside the gate, a mosaic screen, featuring fossil-like amphibian shapes, Will Martin, 1959.

Southeast

Mt. Tabor—Statue of Harvey W. Scott, celebrated editor of *The Oregonian*, Gutzon Borglum, 1933.

Reed College—3202 SE Woodstock. At west end of campus, abstract metal and concrete sculpture, a memorial to William Alderson, who was a professor of literature, Charles Kelly, 1974; center of campus near Eliot Hall, "Wind Passage," 12-foot bronze by Hilda Morris, her largest to date, cast and finished in Italy, 1979, and installed at Reed, 1980; at east end of campus, near the new studio art building, "Trigger Four," rusted Cor-ten steel columns and diagonals about 14 feet high, by Lee Kelly, 1979.

St. Francis Community Park—across street from St. Francis of Assisi School, 1131 SE Oak. A flowing fountain featuring sculpture of steel rectangles and water meandering into a pool, Bruce West.

Northwest

ESCO Corp.—NW 25th & Vaughan. "Flogger" (foundry worker), 11-foot statue of stainless steel, Frederic Littman.

Temple Beth Israel—SW 19th & Flanders. Bronze doors for the Ark, depicting the Burning Bush, Frederic Littman.

Wallace Park—NW 26th & Raleigh. "Silver Dawn," abstract sculpture by Manuel Izquierdo, 1980.

Northeast

Holladay Park—NE 11th & Holladay, near Lloyd Center. Musical fountain with continuous lights and music, Jack Stuhl, 1964.

Intersection—NE 57th & Sandy. Bronze statue of George Washington, Pompeii Coppini, 1927.

Laurelhurst Area—Axis at NE 39th & Glisan. Equestrian statue of Jeanne D'Arc, a replica of one in Paris.

Lloyd Center—"Birds in Flight," dramatic metal sculpture suspended above bridge at east end of ice skating rink, Tom Hardy, 1960; bronze fountain, west mall, George Tsutakawa, 1960; in Ice Pavilion Lounge, "Wooden Ice Skater," Niels Valdemar Fieldskov of Kobenhavn, 1855.

Memorial Coliseum—Lighted memorial fountain, with pulsating cycles, honoring Multnomah County war dead, Skidmore, Owings & Merrill, 1960; in Coliseum's Georgia-Pacific Room, abstract mural, 20 feet long, with recognizable Portland symbols such as Benson drinking fountains, Skidmore and Elk Fountains, Louis Bunce.

Portland International Airport—Mural, "Communication," Louis Bunce, 1960.

North

Beach School—1710 N. Humboldt. Four canvases depicting "The Coming of the White Man West," C.S. Price, 1936. They show a family in a covered wagon, Indians, horses, and men at work in a sawmill.

Jantzen Beach Center—You may question whether it is art, but the ship's propeller fountain just inside the main entrance to this huge shopping complex is worth a look. So is the fine merry-go-round.

Art Footnote

• Additional information about art in public places and art events is available from the Metropolitan Arts Commission, Corbett Building, Room 314, 430 SW Morrison, 97204 (248-4569).

Rugged Oregon coast is year-round tourist attraction. Below, rocky headlands rise from the pounding surf off Cape mears.

Photo: Greater Portland Convention and Visitors' Assn.

GETTING AWAY
FROM IT ALL
(Or Where Tri-Met Doesn't Go)

For VACATIONS and recreation some Oregonians prefer the coast. Others look to the mountains. Portland is strategically located about 1½ hours from either.

Oregon Coast

All roads to the Oregon Coast are mountainous. The most popular routes from Portland arrive at Astoria and Seaside to the north, and Lincoln City, the start of the southern beaches.

U.S. 30 follows the Columbia River to Astoria and is the most beautiful—but longer. No-nonsense U.S. 26 rolls right through Mountain Man Joe Meek's donation land claim near North Plains and then straight over the Coast Range to Seaside with a well-marked turnoff for Cannon Beach and points south.

To reach Otis Junction and Lincoln City, take the valley route, 99W. On this route, consider two stops along the way: one at the *Sokol Blosser Winery* (1-864-3342), 3 miles west of Dundee (turn right off 99W on Blanchard Rd.), and the other at *Nick's Italian Cafe*, 521 3rd St., McMinnville (1-472-7919). The winery tasting room is open from noon to 5 p.m. daily, May–Dec., and weekends, year-around.

All Oregon beaches are public. The weather is temperamental at best, but natives will tell you when an east wind blows in Portland, the skies on the coast will be clear without fail. A temperature of 70 degrees is warm at the beach, but take a windbreaker regardless of the time of the year. For reasons obvious when you stick a toe in the water, the coastal chambers of commerce do not publicize ocean swimming. The water is cold by any standards. However, during the summer months, life guards on duty at Seaside and Cannon Beach protect the hardy.

The beach has always been a retreat·for man, according to the Smithsonian Institution, which sponsors architectural diggings at the edge of the Seaside Golf Course. Their findings have proven that the inland Indian spent summers at the beach with his family, just as we do today.

What to Look for and Where

Astoria, to the north, is the west's first city, established in 1811 as a fur trading post by parties sent out by John Jacob Astor, German-born New York fur trader for whom the settlement is named.

From the top of the 125-foot *Astor Column* on Coxcomb Hill, you'll see the mighty Columbia River join the Pacific Ocean. Unless you are 12 or under, your legs will remember the climb to the top of the tower for at least a week, but it's worth it. Astoria serves as a fishing village, and the docks and moored fishing trawlers make an interesting, if breezy walk.

The *Columbia River Maritime Museum*, on the waterfront, is a new building soon to be housing the Maritime Collection. The present collection is just up the hill in Astoria's first city hall. During the summer months the *Astoria Queen* casts off at Pier 2 for an hour and a half trip on the Columbia River. Tickets are available at the dock for trips scheduled from morning through early evening.

The *Flavel House*, opened by the Clatsop County Historical Society and Museum, 441 8th St., is worth a stop. This Victorian beauty includes a "widow's walk" from which the late captain's wife watched for her husband's return. The rooms are jammed with coast memorabilia, including mint-condition remains of wrecked ships.

If shipwrecks interest you, visit *Ft. Stevens Park*, where the skeleton of the *Peter Iredale* is fast settling into the sand. At low tide you can touch some of the timbers, and part of the superstructure remains for photographs. Ft. Stevens, World War II coastal defense installation, is due a face lifting and will be restored soon for war buffs.

South of Astoria, just off U.S. 101, is *Ft. Clatsop National Monument*. The National Park Service has built a replica of the fort where explorers Lewis and Clark wintered with their expedition in 1805. The children will enjoy the tight quarters and small bunk houses. Adults will wonder how the famous team ever stayed together after being confined in such a small area for an entire winter. If the day is fair, stroll down the well-marked path to the boat launching. There, children can climb into a replica of the Indian canoes used by the explorers.

From Astoria drive south toward **Gearhart**, where Portland's oldest families have maintained beach homes for almost a century, or to Seaside, a beach town with salt water taffy, a main street full of carnival attractions, and the renowned Harrison's Bakery.

Gearhart Beach is known for delivering a wealth of sand dollars and is excellent for razor clam digging. Shovels may be rented at stores and service stations from Gearhart to Seaside. For late risers occasional good clam tides arrive after 10 a.m. in the spring.

If you find your talents do not lie at the end of the shovel, the **Bell Buoy** on the highway south of Seaside will supply you with fresh clams in season; frozen the rest of the year. They also offer excellent kippered salmon (smoked as the Indians did it). Look for chowder clams frozen in pints—a good way to beat supermarket prices.

Cannon Beach also will supply you with razor clams, either at the low tide or at **Malo's** on Main Street. This may be your last stop for fresh clams. Farther south the emphasis is on Yaquina oysters. Most coastal communities, north and south, sell fresh Dungeness crab in season.

The beach at Cannon provides material for a June sandcastle contest as well as periwinkle shells, rather like a mandarin's hat, and perfectly round black stones which are becoming quite collectable. Tide pools at Haystack Rock let the public look into the private life of small marine animals. To learn more about sea life, as well as the fine arts from writing to theater and painting, students of all ages join **Portland State University's Haystack classes** during the summer months. Call the school (229-4800) for additional information.

Year-round theater is available at the **Coaster Theater** on the main street of this active beach community. And a dynamic local woman has opened a restaurant, **The Keeping Room**, which is fast becoming the place to eat on the Oregon Coast. Dinners and Sunday brunch are served year-round with lunches offered in the summer in an atmosphere of mahogany tables, Queen Anne chairs, and Oriental carpets, at this unique restaurant, which offers a round table for single diners. New Year's Eve is a special time to eat here. Wine is served, and reservations are suggested at all times (436-1288).

Indian Beach, at the north edge of Ecola Park, is fast gaining a reputation for surfboarding. The park is furnished with picnic facilities, including fire pits, and provides that much-photographed view of the coastline.

Look for agates farther south. *Road's End* is the best place, since the tides have quit throwing them up on the sands of *Agate Beach*. Agates and other decorative stones tend to arrive in clusters. If you have the sand to yourself, keep walking and squinting. When you see three or more people crouching unnaturally on the horizon, you can be pretty sure that they have found the agate trove for the day. Just grin and work your way into the group.

Driftwood is free for the taking on the beaches and provides excellent fires, if dried, either on the beach or back at your cottage. For some reason the pungent odor, so comforting at sea level, becomes obnoxious in the city, so don't bother to stock up except for ornamental use.

Lincoln City lies immediately to the south of Road's End and represents a consolidation of several old beach towns. The marriage has resulted in a frustrated offspring evident in several miles of shops and enterprises which generally block the ocean front effectively. *Barnacle Bill's* at Lincoln City is legitimate and has a long reputation for fresh seafood on the shell. Take a crab or Pacific shrimp cocktail to go and wait while B.B. takes the backs off your Dungeness Crab. He also sells crab legs and meat by the five-pound can, pressure-packed just as it is shelled. Ask him about oysters also.

About 2 miles south of Lincoln City is *Salishan Lodge*, the widely known "destination" resort with golf, swimming, and even indoor tennis but without easily accessible beach frontage.

Depoe Bay and Newport both offer good beach town browsing with little or no beach walking. Depoe Bay, home of the Memorial Day fleet of flowers, is a little Atlantic City, only the pier is turned sideways. The *Channel Book Store,* one block south of the bridge (765-2352), lends an intellectual air to the town. Old and sometimes rare books are to be found in these cramped quarters. Paperback lovers will have a field day in the back room and save half the price on nearly new editions.

Newport's old town on the waterfront is thriving. Begin with chowder or oyster stew at *Mo's* and rub elbows on the oilcloth covered tables with the locals. The atmosphere is negligible and that's intentional, but the view through steamed windows of fishing boats coming and going sets the pace for the day.

The children will love the strictly-for-fun *Undersea Gardens,* nearly next door, where the brave diver drags out the reluctant octopus several times a day.

Across Yaquina Bay is the Oregon State University *Marine Science Laboratory* where the study of sea life is more serious. The Marine Science museum is open to the public, free of charge, and includes a comprehensive and scholarly assortment of books and charts on every phase of Pacific marine life.

Mt. Hood

Most visitors to Oregon want to see its highest mountain, 11,235-foot Mt. Hood: dormant volcano; one of the nation's most climbed major peaks; rugged setting for the high-altitude baronial resort, Timberline Lodge.

Some Portland visitors come and go without ever seeing Mt. Hood through the clouds, but for most a clear day comes along sooner or later and then "the" mountain dominates the Portland scene.

If you can see it from Portland and want a closer view, hurry to U.S. 30/I-84 and head east to the Wood Village-Mt. Hood exit. Get on U.S. 26 going east.

If you're touring in winter, carry tire chains and check on road conditions (238-8400). Winter or summer, carry coats.

Off the highway at Sandy, about 30 miles east of Portland, is the *Oral Hull* park for the blind, where carefully built trails, signs in Braille, tinkling water, and strong-scented plants combine to give the sightless an experience of Oregon's out-of-doors. Another place with special appeal to the handicapped is *Wildwood Recreation Area,* also on U.S. 26, 39 miles southeast of Portland, where paths are paved and rest rooms have been especially designed so that they can be used by persons in wheelchairs.

Ask at Greater Portland Convention and Visitor's Assn. ★ for "Loop" map. Follow U.S. 26 through Douglas fir forests and past swift streams to *Government Camp,* so named because it was the camp of a detachment of soldiers in 1849. They were forced to abandon their government wagons, leaving them as a landmark and a name for the place.

To see the village, now a resort for skiers and climbers, take the loop through town; otherwise continue on the main road less than a mile to the junction with the **Timberline Lodge** Road, a 6-mile side trip up the south slope of the mountain to the 6,000-foot level.

Timberline, ★ so-called because it is at the elevation where trees stop growing, was built, furnished, and decorated by Works Progress Administration workers during the depression and renovated by the state's artists and craftsmen through "The Friends of Timberline" during the late 1970s. It is a museum of sturdy mountain crafts with massive beams and inspiring interior. Among its treasures is a collection of C.S. Price paintings, executed while the famous artist was employed by the WPA.

Timberline has dining and guest facilities, a swimming pool, and the attractive **C.S. Price Convention Center**, built in 1977 to accommodate conferences, seminars, training sessions, wedding receptions, and other gatherings. A new day-use lodge and hotel addition are soon to open.

Summer tourists and sightseers can travel almost to the top of the state via the Palmer and the Magic Mile Chairlifts. The Palmer spans a permanent snow field, providing year-round skiing at Timberline (see Sports and Recreation). It takes riders from the 7,000-foot to the 8,500-foot level on Oregon's highest peak.

Those who venture above the lodge to climb will encounter a complete mountain climbing experience. Steam heat rises from the fumaroles, the obvious indication that this is indeed a volcano. Oregonians like to say you can fry an egg on a rock on Mt. Hood. Egg-frying is the limit of such activities on volcanic Mt. Hood. Further south in the Mt. Hood National Forest, visitors can soak in natural mountain hot springs, long touted for their restorative values. If you want to soak in a wilderness setting, you have two choices close to Portland:

Austin Hot Springs—Like billiard pockets in a pool table, these hot pools in the cold Clackamas River can be found 35 miles southeast of Estacada in the Mt. Hood National Forest. Take Forest Service Road No. S-46 off Oregon 224 for about 7 miles. Area is maintained by Portland General Electric Co. Free day-use.

Bagby Hot Springs—A 1½-mile hiking trail from the Bagby Hot Springs parking area on the Collawash River, about 40 miles southeast of Estacada, also off Oregon 224, leads to the springs and primitive bath house. (Turn off 224 at Forest Service Road S-46, then follow S-63 and S-70.)

Columbia River Gorge and Mt. Hood Loop

The Columbia River Gorge, carved through the Cascade Mountains by America's second largest river, dramatically blends rock formations and waterfalls. This is the wide watery highway of Northwest exploration.

An hour's travel on U.S. 30/I-84 hits the major sights, but for the full drama of the gorge turn off the freeway at Troutdale for the Columbia Gorge Scenic Route. This, by the way, is a good rainy day trip, because the gorge is most spectacular when storm clouds are dramatic. And, of course, during the rainy season the waterfalls run full force.

Before starting to the gorge in the winter, check the road reports. Freezing east winds sometimes coat gorge roads and scenery with ice and frost.

Suggested first stop on the winding road which used to be the main route east is at *Crown Point,* with its English Tudor vista house. Here the visitor gets the full impact of the job the mighty Columbia has done. Wayside and picnic spots, waterfalls, and rest facilities abound for the next 10 miles.

Don't fail to stop at *Multnomah Falls,* ★ about 8 miles east of Crown Point, where the freeway and scenic route join. This 620-foot falls is considered by many to be among the most beautiful in the United States. A short trail spans the pool between the upper and lower falls. A restaurant and visitor information center are located at the base of the falls.

About 2 miles east of Multnomah Falls (scenic route), look for **Oneonta Gorge,** ★ a narrow cleft in a basalt bluff. A bit beyond Oneonta you'll see appropriately named **Horsetail Falls**. Oneonta and Horsetail are visible from the freeway but reachable only by the scenic route.

Near **Ainsworth State Park** the scenic route merges with the freeway and you're on your way to **Bonneville Dam**, one of many great dams which provide the Pacific Northwest with the larger part of its electric power supply as well as with benefits for navigation, irrigation, flood control, and recreation. For the visitor who is not interested in the engineering spectacle of a dam, there are the fishways.

Sometimes called fish ladders, the fishways, wide stair-steps carrying rapid flowing water, allow passage of salmon and steelhead to spawning grounds above the dam and of fingerlings from spawning grounds to the ocean.

Stop at the new **Bradford Island Visitors Center** for underwater viewing of migrating fish. Best time for fish viewing is between late March and the end of September. The very best, according to guides at the center, is around Sept. 1.

Regular tours of the dam are scheduled daily every half hour from June to September. Group tours can be arranged by calling 1-374-8820.

Bradford Island Visitors Center is open from 8 a.m.-5 p.m. in the winter and daylight to dark in the summer.

When leaving the dam site, you'll have a chance to drive into the Bonneville Fish Hatchery area. This is worth a stop if only to see the primeval-looking 9-foot sturgeon who inhabits a nearby pond with some of his fellows.

Four miles east of Bonneville is **Cascade Locks National Historic Site**. The "Oregon Pony," a little locomotive under a shelter in the park near the locks, hauled the narrow gauge railroad train which portaged goods between steamboat landings above and below the Cascade's rapids before the locks were built.

The **Columbia Sightseer**, a 100-passenger tour boat, cruises the gorge in the summer months, making stops at Bonneville Dam Visitor Center, Cascade Locks, and Stevenson Landing, Washington. Call the Port of Cascade Locks (1-374-8474) for current schedules and fares.

Photo: Greater Portland Convention and Visitors' Assn.

Scenic wonder of the Columbia River Gorge is 620-foot Multnomah Falls, a cool and shady spot on I-84, 30 miles east of Portland. A foot bridge crosses the falls at the top of the lower level. The trail continues on to the top of the falls. Non-hikers may enjoy the water from the grounds below at a restaurant.

Opened as a grand resort in 1921, the **Columbia Gorge Hotel**, overlooking the Columbia River 60 miles east of Portland on I-84, served long quiet years as a retirement home before it was reopened recently as a hotel and restaurant. Visitors flock there for the Sunday Farm Breakfast and a look at what 1920's grandeur was like.

At this point, you may return to Portland or continue on the "Mt. Hood Loop Drive," which returns to the city via Mt. Hood.

At **Hood River** look for the junction with Oregon 35. Pears and apples, the wealth of the Hood River Valley, can be found in many forms—from the real thing to tiny earrings—at the **Fruit Tree**, part of a large restaurant-motel complex near the junction.

Take Oregon 35 south through pear and apple orchard country—blossom time is May—toward Mt. Hood. About 14 miles from Hood River you'll pass through the community of **Mt. Hood**. Consider a stop at the Mt. Hood Country Store, built before Timberline Lodge, where you can mail a card or letter that will bear the unique postmark, "Mt. Hood, OR."

Less than 10 miles south at the Cooper Spur Inn, a turnoff to the right offers a worthwhile fair weather side trip to **Cloud Cap**, 10.5 dusty and bumpy miles up the north side of Mt. Hood. (The road is closed in winter.) On the parking lot at the end of the road are two historic log structures. The larger one, closer to the mountain, is Cloud Cap Inn, erected as a hotel in 1889 and now operated as a climbing base by the Hood River Crag Rats, a mountaineering club.

The smaller building was erected in 1910 and still is owned by the Snow Shoe Club, a private group, mostly Portlanders.

Rest rooms and tent camping facilities can be found at the U.S. Forest Service's nearby Cloud Cap Saddle and Tilly Jane Forest Camps.

On a clear day Cloud Cap offers a breathtaking view of the north side of Mt. Hood—more rugged and spectacular then the more frequently visited south side. To the north also can be seen the Hood River Valley and the great Washington snow peaks—Mt. St. Helens,★ Mt. Rainier, and Mt. Adams.

From Cooper Spur Inn, a small public restaurant, Oregon 35 continues around the east side of Mt. Hood to Government Camp. From there the traveler may complete the Mt. Hood Loop, returning to Portland on U.S. 26.

Willamette Valley

For those who travel to Portland from far places, especially carrying children, a day in the Willamette Valley can bring peace to a family too long cooped up in the confines of a city, even one as nice as Portland.

Oregon's I-5, a total freeway system, running from the northern border to the California crossing, can put you in touch with many small communities. From slow-cured bacon to selected antiques, there is a reason to travel and get off I-5 from time to time.

Heading south from downtown Portland, the freeway splits the rolling hills which begin what we call "the valley."

Champoeg is hallowed ground to Oregonians. It was under these old trees that Joe Meek, U.S. marshal and mountain man, called upon the men to cross his line for the United States and set up a provisional government for Oregon. Once home of the French voyageurs retired from Ft. Vancouver, the property is maintained by the State of Oregon. In addition to excellent picnicking and ball-playing facilities as well as wooded glimpses of the Willamette River, the park includes three museums which are open most of the year.

The home of ***Dr. Robert Newell*** is all that remains of the vast settlement of McLoughlin's former employees. Doc Newell's great house became the refuge for the community during the great flood of 1861 which demolished the area.

The Champoeg Visitor Center, a museum of Oregon's earliest settlers is open year-round. The Daughters of the American Revolution ***Pioneer Mothers' Home*** is open from Feb. 1 to Nov. 30 as is the Newell House. These two charge a small admission fee.

Champoeg is a remnant of many historical firsts: it was the site of the largest village of the Calapooya tribe before the arrival of the white man, a trading post for the Hudson Bay Company in 1828, and the first land purchased for any Oregon park (1906).

Don't miss the turnoff marked Canby-Hubbard, for it is at ***Hubbard*** that you find slow-cured ham and bacon.

Drive into town (don't plan a lunch stop here) and turn right at the old, white church for ***Voget's Meats***. Behind that sterile exterior waft some of the most mouth-watering scents in the state. Sides of bacon, thick with ribbons of lean meat, can be cut into one pound pieces and double-wrapped on the spot to be dropped into your freezer. Voget's chipped beef is close to proscuitto (maybe better), and you should take along a pepper stick to munch on in the car.

A little farther down and to the east is *Aurora*. Keep in mind that all colonists were not without humor and enjoy a visit to the *Aurora Ox Barn Museum*. The museum is open afternoons, Tues.-Sun. The charge includes a well-guided tour.

Dr. William Keil, leader of the Aurora Colony, marched across the United States with a brass band preceding his oldest son, Willie, whom he had promised could lead the trek to Oregon country. Unfortunately Willie died shortly before the departure of the wagon train, so Dr. Keil preserved him in a coffin filled with Golden Rule whiskey. Between the band and the stops to let interested Indians observe the corpse, no one disturbed this gathering as they headed west.

Once there they developed a reputation as furniture craftsmen for early settlers. Much of that furniture remains in Oregon families and is made of ash, maple, and other native hardwoods.

The museum contains a wide variety of the furniture-making equipment, musical instruments from the very band, and gaily colored clothing worn by the colonists. Behind the Ox Barn is an excellent replica of an early settler's cabin and next door is a later home of Aurora.

Aurora today is peppered with antique shops. Naturally, anything of great value is to be found in the museum, but a clever eye may spot some remnant of Oregon history on the shops' shelves.

Meanwhile, back on the freeway, this time prepare for an exit at *Woodburn* to reach *Mt. Angel* and *Silverton*. Mt. Angel Abbey, run by the Benedictine order, sits atop a cliff just like the movie version, with its own farmlands spreading out below. Any time of the year, its library is worth a visit by bibliophiles, but two times are special in Mt. Angel. One is the Oktoberfest, held every autumn when the entire town goes rural Germany with great kegs of beer, homemade sausage, and sauerkraut, and dancing in the streets. A more sober occasion, but equally worth the trip, is Easter sunrise at the Abbey.

Beyond Mt. Angel lies *Silverton,* ★ the start of a do-it-yourself covered bridge tour which follows this section.

The freeway rushes by and the legislature comes and goes, but *Salem* remains a small town. Residents keep it that way by not advertising some of its finest features: history, food and fine shopping.

Take the first Salem exit off I-5, heading south, to reach **Oregon's state buildings**. The state capitol building spreads out its white marble fingers under the gold pioneer who stands, ax in hand, above the lofty tower.

A must to Salem visitors, the capitol building is open 7 days a week and the Capitol Guide Office is open for assistance every day. Stop by, just inside the door, for a pamphlet which will give you a do-it-yourself tour of this historic building, which houses the state's legislative bodies.

During the summer months, groups meet hourly in the rotunda with tower trips (there are 121 steps) offered 12 times a day. Those with ample wind and strong legs will be rewarded by a panorama of the Willamette Valley at its summer best.

Since the Oregon Legislature voted that one percent of the building costs must go toward the purchase of art, visitors have been able to view a permanent capitol art collection as well as revolving displays offered by the Oregon Historical Society.

Almost as historical as the building and its surrounding grounds which back up to the state's oldest institution of higher learning, **Willamette University**, are the "capitol house cinnamon rolls" served weekdays in the dining room. Plan to stop for coffee and rolls by 10 a.m., since regulars fill the tables daily to enjoy these gigantic puffs of cinnamon, raisins, and homemade bread.

Also available at the capitol is a list of some historic homes in the Salem area, all open for viewing. Salem was one of the first Oregon cities to recognize its historic heritage, and visitors will find the preservation efforts rewarding.

The Oak Barbecue Pit, 159 High St. SE, is an old Salem standby for lunches and early dinners. Homemade bread and cream pies lie at either end of the cafeteria style counter and in between great haunches of beef, ham, and pork are drawn juicy and steaming from brick ovens to be cut to order. The atmosphere hasn't changed in more than 25 years.

If you plan your trip for a weekday don't miss the **West Mushroom Farm**, 255 50th NE (581-2471) east of the city. Try touring the mushroom caverns in a lighted miner's helmet. The outlet store sells freshly picked mushrooms.

Peg Fry is the "little woman" who stands 5 foot 8 in her stocking feet behind her **Lemon Tree Boutique**, and she is as charged with style as with energy. Her specialty shop for women is at 345 Owens St. SE (399-1010); her stock is different from any chain store in the state. It takes a while to work your way through her converted house, but you may find yourself with a good cup of coffee in your hand to tide you through a tour of everything from sportswear to formal dress.

Antique shops grow as abundantly as the crops in the Willamette Valley, and two of the best are within Salem city limits. Don't miss *Cynthia Day's "Et Cetera,"* 4721 Liberty Rd. S. (Sunnyslope Shopping Center) for a fine assortment of small pieces including jewelry, china, and rare Willamette Valley Indian baskets. The *Assistance League of Salem's Thrift Shop* is at 533 Commercial St. SE. Open Mon.-Sat., (364-8318) this late Victorian home is jammed with consignment and donation pieces, some of them very nice, all of them collectable to someone.

Covered Bridges

Graft, corruption, and an occasional murder built Oregon's covered bridges, but perseverance has kept them up across rivers in the state much to the delight of photographers and Sunday drivers.

Not long ago, the Oregon Historical Society's 3-day historic bridges outing drew so much interest that Director Thomas Vaughan released the map for others. The actual tour takes 8 hours, allowing ample stopping time for photography and musing.

There are more than 60 covered bridges in the state, most of them usable—all of them worth the viewing. But the Silverton-Cottage Grove tour includes 11 of the best.

The *Gallon House Bridge* at Silverton is a brown wooden reminder of local option days when the bridge was heavily traveled by residents of "dry" Silverton who drove out to a tavern to buy liquor by the gallon. The tavern burned down during prohibition while the bridge remains 84 feet high across Abiqua Creek. Its original cost was $1310. Thomas Creek, out of Lyons, was once nearly covered by bridges. The creek still flows beneath two wooden structures known as the *Jordan Bridges*. The longer one was built in 1936; the shorter, in 1937.

Fourth on the tour is the *Shimanek Bridge* near Scio. It is the latest to be built and was dedicated in 1966. Linn County engineers replaced a storm-damaged covered bridge with a replica since there was no money in the county budget for a steel structure. It is the only red covered bridge in Oregon.

Right in the middle of the farm country, north of Crabtree, is the gothic-style *Hoffman Bridge*, crossing Crabtree Creek and built in 1936.

Larwood Bridge, near the Roaring River Fish Hatchery, sits calmly amid local controversy. Residents insist that this is the only place in the United States where a river flows into a creek, and no one has disputed them.

Off Oregon 212 is the *Crawfordville Bridge*, built over the Calapooya River in 1932. It was bypassed in 1963 but has been maintained and is a variation of the county's open truss sides with a narrow, continuous slit window.

The Mohawk River at Marcola introduces the first Lane County bridge. Lane County has been a leader in bridge restoration and has 21 covered crossings in excellent condition.

In 1904 the *Pengra Bridge* measured 192 feet in span. The newer bridge, built alongside the original in 1938, is shorter but was necessary since the original began to slide into Fall Creek. This bridge holds the record for the longest single chords running the entire length and measuring 126 feet. Since the 18-in. thick chords were too large to be run through a mill, they were rough hewn in the woods, hauled to the bridge site, and resurfaced there.

Unity Bridge, across Big Fall Creek, is 90 feet long with daylight windows to allow drivers to see traffic around a very sharp bend in the road.

For the grand finale, the society picked the *Lowell Bridge*. The original bridge at this site, 210 feet long, was built in 1907 to replace the Hyland Ferry across the middle fork of the Willamette River.

Lane County began to rebuild the bridge in 1945 when they saw that dam control would take out the original. The water began rising in 1955 until the bridge now spreads out much like a giant water lily on the lake. This bridge alone is worth the tour.

Recreational Facilities near Portland

Blue Lake Park—Off I-84, 15 miles east of Portland. A large open Multnomah County park where you can jog, fish, or picnic at one of 900 tables.

Dabney State Park—On the Columbia River Scenic Route,

19 miles east of Portland. A wooded riverside park—the Sandy, not the Columbia—where the river is pleasant for swimming.

Dodge Park—Portland-owned city park on Sandy River, north of Sandy. Day use, picnicking, hiking.

Lewis and Clark State Park—Off I-84, 16 miles east of Portland. Another Sandy River site near the spot where the Sandy joins the Columbia. This is especially pleasant for small children; the water is shallow, the bottom sandy.

Oxbow Park—Off U.S. 26, 20 miles s.e. of Portland. Oxbow has 42 campsites and 44 trailer sites along the swift Sandy River. Facilities include a boat ramp, but swimming is not suggested—and no flush toilets here.

Rooster Rock State Park—On I-84, 22 miles east of Portland. A popular Columbia River park for swimming, picnicking, and boating. Towering Rooster Rock, a landmark of the Gorge, is nearby.

Scoggins Park—Off Oregon 47, 6 miles s.w. of Forest Grove. This Washington County Park on Henry Hagg Lake, created by the Scoggins Dam, offers boating, biking, and swimming. User fees are charged.

Fishing is "advertised" at all these facilities, but you're not guaranteed a catch.

Parks That Can Kill You

The vast recreational opportunities of the Cascade Range, the Columbia River Gorge, the Oregon Coast, and the mouth of the Columbia River are so easily accessible that we tend to regard these areas almost as an extension of the city park system. Unfortunately, each year lives are lost because visitors are unaware of or fail to take precautions against the dangers that exist.

• On the Oregon Coast, don't play on logs and driftwood in the water or on the damp sand. Occasionally, large sneaker waves wash high on to the beach, rolling the logs with sometimes fatal injuries to those close by.

• The mouth of the Columbia River (the bar) can change in minutes from easy rolling swells to a raging maelstrom. A Coast Guardsman said it best: "Everyone who knows the sea is a little frightened when crossing the bar." Wear your life jacket and know your boat and skipper. If you use your own boat, obtain a copy of the Coast Guard's *Bar Guide*.

- In the Oregon Cascades, particularly on "The Mountain" (Hood), be aware that rapid weather changes occur at any time of the year. Go properly equipped, and if you climb, go with a guide.

- The Columbia River Gorge and the Oregon Cascades have many hiking trails for the amateur to expert backpacker, but if you go rock climbing, go with an expert lest you get stranded at an impasse.

- Mt. St. Helens has proven she is a killer volcano. For safe viewing, the State of Washington has designated two special areas. One is about 12 miles north of Vancouver. Take I-5 exit 14 (Ridgefield). The other is at Lewis and Clark State Park near Chehalis. Take exit 68. In Portland, the volcano can be seen from many viewpoints, including the Vista Avenue Bridge, Pittock Acres Park, Council Crest, and the lower parking lot at Lewis and Clark College.

National celebrity, Mt. St. Helens, Washington State's erupting volcano, puts on spectacular shows at irregular intervals.

Photo: Ross Hamilton, *Oregon Journal*

BITS AND ODDMENTS
A *Potpourri of Miscellany*

Annual Events

IN ADDITION to the first crocus, the first tomato, and the two-week winter cold, Portland and the rest of the state host other memorable annual events.

For more detailed information and activities as well as exact dates, good sources for information by the day, week, or month are:

Travel Information, Oregon State Highway Division, Salem, Oregon 97310, and Greater Portland Convention and Visitor's Assn. ★ for activities planned well in advance. Information by the week is available in the "Northwest" and "Leisure" sections of *The Oregonian*, or by the day and week in the "What's Doing" and "Tempo" sections of the *Oregon Journal*. *Willamette Week* runs a week at a glance in its "Fresh Weekly" section also.

For an inclusive look at the state's annual events, from fishing to fashion, from symphony to sandcastles, pick up a copy of *Oregon For All Seasons* by Lampman, Sterling, and Falconer (The Writing Works).

Blinks and Twinkles

If you know where to look, Portland offers some unusual night light sights. Here are some:

• Jackson Tower, on SW Broadway at Yamhill. Hundreds of incandescent bulbs outline this early 20th century building named for the founder of the *Oregon Journal*, which was published there from 1912-1948. Dark outside for many years, the office building now captures Portland's midnight skyline just as it did in its youth.

• A parade of lighted boats cruises the Columbia and Willamette Rivers during the week before Christmas. Check the newspapers for times and locations.

• The red light in the nose of the White Stag, which burns inside a fluorescent outline of the State of Oregon at the west end of the Burnside Bridge. The stag is trademark of a nationally known clothing and equipment manufacturer headquartered in Portland and becomes Rudolph only at the holiday season.

• Standard Plaza Building, 110 SW 6th. Night and day, a weather sphere on top of this downtown tower signals the forecast for the day—red for warmer; white for cooler; green, for no change; flashing for precipitation; steady for dry weather. For example, a flashing white light could mean snow.

• Fremont Bridge (the newest, north of downtown). Two American flags ripple dramatically under spotlights at the highest points in the bridge's sweeping arcs.

• Union Pacific smokestack, U.P. Railroad Yards at N. Interstate, north of the Fremont Bridge. Soft accent lighting on 1887 brick landmark adds distinction to sights seen from I-5 freeway on east side of Willamette.

• Flashing airplane beacon on top of Rocky Butte (see Viewpoints) serves no navigational purpose any longer but is kept in order as a reminder of pre-jet, pre-radar times.

Name Dropping
(or Living With the Willamette Valley Twang)

"Welcome to Oregon"
You probably read that on the sign as you crossed the border or saw it posted prominently at the airport.

It's a sincere, simple phrase with a devilish twist to it, and the natives delight in challenging a foreign dialect by listening for those who fumble and grasp for the proper pronunciation of a local name.

The very name, "Oregon,"(make that Ore-y-gun) is apt to send otherwise solemn matriarchs into unsophisticated snickers when dropped from the untutored tongue of a Bostonian. (Here, it is pronounced Boss-tun.)

Early trappers and traders carried a Chinook dictionary, the inter-tribal Indian language, to speak to our first natives. Oregonians today enjoy living by the word and watching outsiders flounder upon it.

Most Oregon names come easily if you will remember to sit heavily upon the middle syllable or lean firmly upon the last. However, there are many exceptions where you must tramp on the first syllable, sliding down the rest. Oregonians also love to be inconsistent as they turn proper names into "insider" jargon.

In spite of the French Canadians who left Ft. Vancouver to settle land further south and who might have lent a little class to the state with their accents, Oregon has managed to squash any fancy ideas until everything rolls out with the same determined twang. The French made an initial run at upgrading the language by christening La Creole Creek, a beautiful name for a sparkling run of clear water in the Willamette Valley.

Oregonians, even then, snorted unless it was flattened into "Lack-ree-all" (sit on the lack) and finally heeled under any chance of Parisian participation by creating the Willamette Valley version which to this day remains: Rickreall. There isn't a French dictionary which would touch that one with a badly burned crepe (or as most Oregonians say, "crape").

Which is not to downgrade Oregonian speech patterns. They are as much a part of the state as Mt. Hood, the Rose Festival, or the annual rodeos (make that: *row*-dee-ohs).

Take this test: pronounce the name of the eastern Oregon river, the Deschutes.

Unless you said "da-*shoots*" (there is no multiple choice), you are in trouble.

To talk to the natives without their breaking into sporadic guffaws, we have compiled a list of Oregon names to start your Willamette Valley twang to vibrating. In addition are some names which may be universal in pronunciation, but which bear a special part in Oregon history.

If you are inclined to make an occupation out of this game, we recommend reading *Oregon Geographic Names* by Lewis A. and Lewis L. McArthur.

Albina (Al-<u>bine</u>-a)—Now a section of north Portland, was named for Albina Page, daughter of the first mayor of that small community which was laid out in 1872.

Astoria (Ass-<u>tore</u>-ia)—named for John Jacob Astor of New York City, who organized the Pacific Fur Company in 1810. Astoria was the first American settlement on the Pacific Coast.

Aurora (Uh-roar-uh)—is the town founded by Dr. William Keil and named for his daughter. Keil was born in Prussia in 1811 and came to Oregon in 1855.

Calapooya (Cala-poo-ya)—the Indian tribe which lived where Oregon City stands today.

Cannon Beach—as in the armament. Named for a cannon washed up on the beach after the wreck of the schooner *Shark* in 1846. The cannon is still there.

Champoeg (Sham-poo-eeg)—possibly pure Indian, meaning a root or weed. Others believe it could be a combination of the French (champ: field) and the Indian (Pooich: root).

Chinook (Shin-ook) soften the oo—a coastal Indian tribe. Also the universal tribal language as in: ik-poo-ie la-pote (shut the door).

Clackamas (Klak-a-mus)—Indian tribe, part of the Chinooks. Clackamas County was one of the first four districts of early Oregon.

Clatsop (Klat-sup)—An Oregon Indian tribe; original spellings given as Tlatsap or Tschlahtsoptchs. The tribe was part of the Chinook family.

Couch (Kooch)—Capt. John Couch was one of the founders of Portland who built his home upon Couch Lake, a shallow pond which covered approximately 22 city blocks where Union Station stands today.

Dallas (Dallus)—a valley town west of Salem, formerly named Cynthia Ann, but citizens figured the name to be too flighty. Under the administration of President Polk, the county seat of Dallas changed its name to match that of the vice president of the United States. This town is not to be confused with:

The Dalles (Dals)—in Wasco County which comes from the French word "dalle" meaning flagstone. The word "dalles," as used by the French voyageurs, applied to the Columbia River rapids flowing through a narrow channel over flat rocks.

Douglas Fir—as any Oregon school child learns, is named for the Scottish botanical collector, David Douglas, and should not be confused by name with:

Douglas County—which is named for Stephen Arnold Douglas, an American politician and Democratic candidate for the presidency in 1860.

Glisan (Gliss-an)—the most often mispronounced street name in the city of Portland. Rodney L. Glisan was born in

Portland, April 3, 1869, so the pronunciation of his name may not seem important to many of the young. Glisan was an attorney, a member of the Portland city council and the Oregon legislature as well as a very active citizen. He would be pleased to have his name pronounced correctly.

Kinnikinnick (Kinny-key-nik)—also known as bear-berry, this low evergreen plant is thought to have been used by the coast Indians as a tobacco. It is pronounced just as it is spelled, with difficulty.

Molalla (Mole-al-uh)—the name of the tribe of Indians which lived in Clackamas and Marion counties and were the only horse Indians in the northern Pacific segment of the state.

Multnomah (Mult-know-muh)—Lewis and Clark first used this word in their journals to describe the river now called the Willamette. The Mulknomans, as they called them, lived on what now is Sauvie Island. All but two men died during a smallpox epidemic while John McLoughlin was at Ft. Vancouver.

Oneonta (On-ee-onta)—Said to mean "place of peace," this name was probably taken from New York State. A steam boat, built in the tradition of the Mississippi River side-wheelers, was built at Cascades in 1863 and given this name. Possibly the name was transferred to the spot in the gorge.

Oregon (Ore-y-gun)—The history of this name is the most twisted and clouded of any in the state. It is possible that the name originated with Major Robert Rogers (see Kenneth Roberts' *Northwest Passage*), an English army officer who tried to find the fabled Northwest Passage. He used the term Ouragon or Ourigan in a petition for an exploring expedition into the country west of the Great Lakes. The name Oregon was not known to Vancouver or to Gray or referred to by Lewis and Clark.

Oswego (Oss-wee-go)—named by A.A. Durham who operated a sawmill on Sucker Creek (later called Oswego Creek). Durham called his Oregon settlement after Oswego, New York. The Indians called the lake, Waluga, meaning wild swan. Local real estate dealers upgraded the name of the artificial lake on the creek to Oswego Lake, and the town later took the name Lake Oswego.

Portland is a major seaport, but that is not the reason for its name. It might have been named Boston. In 1845 two early settlers, Francis W. Pettygrove from Maine and A.L. Lovejoy from Boston, flipped a penny for the right to name their townsite. Pettygrove won and chose the name of the largest city in his home state.

Sacajawea (Sack-a-ja-<u>we</u>-a)—the Shoshone Indian woman who guided the Lewis and Clark Party west.

St. Johns—James John came to Oregon in 1843, first settling in Linnton and then moving to the community which bears his name. Efforts to change the name to the singular have been turned down. However, John was a pioneer; there is no record that he was ever canonized.

Salishan (<u>Sal</u>-ish-ann)—family of Indians who built houses of planks and beams and lived on salmon. This name has been given to a contemporary plank and beam resort on the Oregon coast.

Sauvie (<u>So</u>-vee)—Lewis and Clark called this island Wapato, the Indian name for a wild potato. The present name is that of the French-Canadian who ran the dairy farm on the island for Ft. Vancouver. Although at one time it was, in fact, Sauvie's Island, perfectionists say that pronouncing it as a possessive puts you in the same class with those who insist the district on lower Burnside is "skid row."

Tenino (Ten-<u>ine</u>-o)—a part of a tribe found in the Columbia and Deschutes valleys, the Tenino Indians are now classed with the Warm Springs Indians. The name means a river channel where the water is held by steep rock walls.

Tualatin (<u>Twall</u>-it-an)—is an Indian word meaning lazy or sluggish. Another meaning is "a land without trees."

Willamette (Will-<u>am</u>-et)—derived from the Indian word "Wallamt," which marked a spot on the Willamette River near Oregon City on the west bank.

Children

One mother of many devised the perfect children's dining room. The tile floor leads to a central drain and above all will be a gigantic sprinkling system. After mealtime the water will be turned on and everything, children and all, will be rinsed squeaky clean. Her idea has merit, but she is not the only one giving original thought to children.

The Portland area offers several restaurants where it is better to be chaperoned by the Little League set, as well as many places of special interest to the young.

Restaurants which help you to relax with children include: Farrell's Ice Cream Parlours, the Organ Grinder, the Carnival,

Ice Cream Saloon, the Old Spaghetti Factory, and The Trees at the Hilton Hotel. All are listed under Restaurants.

Travels with Children

Alphabetically correct or not, all children's lists should start with the zoo.

Washington Park Zoo ★ is part of a large complex at 4001 SW Canyon Rd., which flows into the Oregon Museum of Science and Industry (OMSI) ★ and the Western Forestry Center. ★ Between the three major enterprises, open year-round, there should be enough to keep any family busy for more than a week.

Young ecologists will enjoy the solar house, TERA One, built by Pacific Power and Light Co. for OMSI, and everyone can see the danger of a forest fire in action at the Forestry Center.

Tired parents may wish to book a "sit down" at the Planetarium at OMSI. Once the lights go off and the chairs tilt back, no one will know you are restoring strength unless you snore.

Alpenrose Dairy, 6149 SW Shattuck Rd. (244-1133) offers a day at the farm for all those urban dwellers. Take a picnic lunch to eat on the grassy meadows and visit the cows, ponies, pigs, and ducks. Alpenrose opens its Western Village for an Easter egg hunt, a family day in May, and a rodeo in June. Call for dates.

Crystal Springs Rhododendron Garden, SE 28th just off Woodstock, has wide paved paths, perfect for a baby stroller. Visit here anytime, but the spring is the best, since the rhododendrons are in bloom and the baby ducks are hatching. Take plenty of stale bread. The birds will come up the path to meet you and expect to be fed.

Ride one of the last of the cable-drawn ***ferries*** in the state at Canby. Take 99E and follow the signs out of Oregon City to cross the Willamette River on this free ferry, which is in operation all but the coldest months of the year. As you await your turn to cross the river, look upstream for the blue herons which inhabit the river banks.

Chief Lelooska is awaiting you at his lodge at Ariel, Washington, and just as soon as you've taken your seat in the longhouse, the program will begin. Easterners who long to see the American Indian will delight in this two-hour session of Indian tales and dances complete with intricate wooden masks.

And Oregonians will enjoy having their children see a part of the coast heritage—albeit Alaskan in tradition. Ariel is less than an hour's drive from Portland. Call the Lelooska Foundation, 1-206-225-9522, to schedule a visit with the chief. Living history programs are performed Mar.-Sept. and Oct.-Dec., and special meetings of the "tribe" are often called. Charge for a seat on the bench is reasonable.

The Children's Museum, 3037 SW 2nd (248-4587), is especially geared for the young with two floors of exhibits. Many classes include toddler-parent and parent-child sessions in art, movement, cooking. (Toddlers, 18 months to 3 years.)

Ducks are plentiful at several spots around the city. Take all your bread and visit:

Alpenrose Dairy, 6149 SW Shattuck Rd.

Rhododendron Garden, SE 28th off Woodstock

Laurelhurst Park, SE 39th & Stark

Ledding Library, 10600 SE 21st, Milwaukie

Westmoreland Park, 7700 SE 22nd

Another time take I-5 heading south past the last Salem turnoff for the *Enchanted Forest*, which is commercial but not as bad as it sounds. Children, and adults with strong backs, can go down the rabbit hole just as Alice did, as well as meet many nurseryland characters peeping through the undergrowth. The latest addition is a haunted mansion patterned after the Disneyland favorite. The forest is open May 1-Oct. 1 and includes room for picnicking and a refreshment stand. Admission is charged.

All county fairs pipe the kind of music which draws the young, but the *Polk County Fair* at Rickreall is special. Drive into Salem and take the bridge to Dallas. Rickreall is about 10 minutes west of the state capitol. The entire family is admitted to this last of the small-town fairs for the price of a parking ticket. The entire area is about six city blocks square, all in the open, so parents can find a warm bench while children visit the midway. All concessions are run by local philanthropic organizations, no hucksters here, and the prices are low. The few carnival rides available are for the very young, and the Dairy Association runs the milkshake stand. Check with Tourist Information in Salem for the week, but the fair is always held in August.

The National Park Service is building a precise replica of Dr. John McLoughlin's fort at *Fort Vancouver*,★ just across the Interstate Bridge in Washington. For children who find the written word hard to believe, a trip to the fort may well be worth a thousand volumes. The fort is open year-round.

Students in the Portland public schools form the fine Portland Youth Philharmonic, which performs at the Portland Civic Auditorium.

Parents with budding musicians appreciate the **Community Music Center**, 3350 SE Francis (235-8222), which begins with the 5- and 6-year-old early learner, carrying him on to Junior Symphony level.

The **Ladybug Theatre** has built a sound reputation among the young set for such presentations as "Aladdin and His Wonderful Lamp" and other remarkable tales. The players hold an open sort of theater which encourages even the youngest to listen with good audience manners so that they may contribute at the right time. Productions are held Sat. and Sun. throughout the year, adjacent to the Children's Zoo, 4001 SW Canyon Rd. (228-5648). It is not necessary to visit the zoo to attend the plays, for which a small admission fee is charged.

Oaks Amusement Park, at the foot of SE Spokane, just off the Sellwood Bridge on the east side of the Willamette River (236-5722), offers roller skating all year and amusement rides during the warmer months. The park is responsible for a gigantic Fourth of July fireworks display and offers picnic facilities along the river. Many of the rides are geared for the preschool set.

At the **Oregon Historical Society**, 1230 SW Park (222-1741), young groups may experience the problems of the pioneer in prearranged programs Mon.-Fri., by carding wool and handling artifacts which provide a direct touching point with the past. Call the society to reserve a time for your group. See also Bybee-Howell House.

Just across the street at the **Portland Art Museum** (226-2811), the young will be enchanted with the Northwest Indian artifact room which includes a tour, if prearranged, and the opportunity to press small fingers to a great box of "touchables" used by the earliest dwellers of the Oregon country.

Mothers who frequently trip over miles of unconnected tracks in the kitchen will be relieved to take junior engineers to a magnificent collection of five miles of track (all connected) by the **Columbia Gorge Model Railroad Club** at 3405 N. Montana (281-8591). The club is open for inspection during November.

Dig a few worms and tie some leader to a pole before heading for **Sauvie Island** where the catfishing is still good. The wide sandy beaches provide a good place for children to release a little energy, and they might even bring home dinner.

There comes a time for all children when they prefer to argue that black is white. That is the day to take them, map in hand, to visit the **Willamette Stone**, NW Skyline Blvd., just west of Mt. Calvary Cemetery. The stone marks the meridian line and the 00 base line for surveying all Northwest boundary lines. The Oregon Historical Society will provide you with additional information on the stone and mapping, so stop there first.

Housebound mothers with a toddler or two in tow will find an equally sympathetic and jam-stained shoulder to cry on Mon. and Thurs., Sept.–May at the **Oregon City Indoor Park** at the National Guard Armory, 204 S. John Adams (657-2107). For a nominal charge, which covers the use of the lights and state facilities, mothers with children through age 4 are welcome to pack in the tricycles, toy trucks, and doll buggies as well as lunch and coffee (there is a kitchen) to spend the mornings from 9 until noon in this giant covered area, which provides play experiences for youngsters and an opportunity for adults to meet.

Something is always happening under the auspices of the **Multnomah County Library** children's services programs, and the system steps into a faster pace during the summer months. Check the branch closest to you for events.

Child Care

Babysitting cooperatives thrive in Portland. Members of neighborhood organizations take turns caring for each others' children. Ask in your neighborhood about a cooperative. If there is none and you can't make an informal arrangement with a neighbor, try one of the following:

Family Information and Referral Service—Child Care Coordinating Council (4-C), 1110 SE Alder, provides this service. Call 238-7007 for names, addresses, and telephone numbers of certified child care providers.

Latch Key—The YMCA (223-9622) operates four Latch Key centers (before- and after-school day care; full day care in summer) at:

Creston School, 4701 SE Bush (774-0525)

Vernon School, 2044 NE Killingsworth (287-5405)
Lincoln Park School in the David Douglas District, 13200 SE
  Lincoln (254-4435)
Merle Davies School, 13000 SW Farmington, Beaverton
  (644-6701)

For information about other programs in your area, call 4-C
or the Portland Public Schools (249-2000).

Providence Child Center—830 NE 47th (234-9991). Summer day care program, which augments center's Montessori School program, is open to children aged 2½–5. Extended care for children of working parents is also provided. Other Montessori schools in the area provide similar programs.

AAUW Catalog—Day care, kindergarten, and preschool facilities in Portland area are listed in catalog compiled by Portland Branch, American Association of University Women. Cost is $1. Phone AAUW office, 777-7005, to find out where to obtain a copy.

One private baby sitting agency in Portland is ***Approved Wee-Ba-Bee Attendants*** (252-7183). You might call Wee-Ba-Bee if you're planning a vacation or if you're visiting in a motel and want to do the town—without children. Rates are: $12 for the 4-hour minimum and $2 each hour after. For 24-hour care, rates vary according to number of children, with $25 for 4 or more the maximum.

If You're Over 60

If you're 60 or older and want to know the services and programs available to you in Portland, a central information and referral office for problems of the elderly is as close as your telephone. The number is: 222-5555. The Tri-County Community Council in cooperation with the Area Agency on Aging provides the service.

Community-based support services are also available. Depending on where you live, call these numbers:

Northeast (288-8303)   North (286-8228 or 289-8208)
Southeast (231-4800)   Downtown (227-5605)
Northwest (224-2640)   Near Northeast (288-8338)
Southwest (226-3251)   East County (665-7189)

Following are some programs available to elderly persons in Portland:

Community Schools—Most Community Schools★ sponsor activities for seniors. Call 248-4315 for Community School nearest you.

Congregate Dining and Meals-on-Wheels—These programs are managed in Portland by Loaves and Fishes Corp. Call 777-2424 or your neighborhood senior center (see list above) for the dining center nearest you or to be referred for the meals for the home-bound program.

Discounts—Senior Citizen discounts are given at some movie theaters, certain businesses, and drugstores and for certain personal services. For additional information call the number listed above for your area.

Free Tuition—Any person 65 or older may attend any course free at Portland State University if not taking it for credit and if space is available. For more information call 229-4739.

Grocery Delivery—Groceries are delivered to shut-ins for a nominal charge by Home Bound Services, 533 NE Brazee. Call 249-2875 for delivery schedule and other information.

Homemaker Service—Older persons who need part-time help in the home may be eligible for it under the city program or directly through the agency which provides it, Metropolitan Family Service (228-7238). Call neighborhood senior center for more information.

Northwest Service Center—1819 NW Everett, 97209 (228-6972). This community building in a former Christian Science church houses, among many other services, the *Northwest Neighborhood Nurses* (224-0289), a nonprofit health-care clinic, primarily serving the elderly of Northwest Portland.

Oregon Retired Persons Pharmacy—1501 SW Taylor (226-4141). Caters exclusively to retired persons, offering savings in prescriptions, over-the-counter drugs, and geriatric supplies.

Senior Job Center—Older persons who have talents and skills to develop in retirement can list themselves with this free employment service, which is likely to put them right to work in a part-time job. The center gets requests for all kinds of work, from fixing a leaky faucet to carpentry. Hundreds of persons 45 and older are listed in the active file. For more information call 233-9961. The program is headquartered at 2101 NE Flanders. Another job source is the *Older Worker Program* (229-5513), operated by the State Employment Service.

RSVP—The Retired Senior Volunteer Program, a project

of the Volunteer Bureau of Greater Portland, is for persons 60 and older who are interested in becoming more active and involved in their community. RSVP locates agencies that need volunteers and matches them with older persons who fit the job requirements. RSVP provides limited reimbursement for expenses, and RSVP volunteers are insured against accident and liability. Call 248-5813 or 228-7787 for more information or write RSVP, 718 W. Burnside, Room 504, Portland 97209.

Senior Citizens' Grocery—4707 N. Lombard (285-4141). Prices are lower than general retail prices in this unusual store which is operated by a nonprofit corporation "to enhance the purchasing power of senior citizens."

Swimming—Swim for no charge if you're 55 or older at the YWCA pool, 1111 SW 10th, Wed. and Fri. from 1 to 2 p.m. Senior Citizens' Swims are also scheduled at Columbia Pool, 7701 N. Chautauqua. Call 283-9302 for more information.

Telephone Reassurance—To be placed on a telephone list for a phone check or a friendly visit, call Metropolitan Family Service (228-7238), or neighborhood senior center (above list).

Transportation—Tri-Met issues "Honored Citizen" cards to persons over 65 to qualify for 10¢ fares during weekday non-rush hours and free rides on weekends and evenings after 7.

Washington Park Zoo—A program combining slide shows and live animals travels to senior citizen organizations and facilities by courtesy of the Washington Park Zoo. The zoo also sponsors Senior Citizens' Day, usually in early June. Call 226-1561, extension 26 or 27, for more information.

Other Counties—For senior citizen information in other counties call 222-5555.

Schools

Portland supports an excellent public school system, which is holding its own against the problems of urban transiency and suburban flight.

The Portland Public School District is divided into two geographic areas:

Area I, serving southwest, northwest, and north Portland (244-7541).

Area II, serving the east portions of the district remaining (255-7210).

The district's central phone number is 249-2000. Address is 501 N. Dixon.

Newcomers should inquire about the educational opportunities offered to children from age 4 and up at city-wide public school facilities other than the neighborhood schools.

Early Childhood Education Centers—Preschool programs are offered at some inner city schools for limited number of children who live outside the inner city neighborhoods. The centers generally serve children from age 4 through grade three and provide enrichment programs which most neighborhood schools can't offer. School buses transport children from all over the city to these centers.

Magnet Middle School—Established in 1980 as part of Portland's voluntary desegregation program, this school at 2508 NE Everett (temporary location) offers a high quality program for 6th, 7th, and 8th graders. Children from certain inner city neighborhoods who are assigned to it make up about half the enrollment; children from other areas of the city who attend on a voluntary basis make up the other half.

Specialized High Schools—Several Portland high schools offer specialty or "magnet" programs which attract city-wide enrollments. Performing arts, science/engineering/technology, international studies, business management, and marketing are among the specialties.

Outdoor School—The special natural environment of the area provides the setting for a superior public school program for all 6th graders in Portland and many in the suburbs—a program known as Outdoor School. This is a week-long nature camp experience which the children share with their classroom teachers and with nature specialists. For many a student, Outdoor School is the most memorable public school experience of all.

Private Schools

The Catlin Gabel School, 8825 SW Barnes Rd. (297-1894)
Oregon Episcopal School, 6300 SW Nicol Rd. (246-7771)

Colleges and Universities

Columbia Christian College—200 NE 91st (255-7060)
Lewis and Clark College—0615 SW Palatine Hill Rd. (244-6161)

Marylhurst Education Center—Marylhurst (south of Lake Oswego) (636-8141)

Portland State University—724 SW Harrison (229-3000)

Reed College—3203 SE Woodstock Blvd. (771-1112)

University of Oregon Health Sciences Center—3181 SW Sam Jackson Park Rd. (225-8311); School of Dentistry (225-8311); School of Medicine (225-8311); School of Nursing (225-8311)

University of Portland—5000 N. Willamette Blvd. (283-7911)

Warner Pacific College—2219 SE 68th (775-4366)

Western Conservative Baptist Seminary—5511 SE Hawthorne (233-8561)

Western States Chiropractic College—2900 NE 132nd (256-3180)

Community Colleges

Clackamas Community College—19600 S. Molalla, Oregon City (657-8400)

Mt. Hood Community College—26000 SE Stark, Gresham (667-6422)

Portland Community College—12000 SW 49th (244-6111). Operates centers in southwest, north, southeast, downtown Portland, St. Helens, Newberg, Rock Creek, Vernonia.

Other Schools

Museum Art School, Portland Art Museum—1219 SW Park (226-4391). Grants bachelor fine arts degree for a 4-year course and offers classes for adults and children.

Oregon School of Arts and Crafts, 8245 SW Barnes Rd. (297-5544). Offers wide variety of daytime, evening, and Saturday classes for adults. Soup and homemade bread served at lunchtime for a price.

Center for Urban Education—0245 SW Bancroft (221-0984). An agency of the Ecumenical Ministries of Oregon which offers seminars and workshops at various locations on social problems, concerns, and strategy.

Oregon Museum of Science and Industry—4015 SW Canyon (248-5900). Science enrichment classes from kindergarten through high school and adult.

Chinese Consolidated Benevolent Assn.—315 NW Davis (223-9070). Chinese Language School offers Sat. classes for Chinese and Caucasians.

Publications

If it's in print and recent, the chances are excellent you will find it at Rich's Cigar Store, 734 SW Alder (228-1700), a combination smoke shop and periodical store which caters to everyone. From the *London Times* (one day old) to the most expensive French magazines and those of special interest, Rich's stocks them all, and the print mingles well with the aroma of special tobacco blends. Rich's is as much a part of Portland as that proverbial rose by any other name.

The city itself is the home of a wide variety of newspapers and magazines. Here is a list of the major periodicals.

The Oregonian—1320 SW Broadway (221-8327). Has celebrated its 125th anniversary in the city; obviously here to stay as a morning newspaper.

Oregon Journal—1320 SW Broadway (221-8275). The afternoon daily (except Sunday) paper for the state. While both are part of the S.I. Newhouse chain, the papers are in direct opposition to one another frequently, and the reporting staffs remain aggressively separated.

Willamette Week—320 SW Stark (243-2122). A smart weekly newcomer on the city streets which leans toward critical, in-depth studies of Portland.

Daily Journal of Commerce—2014 NW 24th (226-1311). Handles the business news of the community.

Labor Press—Portland Labor Center (231-4990). Draws a regular readership but particularly at election time when endorsements can mean a vote.

Oregon Historical Quarterly—1230 SW Park (222-1741). Has passed its 75th year of continuous publication, which is unique among historical societies. The *Oregon Quarterly* is available with a membership or by individual copies which may be purchased at the Oregon Historical Society.

Oregon Magazine—208 SW Stark (223-0304). Published monthly, this slick magazine slides across the state uncovering new foibles and twists.

Portland Magazine—824 SW 5th (228-9411). Published by the Chamber of Commerce.

The Portland Guide—4475 SW Scholls Ferry Rd. (297-3050) serves as a tourist information guide to coming attractions in the city.

The Downtowner—published by Community Publications, 6960 SW Sandburg, Tigard (620-4121). Free tabloid, full of free advice and often some good information.

Weather

There is one way to tell a Portlander born and bred, but, it takes patience.

If he says it is too hot when the thermometer on the back porch reaches 85 degrees, he's probably the real thing. If he complains when the temperature drops below 35 degrees, he may belong here. If he owns no umbrella and looks upward as the drizzle comes down to meet him, it's fairly certain he's genuine. If, in March, on a 50-degree day, he takes off his jacket and puts the top down on his convertible because it certainly will be raining by June for the Rose Festival and this is the time to get a head start on a sun tan, you've met a native son.

If the woman, standing at the bus stop, her back braced against a fierce east wind whipping down the Gorge says brightly, "Today I'll set out the pansies, I smell spring in the air," you've spoken with the native daughter.

Weather is a serious topic for Portland.

Like strange Aunt Minnie, Portlanders can talk about it amongst themselves, but should an outsider of say 50 years or less residency in the city dare to criticize the smallest puddle, the retort is likely to imply that he move back home.

CLIMATIC AVERAGE IN PORTLAND

Monthly Averages

	Jan.-Mar.	Apr.-June	July-Sept.	Oct.-Dec.	Annual Aver.
Precipitation (inches)	5.35	2.17	1.0	5.57	42.32
Temperature (degrees)	43.2	57.6	65.8	47.9	53.7
Snowfall (inches)	2.5	Trace	0.0	.4	9.3
No. days 1/100″ or more precip.	17.0	12.0	5.0	16.0	152.0

No. of days in growing season: 251

(Data from Travel Info. Section, Oregon State Highway Div., in *Oregon Climates* folder)

Historic Landmarks

Men and women stood silently as tears streamed unashamed down their faces the day the old Portland Hotel came down. Even now the mention of that turreted building where the city spent its most gracious years (and President Taft was stuck in the bathtub) brings a lump to the throats of those who know its gravestone is a two-tiered parking lot.

Mention of the New Market Theatre, now a parking garage, stirs excitement among residents who hear that it may be transported back into its original glory.

From the greatest building to the smallest surviving cobblestone, Portland has learned the hard way to count its blessings in the form of Historic Landmarks, and most of the credit is due to the Portland Historical Landmarks Commission which annually puts its protective arm around a growing list of moments from the city's past. Many of the landmark buildings and their history are described in the Oregon Historical Society's excellent book *Portland, A Historical Sketch and Guide*, by Terence O'Donnell and Thomas Vaughan. Call the Society for more information on landmarks.

Recycling

Portland Recycling Team, Inc., accepts bottles, cans, bundled newspapers, scrap paper, and aluminum at these locations 7 days a week around the clock:

Southwest—Far south end of 11th on Portland State University parking lot (224-8663)

Northwest—1801 NW Irving (228-5375)

North—2003 N. Portland Blvd. (289-7925)

In addition, glass, cans, and newspaper (only) are accepted any time at Lake Oswego High School.

Call 228-5375 for places and times of the Recycling Team's revolving projects.

Stairs of Portland

Climbing stairs is good exercise, and Portlanders thrive on exercise. If climbing stairs is your idea of keeping in shape, Portland has plenty of steps and not all in the stairwells of tall buildings.

The latest inventory lists 152 outdoor stairways maintained by the City of Portland. Built to take pedestrians, like mountain goats, up or down from one street to another, the stairways range from the old wooden ones to brand new concrete flights.

One, at SW Spring and Vista, is broad, terraced, and landscaped and is more like a park than a staircase.

Probably the longest is a series of stairs, with connecting walkways, from SW Kelly at Custer down to SW Taylors Ferry Rd. (almost to Macadam).

One of the most picturesque and steepest starts at the foot of SW Broadway Dr. and rises to SW Hoffman. To those who know it, it's the "SW Elevator Street" stairway and if Portland were San Francisco, it would no doubt be a street.

One of the newest and nicest connects N. Greeley with N. Going, which is beneath it. This stairway is most likely to serve bus passengers going from one street to the other.

Singles

Parents Without Partners, (246-1925) or (774-7998)
Servetus-For Single Adults, 5314 NE Irving (282-2221).
    Dances, card parties, cocktail parties, lectures, camping.

Private Clubs

In addition to many fraternal clubs and other affiliates of national organizations, these private clubs, some of them having reciprocal guest arrangements with other clubs across the country, are probably Portland's most established:

Aero Club of Oregon, 804 SW Taylor (227-7400). Social, athletic.
Arlington Club, 811 SW Salmon (223-4141). Exclusive, men.
Multnomah Athletic Club, 1849 SW Salmon (223-6251).
Racquet Club, 1853 SW Highland Rd. (223-5460).
The Town Club, 2115 SW Salmon (226-4084). Exclusive, women.
University Club, 1225 SW 6th (223-6237).
West Hills Racquet Club, 2200 SW Cedar Hills Blvd. (646-4106).

Emergency Stops

A good clean restroom can be a blessing. Portland has several, scattered in sometimes unmarked spots around the city. In addition to large department stores and restaurants, there are other emergency stops in the downtown area. Try:

The Main Branch, Multnomah County Library (this is an excellent place to brush your teeth before visiting any one of the many dentists who practice in the Medical-Dental Building just across the street on SW 11th).

City Hall (use the 5th Ave. level entrance; restrooms are located to the left of the council chambers)

County Courthouse

Capt. John Couch Square, 2nd floor.

SW 6th & Yamhill is marked with a green iron cage affair. Although it may seem spooky to descend below the city streets, these city-maintained restrooms are clean and well-kept.

Couch Street Galleries, Old Town, has nonsexist restroom which is clean.

Portland State University's Lincoln Hall (use the campus doors on Park) has large restrooms alongside the auditorium, main floor.

Public restrooms on north side of SW Clay between 3rd & 4th adequately serve Ira's Fountain area.

Don't panic when you find the restroom doors on the main floor of the Pioneer Court House locked. Take the beautiful bird-cage elevator to the third floor for luxurious facilities.

In Lake Oswego, the best emergency stop is found at the Lake Oswego Library, just inside the door off the parking lot, 704 4th. Not only does this library have clean facilities, but it also maintains one of the cleanest and most inexpensive (10¢) copying machines in the main hallway.

Every zoo has restrooms, but the ones at the Washington Park Zoo★ are special. Greeting you as you enter are Peter Giltner's jungle murals (see Art in Public Places).

Telephone Numbers
A Handy Guide to Services

AAA (American Automobile
  Assn.), 222-6700
Air Pollution Control,
  229-6092
Alcoholics Anonymous, 223-
  8569
AMTRAK, ticket reservations,
  1-800-421-8320
Animal Emergency Vet.,
  228-7281
Audubon Society, 292-6855
Auto & Driver's Licenses
  East, 238-8203
  North, 283-5716
  West, 229-5810
Auto Impound, 248-5670

Better Business Bureau, 226-
  3981
Birth & Death Certificates,
  229-5710

Carpool, 227-7665
Chamber of Commerce,
  228-9411
City Club of Portland, 228-7231
City Council Agendas,
  248-4085
City-County, 248-3511
Civic Auditorium, 248-4496

Civic Stadium, 248-4345
Civil Service Board, 248-4352
Consumer Protection,
  229-5548
County Courthouse, 248-3511
Crime Prevention Bureau,
  248-4126
Crisis Intervention, 248-5430

DART, 223-2323
Dental Health Info., 248-3711
DEQ, 229-5555

Energy Outages:
  PP&L, 238-2851
  PGE, 226-8111

FBI, 224-4181
Federal Information Center,
  221-2222
Fire Alarms, 232-2111
FISH, 233-5533
Fish & Wildlife Info.,
  229-5403
Food & Drug Adm., 221-2031
Food Stamps, 238-8424
Forest Service, 221-2877

Gray Line Tours, 226-6755
Greyhound Bus, 243-2325

Historical Society of Oregon,
222-1741
Human Services, Mult. Co.,
248-3816
Humane Society, 285-0641

Lawyer Referral Service,
224-6580
Library—Multnomah Co.,
223-7201

Marriage Licenses, 248-3027
Mayor's Office, 248-4120
Medical Emergency, 232-2111
Medical Services Info.,
248-3816
Medical Society, Mult. Co.,
248-3511
Medicare, 221-3381
Memorial Coliseum, 235-8771
Metropolitan Arts Com.,
248-4569
National Park Service,
221-2877
Neighborhood Assns.:
General Info., 248-4519
Northwest, 223-3331
North, 248-4524
Northeast, 248-4575
Southeast Uplift, 777-5846
Southwest, 248-4592
Neighborhood Environment
Bureau (noise, obstruction,
debris), 248-4465

Ordinances, City, 248-4082,
County, 248-3277
Oregon State Bar Assn.,
1-(800)-452-7636
Oregon Symphony Orchestra,
228-1353

Park Bureau
Recreation Programs,
248-4315
Sports, 248-4325
Physician Referral, 222-0156
Pittock Mansion, 248-4469
Poison & Drug Info.,
225-8968
Police, 248-5730
Port of Portland, 231-5000
Portland International
Raceway, 285-6635
Portland Meadows Horse Race
Track, 285-9144
Portland Opera Assn.,
248-4741
Portland Public Schools,
249-2000
Portland State University,
229-3000
Postal Service, 221-2466

Rape Relief Hotline (Portland
Women's Crisis Line),
235-5333
Recycling Switchboard,
229-5555

Social Security, 221-3381
Social Services—Tri-County,
222-5555
Sport Fishing Info., 229-5222
State Offices in Salem
(Portland number),
229-5700
State Police, 238-8434,
229-5980 (Wash. Co.)
Suicide Prevention, Personal
Crisis, 227-0403

Taxicabs
  Broadway, 227-1234
  Portland Cab Co.,
    256-5400
  Radio, 227-1212
  New Rose City, 282-7707
Tel-Med, 248-9855
Time, 229-1212
Traffic Tickets, 248-3233
Trailways Bus, 228-8571
Translators & Interpreters, 90
  languages & dialects,
    24 hour service
    in emergencies,
    655-5555
Tri-Met
  Route Schedule, 233-3511
  Lost & Found, 238-4855

UNICEF, 287-KIDS

VD Info., 248-3700
Veterans Adm., 221-2431

Veterans Hospital, 222-9221
Visitor Info., 222-2223
Vital Statistics, 229-5710
Volunteer Bureau, 222-1355
Voters Registration, 248-3720

Water Repair, 248-4874
Weather, 255-6660
Weather and road conditions,
  238-8400
Women's Resource Center,
  YWCA, 223-6281
Woodcutting, 221-2400

Youth Services, 248-4356
  SE, 233-1113
  Outer East, 777-3921
  NE, 288-6708
  North, 285-0627
  SW, 245-4441

Zoning & Planning, 248-4250
Zoo, 226-1561

INDEX

DOWNTOWN LOCATION GUIDE

1. Portland State University
2. Oregon Historical Center
3. Portland Art Museum
4. Old Church
5. First Congregational Church
6. First Unitarian Church
7. First Baptist Church
8. Central Library
9. First Presbyterian Church
10. O'Bryant Square
11. Benson Hotel
12. U.S. Customs House
13. Union Station
14. Trailways Bus Depot
15. Import Plaza
16. Portland Police Museum and Architectural Preservation Gallery
17. Waterfront Park
18. Skidmore Fountain
19. Central Police Station
20. Battleship Oregon Mast
21. Meier & Frank
22. Pioneer Courthouse
23. Tri-Met Customer Service
24. Chamber of Commerce
25. Greyhound Bus Depot
26. Hilton Hotel
27. Multnomah County Courthouse
28. Lownsdale Square
29. Chapman Square
30. Federal Courthouse
31. City Hall
32. Terry Schrunk Plaza
33. Green-Wyatt (Federal) Building
34. Civic Auditorium
35. Ira's Fountain
36. Red Lion Inn
37. Galleria
38. Willamette Center (Convention & Visitors Information
39. Marriott Hotel
40. County Justice Center (completion 1982)
41. City Office Building (completion 1982)